ARCHDEACON TOM DUGGAN

IN PEACE AND IN WAR

Dr. Carthach MacCarthy

BLACKWATER PRESS

Editor
Rachel O'Connor

Design & Layout
Paula Byrne

ISBN
0 86121 509 5

Produced in Ireland by
Blackwater Press
c/o Folens Publishers
8 Broomhill Business Park,
Tallaght, Dublin 24.

The author and publishers wish to thank: The Mercier Press; Victor Gollancz Ltd; Hutchinson; Weidenfeld and Nicolson; Bertram Books; Pan Books; Macmillan; University Press of America and New South Wales University Press for permission to reproduce material used in this book.

While considerable effort has been made to locate all holders of copyright material used in this text, we have failed to contact some of these. Should they wish to contact Blackwater Press, we will be glad to come to some arrangement.

This book is respectfully dedicated to the Bishop, Priests, Nuns and Laity of the Dioceses of Cork and Ross.

ACKNOWLEDGEMENTS

My sincerest thanks are due to the following: Dr. Michael Murphy, Bishop of Cork and Ross for moral and financial support; Sister Angela Bolster for her invaluable help in regard to the Duggan papers in the Cork and Ross diocesan archives; Ruth Flanagan, Librarian, Cork County Library and her staff, particularly Tim Cadogan and Kieran Wyse; The staff of the archives department in the National Library, Dublin; The staff of the archives department in University College, Dublin; Fr. Anthony Gaughan for allowing me to go through the Alfred O'Rahilly papers; Ian R. English for invaluable help very freely given regarding Tom Duggan's service with the 8th Batallion, Durham Light Infantry; Ursula O'Reilly, for typing the final draft of the book and putting it on disk; Michelle Ryan for typing the first draft of the book; Tom O'Doherty of the Muskerry Leader for his generous co-operation and Sister Mary Patrick Quinlan, John Thuillier and Terry Connolly who were a great help when I was writing the chapter on Kinsale.

I would also like to thank the priests of the dioceses of Cork and Ross who helped, particularly the following: Canon Timothy Crowley, Canon Michael Cahalane, Canon Kevin O'Callaghan, Dr. Padraig Corkery, Fathers Pat O'Brien, Michael Nyhan and Joe Murphy of the Cork Mission in Trujillo, Peru.

A special word of thanks to Fr. Michael Crowley, P.P. Curraheen Road, for valuable information about the Archdeacon's funeral; Fr. Michael Fitzgerald, Columban Fathers, Lima; Fr. Rodolfo Masciarelli, Fr. George Flynn and Fr. Mario Carty of the Society of St. James the Apostle in Lima; Rachel O'Connor and Anna O'Donovan of Blackwater Press for their many acts of kindness and Walter McGrath for his kind help regarding the Archdeacon's Fenian grandfather.

Dr. Carthach MacCarthy

CONTENTS

PROLOGUE

Dr. Walter McDonald, Tom Duggan's mentor in Maynooth, once wrote:

> Every man, they say, has in his life the materials of a first-rate novel, if he will only tell the story faithfully and simply...without vain attempt at ornament and without deviating from the truth.

In a word, every man has a story to tell. Having considered the matter carefully, Duggan decided against writing his life story. Perhaps he found McDonald's criteria too stringent. He wrote in self-justification:

> The stuff is there. If I could write in the carefree way I talk I'd have something. The difficulty is I talk not Irish and certainly not English, rather that powerful patois that Somerville and Ross have made famous.

With all due respect I think that he was off beam when he claimed that he spoke the patois made famous by Somerville and Ross in their little masterpiece *Some Experiences of an Irish R.M.* and other stories with a West Carbery Ascendancy background.

Duggan spoke a language that was all his own. There was an old-world flavour about his utterances, a hint of pedantry, a schoolmasterly affectation, a fondness for circumlocution. Victorian gentlemen rather that the characters in Somerville and Ross would have recognised the style as not far different from their own. The late James Dillon, T.D., spoke more or less the same kind of language and nobody would ever accuse Dillon of speaking in dialect.

Duggan's style may not have been ideal for autobiographical purposes but the important point is that he had a story to tell, a story which would have come through regardless of style, a story which needed his personal stamp. There was only one Duggan and only one genuine Duggan story. Though he decided against writing the story, many people felt that it should not remain unwritten. Acting on the principle that even a badly told story is better than no story, I took my courage in my hands and set about writing the Tom Duggan story as best I could.

It is my hope that the dwindling band of those who knew him well and indeed the wider public may not find the book entirely unsatisfying.

THE BEGINNINGS

Thomas Francis Duggan, the subject of this story, was born on the seventh day of May, 1890, the eldest child of Thomas and Hannah Duggan, both teachers in the local school at Ballyheeda in the parish of Ballinhassig in the County of Cork. To be more precise about his place of birth, it was at the Half Way, a tiny village situated at the western end of the steep Liberty Hill which overlooks Cork city to the east and is half way between the city and the town of Bandon.

The Half Way nestles beside the Owenabue river, immortalised by Denny Lane in his lovely ballad *Carrigdhoun:*

> On Carrigdhoun the heath is brown,
> the clouds are dark o'er Ardnalee
> and many a stream comes rushing down
> to swell the angry Owenabue.

Truth to tell, the Owenabue, even in winter, is never very angry as it passes the Half Way. It is little more than a placid stream in the midst of a marshy plain. According to local folklore this swampy terrain hampered the advance of O'Neill's cavalry on their way to fight the battle of Kinsale. A later ballad, not quite as famous as Carrigdhoun, describes the local landmarks in more homely language:

> It's pleasant to be in Ballyheeda and likewise Rigsdale.
> From the Rising Sun south to the lovely Half-Way.
> There's beauty in the Mountain, for all men to see,
> and Ballygarvan sits happily on the grand Owenabue.*

The rented house in which Thomas Francis was born still stands, externally unchanged; it is the first two-storey house on the left side of the village as one enters it from the city end. The house consisted of two rooms downstairs, a kitchen at the back with the large open fireplace of the time which served as the living room, and at the front was 'the room', a little parlour used only on special occasions. Upstairs there were three small bedrooms, in one of which all the Duggan children were born. As was the case with the great majority of rural dwellings at the time, the house was without such modern conveniences as a bathroom or running water.

* Quoted by John L. O'Sullivan in *By Carrigdhoun and Owenabue.*

This was Thomas F.'s home for the first thirteen years of his life. There was little space for a growing family and there were few luxuries. The school at Ballyheeda was a couple of miles away and the Duggan parents saved every penny they could with a view to acquiring a house of their own nearer to the school. An added reason for wishing to get away from the village was the proximity of two public houses which might constitute a temptation to their growing children. The parents achieved their objective in 1903 when a new school was built at Ballyheeda and they availed of the builder's presence to build a fine commodious dwelling, situated on a hill-side, overlooking a lovely wooded glen.

As in most rural communities of the time, the great bulk of the people had no more than a primary education, if even that, and so the teacher was a person apart, and the principal teacher called 'the master' was a sort of father-figure, equal in rank almost with the parish priest. The whole scene in fact was not far removed from Goldsmith's idealised picture of the *Village Schoolmaster*.

If the teacher was seen as different from the others, so also were his children. The education they received at school was supplemented by more intensive coaching at home; they had greater access to books, they got more encouragement to learn and they even received a certain amount of discreet career guidance with an eye towards qualifying for one of the professions. All these factors gave these children a head-start when it came to beginning their post-primary studies. The number of priests who came from such a background was exceptionally high.

Most of the Duggan children's contemporaries lived on farms and consequently much of their time was spent on farmwork, in the seasonal tasks of saving the hay, harvesting the corn or thinning turnips, that most boring of all agricultural tasks. At busy times on the farm, schoolwork was definitely relegated to second place and often indeed only a grudging acceptance of the system made parents send their children to school at all. Very often when the roll-call was made, one heard the excuse from the small brother of an absentee, 'He's wanting, sir'.

And so among the boys of farming stock there was constant interaction with the neighbours; farmers worked in co-operation, and their sons shared in the communal labour and in the meal and general entertainment which followed.

It was different with the teacher's son. Normally the teacher did not own any land except for a field beside the house. And so his children missed out on a good deal of the work and play of local farmers' children and the darker secrets of the parish were not shared with them. The local lads tended to be a little wary of the master's son.

This was the case with young Tom Duggan. For instance, writing to his mother from the Western Front in 1918 he described his efforts to become a horseman while on a few days' leave. He was twenty-eight at the time and so his experience was very different from that of the ordinary young Ballyheeda boys, most of whom were riding horses before they entered their teens, and certainly very different to that of the young Hydes down the road at Knocklucy who learned to ride nearly as soon as they could walk; one of them, Tim, destined one day to win a Grand National on 'Workman'.

Tom laboured under another handicap as compared with his peers. All through life he had trouble with his eyes and as a rule he wore spectacles and had to receive periodic treatment for his malady. This prevented him from taking an active part in competitive games, and in a community where proficiency in the game of hurling was highly regarded it was hard to resign oneself to the role of 'hurler on the ditch'. There was one pastime, however, in which he participated enthusiastically, the popular Cork sport of bowling.

But the young Duggans excelled in the academic sphere. All four children were very bright and none of them experienced any difficulty in school subjects. Tom excelled in mathematics which became a life-long interest as is proved by one of his last letters from Peru in the course of which he presented Ned, his brother, with a mathematical problem.

The young Duggans had another boast. Their grandfather, Thomas Duggan had been a well-known Fenian, and though the Fenians had not ranked highly in the estimation of Church or State, it was a different story in the homesteads of West Cork.

Thomas Duggan, the Fenian, had been dismissed from his post as national teacher in Ballincollig for the crime of trying to recruit and train young Fenians under the very noses of the police and military in Ballincollig and of his very embarrassed parish priest, Canon David Horgan. His methods showed considerable ingenuity and perhaps a certain lack of scrupulosity, traits which were to be repeated in the story of his grandson's life. He decided that the local branch of the Catholic Young Men's Society offered ideal cover for his Fenian activities. The parish priest must have wondered why all of a sudden this usually innocuous body, politically speaking, began to attract an inordinately high number of strapping young men. Eventually the subterfuge was discovered and he was reported by the local Protestant clergyman to the Commissioners of

Education in Dublin, as the following report of the Commissioners' meeting of 14 February 1862, shows:

> The Secretary acquaints the Board that information of a confidential nature has been communicated to the Office of Government that Thomas Duggan, teacher of Ballincollig N.S., County Cork, has been in the habit of attending a secret and seditious society. The Secretary also read a copy of his letter of the 24th January conveying this intelligence to the Head Inspector and instructs him to proceed to Ballincollig to ascertain and report whether such a society exists, whether Duggan has been or is a member of it and what part he has taken in its proceedings. And he also submits Mr. Sheridan's letters in reply dated respectively the 1st, 5th and 8th of February, reporting so far as he has been able to ascertain the facts as to the illegal connection of Mr. Duggan with the society in question called 'The Young Men's Society'.
>
> Ordered that the Commissioners are of the opinion from a perusal of Mr. Sheridan's letters that before coming to a final decision on the case, further enquiries should be made, and an opportunity should be afforded Mr. Duggan of giving such explanation as he may wish to offer and that Mr. Sheridan be therefore directed to call on Mr. Duggan on Monday 17 for an explanation with reference to his alleged connection with 'The Young Men's Society' and to ascertain if he attended its meetings or frequented any of the suspected 'Public Houses' since it was denounced by the Rev. Mr. Cahill as dangerous and disloyal – further if he did so, did he continue to attend after the President and the 'Spiritual Director' Rev. Mr. Horgan, withdrew from it.*

The sequel came at a further meeting of the Commissioners on 21 February, 1862, and this date marks the end of Thomas Duggan's career as a national teacher in Ireland:

> The Secretary read letter No.12 dated 18th February from Head Inspector Sheridan reporting the result of the enquiries he had made both of Mr. Duggan and the Rev. Mr. Horgan in conformity with the foregoing instructions:

* Record of the minutes of the meetings of the Commissioners for National Education.

> Ordered that as Mr. Thomas Duggan appears to have continued a member of The Young Men's Society of Ballincollig after it ceased to be a religious and had become a political society, he be dismissed from service of the Board and his salary withdrawn from this date.*

At the time of his dismissal Duggan was aged forty, a married man, having wedded Lucinda O'Driscoll some years previously. She had borne him five children: Thomas, born 8 October 1851; Ellen Maria, 13 November 1853; Mary Anne, 2 December 1855; Edmond, 20 February 1858 and Frederick, 6 March 1860. A sixth child, Michael, was born on 24 April 1862, some two months after his father's dismissal.†

In a garrison town like Ballincollig there was little chance of employment for a dismissed teacher. Thomas decided to emigrate to the United States, then an important centre of Fenian activity. It is believed that he fought on the Confederate side in the Civil War then being waged. He returned to Ballincollig in late 1864 or early 1865, having heard whispers of an armed rebellion at home. Apparently, like the Bourbons, politically speaking he 'had learned nothing or forgotten nothing' – he immediately resumed his Fenian activities. Irishmen serving in the British Army were special targets for Fenian recruiting officers and consequently the large military garrison in Ballincollig with a high proportion of Irishmen must have seemed to Duggan a fruitful field for Fenian indoctrination.

Unfortunately, two private soldiers named James Kane and Thomas Murphy with very poor records turned Queen's evidence, possibly with a view to currying favour with higher authority. As a result of their information, Duggan was arrested in November at Moxley's bar and along with Jerry O'Donovan of Tower, an employee at the Hydro in Blarney, was returned for trial before the Special Commission set up to try the Fenian prisoners in Cork.

Amid unprecedented security the two judges, Keogh and Fitzgerald, were brought to Cork on 13 December, 1865 following the trial of the Fenian leaders in Dublin. Still smarting from the humiliating verbal castigation to which they had been subjected by O'Donovan Rossa during his trial in Dublin they were in no mood for trifling. The reception afforded them by the citizenry of Cork was not likely to be a help. According to *The Cork Examiner*: 'Every night the crowd collected outside the Courthouse hooted, hissed and yelled as their lordships drove off.'

* Ibid.

† Taken from Ballincollig Parish Records.

On 19 December it was the turn of Thomas Duggan to stand in the dock jointly with Jerry O'Donovan. Both were found guilty and sentenced to penal servitude, Duggan to ten years and O'Donovan to five. A letter written by Duggan to the Fenian journal *The Irish People* was of so fiery a nature that in the judges' eyes it constituted a felony and led to his conviction, as is apparent from their reference to the evidence of the informers: 'We don't at all intend to suggest that the evidence of Kane and Murphy is not open to suspicion.'

In sentencing Duggan, Fitzgerald said:

> Thomas Duggan, it certainly is not without some astonishment that we hear of a person of your position and intemperate habits occupying the position of centre of this society. It appears that you were brought up a national school master, but that in 1862 you were most properly removed, you having then connected yourself with some illegal body. You are, it appears, from the letter, a man of education, a man who ought to know better.....Were it not for your comparatively humble position we would have sentenced you to still severer punishment. We consider that although not one of the leaders, you were deeply engaged in the conspiracy.*

Not at all abashed by his surroundings Duggan, whose speech is to be found in the famous collection of *Speeches from the Dock,* poured scorn on the jury, Protestants almost to a man, who had found him guilty:

> I do not state these things in order to change the sentence I am about to receive. I know your lordships' minds are made up on that. I state this merely to show what kind of tools the British Government employ to procure these convictions. I have only to say and I appeal to any intelligent man for his opinion, that the manner in which the jury list was made out for these trials clearly shows that in this country political trials by jury are a mockery.

In its leading article on the following day, 21 December 1865, *The Cork Examiner* spoke of Fenian 'madness':

> The letter of one of them Duggan, which established his connection with the 'Irish People' was a production of remarkable ability. How then can we explain the mode in which these men deliberately rushed upon their ruin.

* *The Cork Examiner*, December 20, 1865.

> It is absolutely inexplicable, unless upon the supposition that this Fenian movement has become in some minds a species of madness, rendering them insensible alike to chances of success or consequences to themselves.

The charge made by Fitzgerald against Duggan of 'intemperate habits' was apparently grounded on the evidence of the informer, James Kane, who swore that when he met Duggan by appointment in Barry's public house in Ballincollig 'he was sitting by the fire on a chair, apparently in drink'. The only other reference to Duggan's alleged intemperance is in a viciously anti-Fenian book written under the name of John Rutherford and entitled *The Secret History of the Fenian Conspiracy*. According to the writer: 'Duggan, one of the principal centres for Cork, was probably the most profligate man in the county.'

This assessment is comparatively mild as compared with his pen-picture of Rossa: 'O'Donovan Rossa was notoriously intemperate – that eminently truculent, vulgar, and illiterate demagogue wrote largely, handling his pen with the rough paw of an unlicked bear, but always with coarse vigour and often with effect.'

When the sentence had been imposed, Duggan and his comrades were transferred to Mountjoy prison in Dublin and a few days after Christmas they were transferred to Pentonville prison in London and some months later to the island prison of Portland. Their companions included the Fenian leaders sentenced in Dublin; Rossa, Thomas Clarke Luby, John O'Leary, Charles Kickham and 'Pagan' O'Leary. Conditions, as described by Rossa, were inhuman, especially in Portland where their forced labour consisted of hewing the famous Portland limestone from the quarries on the island. In his book *My Years in English Jails*, Rossa mentions Tom Duggan:

> They prohibited us from speaking in our mother tongue even on the days when we were allowed to talk. They called it 'slang'. I think it was Thomas Duggan of Ballincollig that was severely reprimanded once for speaking in Irish and threatened with severe punishment if he repeated the offence.

Rossa seems to have taken a special interest in the welfare of the families of fellow-Cork convicts, Tom Duggan and Cornelius Dwyer Keane of Skibbereen. Writing to his wife on 23 August 1866, he inquired of her: 'Do you write to Mrs. Keane and to Mrs. Duggan of Ballincollig. You should.'*

* O'Donovan Rossa, Jeremiah, *Irish Rebels in English Prisons.*

In October 1867, word arrived that a number of Fenian prisoners were to be transported on the convict ship, the *Hougoumont,* to Western Australia. Tom Duggan was delighted to be one of the numbers because of his hope that it might lead to a more benign form of servitude in the colony, unlike the fiery young John Boyle O'Reilly who viewed it solely as a step towards escaping from prison and continuing his Fenian activities: 'Australia. The ship. Another chance for the old dreams'.

Keith Amos, author of a volume on *The Fenians in Australia*, mentions Tom Duggan among the Fenians of note:

> Thomas Duggan, a national schoolteacher from Ballincollig, County Cork, and John Kenneally, a clerk from the same county – two Cork 'centres' who were responsible for the recruitment of several thousand Fenians; Cornelius Keane, a lawyer's clerk from Skibbereen, who was one of the first to assist O'Donovan Rossa and became 'centre' of Skibbereen.*

The *Hougoumont* set sail on 12 October and the convicts on board included 62 Fenians. One of the prisoners, John Sarsfield Casey, known as 'The Galtee Boy' kept a diary of the voyage. To occupy their minds the Fenians decided to produce a manuscript journal to be called *The Wild Goose*. The entry in Casey's diary for 31 October is as follows: 'Meeting about project of starting a newspaper while on board. T. Duggan, Chairman; Mr. John Flood appointed Editor; Mr. J. O'Reilly, Sub-Editor; Mr. C. Keane, Reader.'

Tom Duggan contributed four instalments of a serial in the manner of the old Irish folk tales. The writers chose pen-names, Duggan's being Mushra, surely a clue to his West Cork roots; he was born at Parknamore in the parish of Kilmurry, from which Mushra is clearly visible.

After a voyage of eighty-nine days the convict ship arrived at Freemantle in Western Australia, just two years after Duggan had been sentenced in Cork. After a few days in prison, the prisoners were organised into work-parties for road-making. Duggan's party of twenty were sent to a camp at West Guilford near Perth. In a letter which Duggan wrote to *The Nation* and subsequently published in *The Cork Examiner* on 12 December 1868, he described his experiences:

> Our party which now consists of nineteen men are employed quarrying stones. John Keneally and I are employed loading a cart with them. It is heavy work under the burning skies of this country

* The figures quoted seem to be exaggerated.

> but still it is preferable, as far as prison life is concerned, to Portland. The winter which is the rainy season here, is now over and what a winter, like a wet July in Ireland...
>
> This colony is a miserable place to live in, though notwithstanding the great heat, it has a fine healthy climate. The prevailing diseases of the country are diarrhoea and opthalmia. I had an attack of diarrhoea since I came here, which stuck to me for three months. I am also troubled with eye sores; though they are not very bad, still they give me some uneasiness.

Following some agitation regarding the treatment of the Fenian prisoners, a number of those in Australia were released including Tom Duggan on 15 May 1869. By then he had served three years and a half of his sentence. He was one of a handful of prisoners who stayed on in Australia and tried to make a livelihood there. After some difficulty he succeeded in taking up his old profession of teaching, first in a private capacity and later as a government employee in a state school. His last years were clouded by disease and lack of means. He spent the final eight years of his life in a home belonging to the St. John of God nuns in Subiaco, a suburb of Perth, and died there on Christmas Eve, 1913. He was buried in the local cemetery, since closed, and after the lapse of so many years it is unlikely that his grave will ever be located.[1]

When the doors of the courtroom closed behind Tom Duggan, his wife and children never saw him again. As often happens with the wives of patriots, very little is known of Mrs. Duggan. After that black Christmas with their little world tumbling down around them they retired into the shadows and it is difficult, if not impossible, to piece their story together. It must have been a grim struggle to survive for Lucinda and her four children, whose ages ranged from fourteen to three.

All that is known is that the eldest child, Thomas, somehow managed to follow in his father's footsteps as a teacher, that he secured a post in Ballyheeda national school, that he married a lady-teacher in the school named Hanora O'Driscoll from the parish of Drimoleague. Their eldest child, Thomas Francis, was born on 7 May 1890. To distinguish him from his father he was known in the family as T.F. There were three other children, Jeremiah, Edward and Lucy.

Did they ever seriously consider bringing the old Fenian home? One can only guess, but the probability is that they did not. In the early years it would have been impossible financially: they had a young family and were trying to pay for a new house. But there probably was a more fundamental reason. Both were teachers, servants of the Crown. Thomas was in indifferent health. He had already suffered greatly through the political involvement of his father. Would it be right to attract attention to their Fenian background and compromise themselves and their children? All things considered, it probably seemed a more prudent and responsible approach not to arrange for the old Fenian to come home and thereby risk reopening old wounds.

But they kept in touch with the old man, and Lucy, his granddaughter, remembers how careful her mother was to send him a copy of *The Weekly Examiner.* Thomas Francis was intensely proud of the grandfather he had never seen, and in a place of honour in his study he always kept a framed copy of the decree of the Commissioners of Education dismissing his grandfather from his teaching post.

Nothing is known of the Fenian's ability as a teacher. But Thomas, his son, is reputed to have been an excellent teacher who tried hard to give his pupils as comprehensive an education as was possible within the curricular constraints of the time when, for example, the Irish language could not be taught and the text books for the teaching of history exhibited a pronounced colonial flavour.

Thomas Duggan was a quiet, easy-going, frail man who left the running of the home and the management of the children to his wife. It was she who controlled the purse-strings and bought the 'messages', the country phrase for the weekly provisions. She had her hands more than full, especially after her husband's premature retirement owing to ill-health and his death on 16 April, 1909 at the age of fifty-eight.

Somehow she managed to cope and her children eased the burden somewhat by winning scholarships and exhibitions; she lived to be a very old woman, outliving her husband by more than thirty years.

According to the common custom of the time, Tom stayed on at primary school till the age of fifteen. Not surprisingly, seeing that his parents were teaching in the school, we learn from a perusal of the roll-book that his attendance record was exemplary. So well had his primary education been catered for that he experienced little difficulty in fitting into the post-primary system.

Jer was the second boy; they called him 'Son'. He turned out to be the wild one of the family and gave his mother more trouble than all the rest combined, but she kept forgiving and spoiling him. Drink was his problem. One of the aims of the other children as they grew up was to keep their mother from making a will because it was a certainty that she would leave everything to Jer, thereby ensuring a rapid dissipation of the money. Jer died at the early age of thirty-nine.

Ned was next in the family. He seems to have taken after his father in that he was a man of few words, soft spoken and reserved and less restless than the others. He was a good student and won a place in the British civil service.

One of the few recorded memories of Tom's early childhood concerns Ned. It is found in a letter he wrote to his mother from a prison-of-war camp in Germany in 1918. It happened to be the anniversary of Ned's christening and he recalls the occasion:

> Congratulations to Ned. I remember this day 23 years ago very well. About this hour, I think, I got into the covered car outside the door and the horse ran away with me. Felt quite a hero when I was brought back, particularly when I realised that there was no one to spank me.
>
> I said Mass for him this morning.

Lucy was the youngest. She became a national school teacher and eventually Professor of Education at U.C.C.

Ned, Jer and Lucy did not marry and consequently with their deaths this branch of the Duggan clan became extinct. They are all buried with their parents in Ballyheeda except Tom whose remains lie in far-away South America.

Farranferris and University College, Cork

> I am passing over my early years. Nothing very interesting, nothing particularly edifying, nothing the reverse.

So Duggan summed up his youth in a rather dismissive manner. Perhaps he was right, if speaking relatively: compared to the life which followed, his youth, it seems, was comparatively normal.

After a term or two in the Christian Brothers College, Cork, he changed over to the Seminary at Farranferris, probably experiencing the first stirrings of a vocation to the priesthood. He arrived in Farranferris in 1907. Unknown to him it was a particularly good time to arrive there for a boy who was interested in preparing for his future. The rather casual reign of Dr. John B. O'Mahony as President had just ended and Bishop O'Callaghan had appointed Dr. Patrick Sexton, then Professor of Dogmatic Theology in All Hallows Seminary in Dublin, in his place. Sexton was a man of many gifts; besides intellectual brilliance he possessed other more important qualifications for his new post: he was a charismatic figure, a natural leader, a man of boundless energy.

His first step was to make changes and additions to his staff. He inherited two excellent teachers in Dr. Joseph Scannell and Fr. John Murphy. Looking around the diocese for available talent he decided that the men he needed most were Fr. John O'Kennedy, Fr. Cormac Walsh and Fr. Christy O'Flynn. Bishop O'Callaghan was a relative, and so there was no great difficulty in securing the appointment of these three men. The three shared one common factor, they were all involved in the Irish-Ireland movement; O'Kennedy in the Irish language area, Walsh in Irish games, especially hurling, and Christy O'Flynn in Irish traditional music and culture.

It was the beginning of a renaissance for the Seminary. The new broom swept very cleanly indeed. Sexton set as his priority the creation of a more mature and responsible attitude among the students towards both the spiritual and academic life. He was determined that the Seminary students would be able to hold their own with the best. At the time, and for many years afterwards, boys intending to become priests stayed on at Farranferris on completion of their secondary course to study for an Arts Degree at University College, Cork before going on to a major seminary. It was important in Sexton's eyes that they should be seen as in no way inferior to their lay peers. His drive and enthusiasm quickly bore fruit, and the students responded readily to the new approach.

Farranferris at the time was a minor seminary in a much more real sense than now. Its numbers were made up of boys who were looked on by their local priests as likely aspirants for the priesthood. The atmosphere, the time-table, the curriculum were all meant to be a help towards preparing for life in a major seminary like Maynooth.

The student numbers were small, no more than about fifty in Duggan's time. The pupil-teacher ratio, such a vexed question in the modern context, presented no difficulties: there were five or six priest-teachers and one layman. This meant that each student received individual attention and also that discipline did not have to be over-strict. The relationship of staff to students, therefore, was paternal in the best sense of the word.

Tom Duggan fitted easily into this *milieu*. He had been accustomed to discipline in the home and so found little difficulty in adapting to the rules of the Seminary. Many of the other students came from similar backgrounds and he quickly settled in to the Seminary way of life. He participated as best he could in extra-curricular activities though his poor eye-sight continued to prevent him from taking an active part in the game of hurling. By way of compensation he was very active in the debating society as the extant minutes of its meetings show. His interventions show that even then he took an interest in the national question. For instance, speaking on 3 December 1910, on the topic of 'Whether internal dissension has been more detrimental to the interests of Ireland than English oppression', his view was that it was natural to have internal broils in the development of a country. However, in spite of party squabbles, the country would never be in such a sorry state only for English oppression.

It was through the debating society that he first came into close contact with Fr. Christy O'Flynn. It proved an enduring friendship. Fifty years later when Duggan died in Peru, Christy was in hospital in Cork and died a few weeks later. He told a friend, 'I was bad when Duggan died but his death finished me'.

When the time came to begin his university course, Duggan welcomed the change. University College, Cork, at the time was a comparatively small establishment. The atmosphere was homely and personal; it was uncrowded, and life was unhurried. Its range of faculties was limited but sufficient for the time. Comparing it to the massive modern university is like comparing the little old-time corner-shop with the mammoth mega-markets of today. It was more in line with Cardinal Newman's vision of a university, 'An *Alma Mater*, knowing her children one by one, not a foundry, or a mint, or a treadmill'.*

During term, the Farranferris students walked the couple of miles to the University each day, dressed in their sober black suits and carrying their little attaché-cases – it was before the advent of the brief-case! This widening of their horizons at an impressionable age benefited them greatly; again to quote Newman:

> When a multitude of young men, keen, open-hearted, sympathetic, and observant, as young men are, come together and freely mix with each other, they are sure to learn one from another, even if there is no one to teach them; the conversation of all is a series of lectures to each, and they gain for themselves new ideas and views, fresh matter of thought, and distinct principles for judging and acting, day by day .... It is seeing the world on a small field with little trouble; for the pupils or students come from very different places, and with widely different notions, and there is much to generalise, much to adjust, much to eliminate, there are inter-relations to be defined, and conventional rules to be established in the process by which the whole assemblage is moulded together, and gains one tone and one character.

* John Henry Newman, *Discource Vi in the Idea of a University.*

This was Duggan's experience of U.C.C. He mixed freely; he even sought out those of unusual or unorthodox views for his own enlightenment. In the process he became a more mature and rounded person. At the time there was little of the feverish competitiveness which distorts the modern educational process, and takes away the enjoyment. There was a relaxed atmosphere which allowed students to think and to observe. No wonder Duggan had very happy memories of his time in U.C.C. It was the start of a relationship which lasted until he left for Peru in the last months of his life.

Academically, he had few problems. He studied Classics and on 14 August 1909, his name appears among the list of successes in First Arts on the first-ever list of examination results published by Farranferris. His name appears again on *The Cork Examiner* of 15 August 1910, as gaining First Honours in Latin and Second Honours in Greek, as well as a scholarship of £24. Again in 1911 he won a third-year Classical Scholarship of £30 and an Exhibition worth £12. When considering the apparently paltry value of these scholarships, one should make allowances for the differences brought about since by monetary inflation: doubtless the money was very welcome to the struggling widow in Ballyheeda.

Duggan always lamented the break which occurred in the Farranferris-U.C.C. relationship in the late twenties. He considered it a mistake to send students straight from Farranferris to a major seminary such as Maynooth. He raised the matter with Bishop Lucey but to no avail. The throwing-open of Maynooth's doors to lay students, male and female, in comparatively recent times would seem to bear out his view. As in many other matters, Duggan was ahead of his time in this very important question of the formation of future priests.

St. Patrick's College, Maynooth (1911 - 1915)

The Maynooth College which Duggan entered in September, 1911, was no place for faint hearts; it certainly bore little resemblance to the Maynooth of today. Discipline was over-severe, even allowing for the fact that with six hundred students some degree of regimentation was necessary. Some of the rules made little sense. For instance, the solemn rule of silence from night-prayer until after breakfast in the morning was supposed to apply even to students who shared the one room. Delicacies like chocolates were forbidden, lest, as one President put it, 'the students might turn into chocolate priests'. Newspapers were not allowed and the only source of information was the occasional newspaper-clipping enclosed in letters from home.

There was a great emphasis on conformity and a corresponding dislike for singularity in any shape or form. This inevitably led to a certain degree of eye-service, and placed a premium on playing safe or 'navigating' as the Maynooth phrase went. It seemed as if the old Jansenistic spirit still haunted the place. It wasn't quite that man was still a fallen creature but he needed to be watched!

To one who had experienced the benevolent rule of Dr. Sexton in Farranferris and the freedom of U.C.C., the Maynooth system seemed strange and childish in many ways. Tom Duggan had become accustomed to being treated as an adult and he felt a certain sense of shock that this did not seem to be part of the Maynooth tradition. But he gradually came to terms with his new environment and settled in happily to life in Maynooth. The place seemed to grow on him; he became proud of being part of it and the few honours which came his way in later life pleased him as much as being made president of the Maynooth Union, the association of Maynooth-trained priests.

The basic units of Maynooth student society were the class and the diocese. The class consisted of about one hundred students from all parts of Ireland. At the beginning of each student's time in Maynooth his name went into a hat along with those of his classmates to determine the order of seniority; the order in which the names emerged was as immutable as the laws of the Medes and the Persians. As a result, each student spent most of his daylight hours in the immediate company of his two neighbours on the seniority list who were called his 'immediates'. Naturally one could be either lucky or unlucky in this respect, it was all a matter of pure chance. Such minor matters as incompatibility of temperament did not enter into the question.

The other unit of Maynooth society, the diocese, consisted in Duggan's case of about forty fellow Cork students. Normally one met one's diocesans only at recreation times during which they either played games in their own little section of the huge park (called Sinn Féin for some strange reason) or walked around within the precincts of the park.

This type of segregation according to class or diocese was quite rigid and any departures from it were viewed with suspicion. The system had the advantage of welding together the members of one class-year or one diocese but it had the disadvantage not only of isolating them from the outside world but of creating artificial barriers between the students themselves.

Academically speaking, like other students who had completed their pre-Theology courses outside of Maynooth, Duggan found himself at an initial disadvantage. As well as trying to master a completely new branch of learning he had to acclimatise himself to a comparatively new way of life in new surroundings.

Not surprisingly, therefore, he failed to reach the top rungs of the academic ladder in his first year in Maynooth. True he figured on the prize list, read out with a flourish in sonorous Latin in the presence of all the Irish bishops at the end of the academic year, but only in a minor capacity. He was among those who *proxime accesserunt* in Dogmatic Theology; in other words, he was a little below the top-notchers. His only other distinction was in Patrology, the study of the early Fathers of the Church, which did not rank very highly in the students' list of priorities.

He was not long in putting matters right. In his second and third year examination he led the class in Dogmatic Theology, a distinction, the magnitude of which only a Maynooth student of the time could appreciate, Dogma being the subject that calls for the most acute mind. It may have helped his concentration a little that the senior professor of Dogma was none other than Dr. Daniel Coghlan, future Bishop of Cork and a tower of orthodoxy. It was an auspicious beginning to a relationship that was destined to have many ups and downs.

His intellectual rivals, if one may use the term, consisted of two future bishops, Austin Quinn of Kilmore and Patrick O'Neill of Limerick. In the final examination for the Baccalaureate of Divinity degree, which took in the whole four-year course, the order at the top was Austin Quinn, Tom Duggan and Paddy O'Neill. According to the system of the time, all three were invited back to Maynooth for further studies.

Spiritually, during those years before becoming a priest, Duggan was at ease and content. For the first time he had the benefit of continuing expert spiritual direction provided by two Vincentian Fathers. He was fortunate insofar as he did not suffer any major spiritual crises as regards his vocation to the priesthood, unlike others who agonised deeply and had frequent doubts and scruples about their vocation.

Much later in life he looked back on his days in Maynooth at the invitation of *Vexilla Regis*, the journal produced for many years by former Maynooth students who did not become priests. This article provides a precious insight into Duggan's spirituality and sense of compassion:

> Forty years ago we were all at Maynooth together. The majority of us had no doubts and no forebodings. God wanted us for the priesthood and we were his to serve. That was the background of our astonishingly happy lives.

> Humbly we set ourselves to put edge and temper on the metal which composed us; we studied, we said our prayers, we kept our silences (habitually if not bigotedly). We accepted our environment quite naturally. Why God selected us we did not overmuch enquire. Very properly we left it as part of the incomprehensibility of the Deity. One thing we did know. This was not humility, it was stark common sense and realism. We recognised that our acceptance by God for the priesthood had little to do with our power of mind or of our strength of character.
>
> We had to see an unhappy minority in our midst. They had all the virtues and all the talents; they were in Maynooth but God wanted them elsewhere. We saw them leave us one by one and our hearts went out to them in their agony. Sometimes we had the task – the impossible task of breaking the news at home. A godly family had made the focal point of life the day it would see a son of the household ascend the altar of God – disruption and chaos and ruin of twenty years of striving.
>
> We tried to tell these parents, these brothers and sisters that God did want this son of their household but he wanted him in a different way. That boy was not wanted in formal sacerdotal service but he was wanted. On him was laid the high and weighty duty to proclaim the Glory of the God who made him – to proclaim it in the beauty and the grace of a well-spent life. And thus proclaiming God, he was to have an influence for good as high as any ordained priest.
>
> These were the things we tried to say. We were self-conscious and inarticulate, and a poor family in broken-hearted concentration on its grief was in no mood to listen... But the vision we had and could not communicate, the vision of lives lived spaciously and unto edification became in the years to come veritable and glorious reality.

Duggan had died before this beautifully-expressed vision of the lay apostolate became the official teaching of the Church through the Second Vatican Council.

Tom was ordained a priest on 21 June 1915. The annual ordination ceremony which used to be the great liturgical occasion of the Maynooth calendar was carried out in its full glory. The large number to be ordained, roughly a hundred, meant that invitations had to be cut to a minimum because space was very limited in the lovely Maynooth chapel. In Tom Duggan's case, his guests were his mother, brothers, Jer and Ned, and his sister Lucy. The little group must have thrilled to the beauty of the ceremony, the laying on of hands that goes back to Jesus himself, and the emotional finale as the procession of newly-ordained priests wended its way down the length of the chapel to the accompaniment of a mighty salute from the magnificent Maynooth organ.

The following day Tom celebrated his first Mass in the much humbler surrounding of the little church at Ballyheeda where he had been baptised. In all probability it was a very homely ceremony without the frills nowadays associated with such occasions.

A Post-Graduate Student (1915 - 1917)

Following the completion of his ordinary theological course, Duggan was recommended to his bishop as a suitable candidate for further studies, and in September, 1915, he found himself back in Maynooth as a post-graduate.

The building set aside for such students was known as Dunboyne House. Outwardly it was no different from the other houses on the campus. As one enters the College and walks through the very beautiful St. Joseph's Square it is the unpretentious building on the far left.

Technically it was simply the building where post-graduate priests lived and studied, each with a bedsitter which just about provided room for a bed and a shelf of books and a table. In reality it was a great deal more than that, it was an essential part of the intellectual core of the Irish Church of the time and a sort of training-ground for future Irish bishops at a time when intellectual ability was regarded as a far more important requisite for bishops than mere pastoral experience.

When Tom Duggan entered the Dunboyne in September, 1915, Dr. Walter MacDonald and it were regarded as almost synonymous. MacDonald's official title, Prefect of the Dunboyne, in no way covered the vast field of influence which made him a key figure in moulding the Irish Church of that era. He personally directed the small group of specially selected students in the strictly theological areas of Dogmatic and Moral Theology but in addition he was in many ways their 'guide, philosopher and friend'. It could be said of him that he dominated the Dunboyne by sheer intellectual ability and force of character.

In a sense MacDonald governed the Dunboyne as an independent fiefdom. The professors in the regular theological faculty viewed that situation with some misgivings but there was nothing either they or the bishops could do.

Duggan found MacDonald's method of teaching completely different to the system he had known in his under-graduate days. Then one sat passively in class, listened to the professor and tried to take down verbatim what he said, and the only personal contribution a student made was to answer a question put to him by the professor.

MacDonald's methods could not have been more different. He assumed that his students knew their theology as otherwise they should not have been in his class. Consequently his aim was not so much to impart fresh knowledge directly as to train his students how to use their minds. To that end he used his class periods not as occasions for lecturing but as a forum for discussion. His method was to propose some disputed theological problem as a subject for discussion at the start of class, rather in the manner of throwing in the ball at the start of a game. He gave his own view but did not impose it, and any of the students was quite free, even encouraged, to challenge it. His classes as a result were lively affairs and kept both him and his students on their toes. Not many professors would have the competence or the confidence to put such a system of instruction into operation.

In his book *Reminiscences of a Maynooth Professor* MacDonald looked back nostalgically on those happy days and on the intellectual benefit and satisfaction gained from them:

> Few professors, I fancy, have had anything like the advantage I have had in hearing my teaching criticised in this way, year after year by a number of clever young men, who, if they accepted it at all, did so only with great reluctance. I have always welcomed this criticism and tried to profit by it, lopping off or modifying any part of my teachings which I could not defend to the satisfaction of my own conscience.

Duggan was greatly enamoured of this system with its underlying current of intellectual honesty. MacDonald's approach was in tune with his own sharpness of mind; he admired the way MacDonald strode into class without book or note to buttress his arguments. All through life he remembered him and shared his love of dialectic, the testing of truth by discussion.

Unfortunately there was another side to this brilliant man, Walter MacDonald, known affectionately to his students as 'Watty', which may also have left its mark on Duggan. Somewhere the mixture seemed to have gone wrong in MacDonald's personality, and this made his life something of a tragedy.

Almost from the start of his teaching role at Maynooth he was in conflict with authority and by the time Tom Duggan arrived on the Dunboyne MacDonald had long been an embarrassment to the conservative Irish Church.

His troubles began with his unorthodox views about physics which he tried to apply to philosophy and Catholic theology. His Kinetic theory on motion was the fulcrum on which he hoped to apply the findings of science to a better understanding of Dogmatic Theology. His book on Motion and subsequent books with a similar scientific background were never published as he failed to gain the necessary *nihil obstat*, or ecclesiastical licence to publish. For this he blamed the influence of his fellow-professors in Maynooth, particularly Dr. Coghlan; he blamed Maynooth and ultimately the Irish Bishops, and as a result he embarked on a course of confrontation with authority which left him bruised and embittered.

This stands out clearly in what has become known as the O'Hickey case. Dr. O'Hickey was professor of Irish at Maynooth when the agitation started to make Irish a compulsory subject for entrance to the newly established National University of Ireland, and he became passionately involved on the side of Irish. This was not welcomed by the Irish Bishops, many of whom were members of the Senate of the National University. Maynooth itself was also directly involved as its pre-Theology faculties formed a constituent college of the University.

The Standing committee of the Bishops declared that 'in existing circumstances, compulsion, instead of being a help, would be a hindrance to the language movement'.* O'Hickey reacted violently, comparing the Bishops to some clerics in the past who betrayed their country in its hour of need and referring to them as 'recreant Senators'. Considering that Cardinal Logue, Primate of All-Ireland and Dr. Daniel Mannix, the President of Maynooth were two of those thus stigmatised, these were very provocative words. Soon the Maynooth students were brought into the fray and, addressing a meeting of the student-body, O'Hickey spoke scathingly of the Irish Bishops whilst exonerating Archbishop Walsh of Dublin from blame. 'As for the rest,' he said, 'I shall say no further than to recommend them to your earnest prayers.'

It was too much for the Bishops to tolerate but they moved cautiously, staying well within the law. Eventually O'Hickey was asked to resign his chair. In his hour of trial he turned to MacDonald for advice. MacDonald advised him to sit tight; he did so and the Bishops dismissed him from his post. MacDonald advised him to appeal to Rome and took over the prosecution of his case. Dr. Leon O'Broin summed up MacDonald's part in the affair in an unfavourable light, referring to him as 'a fellow-Professor who planned O'Hickey's strategy and fed

* Leon O'Broin, *The Gaelic League and Chair of Irish Studies in Maynooth*, Winter 1963.

fuel to his discontent from his own sense of grievance!' In other words, he was using the O'Hickey case as a stick to strike the Bishops.[2]

Professor P.J. Corish in *The Irish Catholic Experience* commends O'Broin for his fairness:

> The account given by Walter MacDonald in his Reminisences has become widely known but it is very partial. The balanced assessment by Lóin Ó Broin is rightly severe on MacDonald not only for his account of the affair but for his part in it.

But MacDonald was no expert in Canon Law. O'Hickey spent years in Rome trying to further his cause and eventually returned home in 1916, a beaten and broken man, having lost his case through default by failing to produce the requisite documentation within the statutory time. Soon afterwards he died.

Ostensibly, MacDonald had been fighting for O'Hickey, and on a wider front for the principle of academic freedom of expression and security of tenure for Maynooth professors, but shorn of high principle, it boiled down to a vendetta against the Irish Bishops.

Duggan was one of MacDonald's students during the final stages of the O'Hickey case. Seeing that much of the famous *Reminiscences* is devoted to defending O'Hickey it would be too much to expect of human nature that MacDonald keep silent on the matter in the presence of his students.

MacDonald died in 1920, leaving behind a file of reminiscences which he had written over the years and which he left in the care of his literary editor, Denis Gwynn. These were later published by Gwynn under the title of *Reminiscences of a Maynooth Professor*. The book greatly displeased many of MacDonald's former students. In the 1950s when Gwynn was based in Cork and had become friendly with Duggan he published a new edition of the book under the old heading but this time it was made up of only part of the original book with the addition of a long memoir written by Gwynn in which MacDonald is depicted as a martyr to truth, a sort of modern Savonarola! He sent a copy to Duggan for his comments but must have been very disappointed with the response. Duggan wrote a scathing criticism of the *Memoir*:

> In a collection of essays of evanescent value, a *Memoir* as long and as elaborate as yours will be very much the tail that wags the dog. As I often told you, if they who loved Watty MacDonald had known in 1922 that the *Reminiscences* were under their hand in Dublin, they would undoubtedly have taken advantage of the lawlessness of the

> times and burned them. The Watty who taught us and the Watty of the *Reminiscences* are two separate persons.
> One could draw two different portraits of MacDonald:
> (1) As a forward-looking, progressive scholar who found himself impeded on all sides by obscurantists in his life-long dedication to the synthesis of Science and Philosophy, in a word, an *Athanasius contra mundum*.
> (2) As one whose over-burden of work left him no scope for the deep study that would have been necessary to propound convincingly theories that would challenge much of the generally accepted theology of the Church – a man of extraordinarily intense spiritual life, yet an iconoclast to the roots of his being.
>
> The theories in Physics which to make the background of our Philosophy Dr. MacDonald strove so vigorously – these theories have been more thoroughly abandoned than anything of Aristotle. *Motion* examined under the postulates of modern Physics, is more anachronistic than the *Principia*.
>
> His imprudences continued over a quarter of a century...He escaped the weightier consequences because Bishop O'Donnell, with more credit to his heart than to his head, was always prepared to intervene, and Bishop O'Donnell was the potent force in the Irish Hierarchy of that period.
>
> There were two ways of looking at MacDonald and his activities. Fifty years ago around the Park of Maynooth the students of my generation argued the pros and cons. We tended to be for Watty; the man's personal charm ensured our love and admiration. Yet though we were hero-worshippers we were not fools. We did recognise that there was another side to the picture which Denis Gwynn has done very little to present.
>
> In everything non-essential, the Memoir is satisfying.

Others of MacDonald's former students adopted the same attitude as Duggan. Perhaps the fairest comment was made by Austin Quinn, bishop of Kilmore: 'It is too bad that one of his sanctity, brilliance and honesty has bequeathed to posterity but his one blind spot.'

The tragedy of Walter MacDonald was that though he held a position of great prestige in the Irish Church over a long period, he saw himself as labouring for an ungrateful Church which gave him, he complained, 'no badge to wear in token of being recognised'.* He never came to terms with the simple fact that when it comes to filling its top positions academic brilliance is not the only criterion demanded by the Church. Undoubtedly he had to endure the fact that men of lesser intellectual calibre were more than once preferred for non-academic posts both inside and outside of Maynooth. His tragedy was that he could not understand the reason.

Of what did the flaw in his personality consist? Duggan speaks of his 'imprudences'. Austin Quinn refers to his 'blind spot'. But neither of them was prepared to be specific. But reading the *Reminiscences* as detachedly as possible one cannot escape the conclusion that his trouble was intellectual pride which led him to make serious errors of judgement. Take, for instance, the following passage in his book, pathetic but also revealing and damning:

> What is the use of one like me trying to be safe? May not one as well go for the truth bald-headed? I must, after all, have been asking questions that should not be asked. Or is it that one may not ask a question of any kind, except, of course, of the enemies of the Church? Or, at least, that, when you have got your answer – such as has been found satisfactory hitherto – you are to put no supplementary question, but must, if you do not feel justified, beat your breast humbly and penitently, with a 'What a conceited and withal, stupid, theologian I must be!
>
> How many a rough, honest poor fellow – the Dobbins of life – has served and worshipped a mistress for years and years, living on a smile now and then, and content to wear away his life – ever so many lives – in her service, if only she will allow him to serve her, even without the reward of a smile....
>
> But how much more than crown and sceptre it would be if one heard her say occasionally, 'Well done; thou good and faithful' or if she gave one small badge to wear in token of being recognised as hers'.

How is it that Duggan in referring to MacDonald's imprudences never went on to investigate the cause? Was it out of respect for his former mentor or was it because he was blind to MacDonald's basic defect because he suffered from the same handicap himself? Perhaps there was more than a trace of intellectual pride in Tom's own make-up. One way or another, it would seem that perhaps more than any other human being MacDonald influenced Duggan's formation.

* MacDonald, Walter, *Reminiscences of a Maynooth Professor.*

In the final examination for the degree of Licentiate in Theology (S.T.L.) which took place at the end of the course, the order of merit was Paddy O'Neill of Limerick, Austin Quinn of Kilmore and Tom Duggan of Cork. The story goes that in the course of the examination Tom became involved in an argument with the senior professor of Scripture, Fr. Patrick Boylan whom he would have admired as a scripture scholar but not as a theologian.

Surprisingly, he was not invited back for his doctorate. It may not have been entirely for academic reasons. The alleged disagreement with Boylan may have been regarded by the authorities as evidence of intellectual pride. It may also have been that Daniel Coholan, by then Bishop of Cork, thought it was time to remove him from the influence of Walter MacDonald.

Duggan's friend, Paddy O'Neill, was invited back and in due course became a professor, Vice-President of Maynooth and Bishop of Limerick.

A humble man, he gave it as his opinion that Tom Duggan was better suited to the professorship than he. It is idle to speculate how the whole course of Duggan's life might have been very different had he been given the opportunity of further study in Maynooth.

During Tom's time in Maynooth as a post-graduate student, two notable events took place which interested him deeply; the Easter Rising of 1916 and the founding of the Maynooth Mission to China, later known as the Columban Fathers.

Under the Maynooth system of the time the students did not return home for Easter but stayed on at the college and entertained themselves with the college sports, normally a highlight of the Maynooth athletic programme. But in Easter 1916, there was little interest in sport. The solemn rule of silence was tacitly suspended. It could hardly have been otherwise when from points of vantage such as the top storey of St. Mary's they could plainly see the red glow over Dublin. Walter MacDonald gives a graphic description in his book:

> All that week guns could be heard thundering away. By day one could see great columns of smoke rising from the city, twelve miles away; by night it turned into a pillar of fire, and the whole inter-eastern sky was lit up by the burning.

The President of the time, Monsignor Hogan, known to the students as 'Allez' was a graduate of the Sorbonne and as one might expect from a French-trained priest of the time he abhorred the very words 'rebellion' and 'violence'. One can imagine his horror, then, when on Easter Sunday he heard the tramp of armed men moving up through St. Joseph's Square and coming to a halt underneath his window. It transpired that they were a company of the local Volunteers on their way to join in the fight in Dublin. Hogan was in a quandary. What these men had in mind was totally against his principles but on the other hand they were neighbours and were led by Donal O Buachalla, the most prominent man in the town and a supplier of the college. It would have been very poor public relations to refuse them a blessing. Hogan compromised: he gave them his blessing as individuals going into danger but not to their cause.

A day or two later Hogan came upon a large group of his students being put through their paces in a drilling practice in the Junior Garden. In fairness to Hogan he kept his feelings under control and contented himself with the mild admonition: 'Gentlemen, you would be well advised to disperse!'

Information as to Tom Duggan's movements during the week are sparse. Normally as a post-graduate he would have been entitled to spend the Easter holidays at home. Whether 'the close contacts he had with the upper ranks of Sinn Féin', which he referred to later, meant that he had some inside information about the Rising is unknown, but it is known that Ned, the quiet man of the family, became involved. A civil servant in London he happened to find himself in Dublin on Easter Monday on his way to Cork. He never got there. He calmly walked up to the first Volunteer outpost he saw and asked for a gun. He was captured, imprisoned in Kilmainham and later transferred to Wakefield. On his release, naturally, there was no question of returning to the British civil service. A *persona non grata* in England, he set up a consultancy business in Dublin and after the Treaty secured a post in the Irish civil service.

Duggan's attitude to the Rising is revealed in a letter written on 16 June 1916, to a friend living abroad:

> It may interest you to know that anything you have hitherto heard about the Rising is a lie. I warn you not to believe one single word against the Volunteers. We are not beaten yet when we can produce men like them.

The founding of the Maynooth Mission to China, later known as the Columban Fathers, was another event which upset the even tenor of life in Maynooth in those years. The founders of the Society were Dr. John Blowick, a professor in Maynooth, and Fr. Ned Galvin, a priest of the Cork diocese on loan to the diocese of Brooklyn. Their dream was of another great missionary movement in the Far East akin to the vision of Columban and Killian in the Europe of their time.

When the first house of the Society was opened in 1918, it had already attracted ten Maynooth students. It nearly gained Tom Duggan also as we see from a letter written to a friend who had joined:

> I hope you are having a happy and successful mission. I am sure God is rewarding you even in this life for your sacrifice. About myself, I am no nearer to going than last year. The only thing that makes any appeal to me is to find Irishmen and dear friends with their backs to the wall, fighting God's battle against fearful odds. It seems to be up to one's manhood to strike in and help. But surely that is not sufficient. If you and Galvin and to a lesser extent Reilly were not fighting out there it would never occur to me to go.
>
> After the most searching introspection, that is the nearest thing to a call I can discover. I am afraid to go on such an arduous work without a more definite vocation. Will you please pray for me that God may deign to reveal to me where he wants me. I hope to talk the whole subject out with Galvin when I see him. I believe he is coming home.

At the time then it appears that he concluded that he had not received a clear call for that particular mission. But all through life he kept up his contacts with the Columbans and for Bishop Galvin in particular he felt a great sense of reverence and admiration.

Very few items remain of the correspondence received by Tom whilst a student at Maynooth. There are two letters from John Hennessy, a great family friend who had succeeded his father as principal of Ballyheeda school. Both refer to the history of the game of hurling. There is also a very droll letter from Ned about the game at local level:

> Did you hear that Ballinhassig are playing for the Cork and Bandon Shield. We played the first match last Sunday – against Knockavilla. I was in goal. Luckily I got scarcely anything to do. Knockavilla were useless and we had great backs – Butler and Jerome Crowley could play for the county. Needless to say I won't remain in goal: I stayed there last Sunday very much against my will and because no one else would take the job.
>
> I suppose you heard of the great Jack Lucey. He used to live in Waterfall about 50 years ago, the terror of the county in hurling. He used to practise very hard – not much else indeed. Every year when

> the stones were being picked out of his fields and heaped in a corner, he hired two young fellows for a week – the best shots he could find. Then he stood up on the ditch and the young fellows fired at him as hard as they could. Lucey used never simply stop the stones but swung on them with the full length of his hurley.

The fact that he was not recalled for a doctorate in Maynooth did not worry Tom unduly. At heart he was not an academic – it would tie him down too much. By nature and inclination he was a freelance. It was the summer of 1917 and he was aged twenty-seven. He was not yet ready mentally or psychologically to go home to his diocese – he felt he needed to broaden his horizons a little before settling down.

An appeal for Irish priests willing to serve as chaplains with the British Forces engaged in World War I had recently been made by Cardinal Logue. It seemed providential, an answer to prayer as far as Tom Duggan was concerned.

Before leaving Maynooth his mind was made up – he was going to volunteer.

1 Keith Amos, *The Fenians in Australia*, page 279 gives a rather harrowing picture of the old patriots last years:
'Duggan had returned from his Goomalling teaching position at 82 years of age, then entered an old men's refuge as a pauper.... Within a few months funds were on hand to settle Duggan and Kelly in a cottage in North Perth... The Celtic Club had planned to assist Duggan to return to the care of his relatives in Ireland, but a sudden decline in his health – from Parkinson's disease – caused arrangements to be abandoned. He was admitted in 1905 to St. John of God hospital, Subiaco.'
Fortunately Mr. Walter McGrath, through the good offices of Fr. Senan, O.F.M. Cap. has been able to publish a somewhat brighter account of Duggan's last years in the care of the St. John of God Sisters. (Hunting up the Last Years of 'Australian Tom Duggan', *Cork Evening Echo*, 4.VII.1969.)
'In hospital he was a great favourite. Although held in affection he was also regarded with respect and some little awe, as befitting a literary man who had suffered for his patriotic views, and he was always referred to as "Mr. Duggan", never "Tom" or "Duggan".'

2 Leon O'Broin, *Studies*, Winter, 1963, page 358 - Professor P.J. Corish agrees with O'Broin:
'The balanced assessment by Leon O'Broin is rightly severe on MacDonald, not only for his account of the affair but for his part in it: as he sums up, MacDonald fed fuel to O'Hickeys discontent form own sense of grievance.' (Patrick J.Corish, *The Irish Catholic Experience*, page 240.)

WAR CHAPLAIN

CHAPLAIN TO THE BRITISH FORCES IN WORLD WAR I

It may appear strange that a person of Duggan's Fenian background and of strong nationalist views should volunteer for a military chaplaincy with the British Forces. His former professor, Dr. Daniel Coghlan, then Bishop of Cork, must have been surprised when he sought permission although he was well aware of Cardinal Logue's appeal for chaplains and that in fact a number of his priests including Dr. Joseph Scannell of Farranferris were already serving as chaplains.

Duggan himself has given different answers. In an early account he implies that his motives were purely spiritual:

> My generation in Maynooth embraced the ideals of Easter Week, 1916, with a hundred percent fervour. This did not prevent us from becoming chaplains in the British Army. In the first World War there were well over 100,000 Irish Catholics in the fighting ranks. (The casualties alone were 50,000.)
>
> Everyone admitted that these boys were spiritually intractable to anyone save an Irish priest. Hence, when Cardinal Logue issued a special appeal for Irish Chaplains, I volunteered. And I went off to France with the blessing and encouragement of every friend I had in advanced Sinn Féin circles in Dublin.

This seems clear enough but judging from another account which he wrote when President of Farranferris it would appear that there were several motives:

> I left Maynooth in 1917, and partly because Dr. Watty MacDonald recommended it, wholly because I liked it, I sought and obtained permission to become an Army Chaplain.
>
> Why did I go? There was the ordinary priestly motives of being in a position to do good. There was the glamour of war. And, to be frank, I must recall that the idea of seeing the world at John Bull's expense did weigh with me.
>
> Anyhow I joined. I had some qualms as a hot Sinn Féiner. I rather think it was to Alfie Manahan* I submitted this scruple and I

* Fr. Manahan was one of the Vincentian spiritual directors.

> promptly got Alfie's *congé*. I really had no difficulty. It was a non-combatant service and if poor fools of Irishmen, through choice or necessity, went to fight for 'the rights of small nations' someone had to follow them to look after their souls.

His associates in the national movement had no difficulty in coming to terms with a Duggan in British uniform. For instance, Todd Andrews in his book *Dublin Made Me* has this to say: 'Fr. Tom Duggan, himself a staunch Republican, had been a British Army Chaplain because he believed that souls had neither nationality nor politics!'

Duggan has left a written account of his actual departure. It is so dramatised that it is hard to regard it as entirely factual.

> In Cork, on Saturday, 16 September, I very furtively got into poor King George's uniform and made a dash for the mail train. I went down to Maynooth that night. I well remember everyone seemed to sneer at my uniform. Probably all my imagination but anyhow early next day I borrowed a bicycle and made for Dublin. I called to the North Dublin Union (since absorbed), and the holy nuns there nearly threw me out first. They were seething with patriotism at the time and the sight of me in my uniform gave them sore distress. However, after a struggle, holy religion triumphed and they gave me coffee.
>
> God help us! It is hard to say who were the more innocent. They proposed and I agreed that being a Captain in the King's Army all prison doors without doubt would fall before me. I ought to explain that poor Tom Ashe's hunger-strike was on and they had heard nothing of him for days. Therefore the brainwave! I was to present myself at Mountjoy gates and demand admittance.
>
> So I abandoned the bicycle. (Incidentally in the excitement I forgot to write to the Revd. owner and he did not recover it for months.) I hied away to Mountjoy. To my relief (and surprise) no one embarrassed me by turning out the guard. I might have been the bread man for all the notice anyone took of me. Needless to say, I did not get to see poor Ashe, and when I heard of him next (in France) he was dead.
>
> So I returned to my holy nuns. The poor ladies sang another hymn of hate – confirmed all their worst suspicions of poor John Bull.

There seems to be a certain insensitivity towards the feelings of others in these lines. For instance, did it not occur to him that Ashe, then close to death, might not welcome any visitor arriving in British uniform, even a priest? But then there was a trace of naivety in Duggan, an insensitivity towards the feelings of others: it was as if he believed that people would know instinctively that his motives were always the best.

Did he misread the signs of the times and fail to foresee that a turning-point was near in the struggle for Irish freedom? In fact, within a few days of Tom Ashe's death, standing at his graveside, Michael Collins delivered what must have been the shortest oration in history as he pointed the way ahead: 'Nothing else remains to be said. The volley which you have just heard is the only speech it is proper to make over the grave of a dead Fenian.'*

Had Duggan waited a few more days, might his resolve to make his way to the Western Front have weakened? We shall never know.

The war situation in Flanders was grim when he arrived there in early October, 1917. The war had proved a disaster for all concerned. It had largely been an artillery, a heavy-gun, war. Very many of its participants would carry the painful effects of shell-shock with them for the rest of their lives.

Each side had launched major offensives, beginning with the great German offensive of September, 1914 which all but finished the war. This was followed by the first battle of Ypres, ending in stalemate, followed in 1915 by the equally inconclusive second battle of Ypres.

Then came 1916, the year of the slaughter, massacres on the French side at Verdun, on the British side on the Somme, for the Germans in both battles, each of which lasted for months.

1917 was not quite so bad but it was still brutal. It had begun with a Spring offensive with high hopes of success by the British and French with a series of battles known as the third battle of Ypres. It continued right through the year with fearful losses on both sides, particularly for the British at Paschendaele, a name that for years after sent shivers down the spines of the survivors. It had been a year of high hopes and grim despair, especially in its final phase around the town of Cambrai where the British introduced their new mechanised weapon, the tank, only to see it ending in failure like all the others.

Coming towards the end of 1917, therefore, after three years of deadly war, both sides finished up almost as they had started, facing each other across a muddy and barbed-wire hell called *No Man's Land*. High hopes and miserable defeats, a depressing Christmas surely.

* Dwyer, T. Ryle, *Michael Collins*.

The war had become a war of attrition, a dirty, grinding, monotonous, soul-destroying experience that seemed endless and pointless. After three years of massive losses on both sides, the territorial gains were minimal. Conditions in the trenches were primitive in the extreme and shell-shocked soldiers abounded. Morale was at a low ebb and the French in particular were at times very close to open mutiny. The 'war to end wars' had turned very sour.

All in all, it must have been a shattering experience for Duggan when he arrived in Flanders in 1917. It is true that he was spared the more brutal aspects of the fighting for some time because initially he was posted to a C.C.S., (a casualty clearing station) some distance from the front line. Nevertheless the reality of war must have been a rude shock.

If one can go by his letters, however, he did not allow the experience to dampen his spirits. He writes so light-heartedly and cheerfully that at times it actually seems as if he was enjoying the war. But on reading through his letters carefully one detects an underlying but very definite current of suffering, of compassion for the wounded and of a great distaste for the savagery that abounded, the overwhelming visual impact of 'man's inhumanity to man'.*

One must remember also the constraints within which he wrote. Most of his letters were to his mother and naturally in them he did not dwell on the unpleasant side of war. He also had to be careful about security restrictions, of talking about place-names, for instance, or where the different regiments were operating. His letters, therefore, do not give the whole picture but nevertheless they provide a wonderfully live portrayal of Duggan in a war-time situation.

His earlier letters were written from 15 C.C.S. but there is no indication of his whereabouts. His first letter was written to his mother on 11 October 1917.

> Nothing doing here. We only get the slightly wounded. I go to bed at 10 o'clock and get up at 7.30 as regular as clockwork. The Village Curé was very incensed with me because he heard that I knelt down and said a prayer for the poor German who died here. According to the Curé, he was no fit subject for anyone's prayers, sharing as he did in the Kaiser's sin in the same way as we share in Adam's.

Apparently his predecessor as chaplain had failed to draw in the crowds:

> I had Mass yesterday at nine o'clock. At 9.05 I had to look for the server. Then I found we had no breads so I had to send him to the

* Burns, Robert, *Man was made to mourn*.

> village. In the meantime my congregation (one) turned up. If Mass had been punctual he would have missed it altogether.

After a while under his urgings the pastoral situation began to improve.

> I heard about 30 Confessions and gave Communion, superintended by the Curé. The latter suggested that I should advise the men to contribute to his poor box. Am afraid I did not try to make my charity sermon very moving.

He did not find much sign of war 'hype' among the troops:

> I hear a good deal less war news than you do. I haven't met a soldier yet who isn't hungering for peace. The fight to a finish people one knocks across are in nine cases out of ten in nice comfortable billets.

He found that caring for the wounded can be a harrowing experience:

> A young officer came in this morning very badly wounded in the abdomen. I gave him absolution and anointed him. He died during the night. There is a chap here named Murray, he is another of my men. His brain was touched by a bullet. For a week he was doing well but he has relapsed.
>
> We don't get the bad cases but even here things are pitiful enough. It is awful to see fine young lads deaf, dumb and practically senseless from shell-shock. If you like, that is anti-climax for the poor women who brought them into the world.

He seemed to be moving around constantly:

> I never read, never stay indoors – back to the land isn't in it with this life.
>
> I had occasion to go to a spot the other day about five miles from the line. I was amused to see a merry-go-round. It reminded me of the day Strip Murphy got sick in the swing boats with me and my penny went wrong.
>
> I was around this evening and people have a habit of pairing off on a fine evening like at home. The only thing I notice is that people here are not so easily non-plussed. Their hands are far more tenacious on their neighbours' waists.

Sometimes distinguished visitors arrived, like Cardinal Bourne, the Archbishop of Westminster:

> Cardinal Bourne is coming over and there is tremendous excitement. He is to meet all the chaplains of the area next week. I'll turn up there if I can, not to see him but on the off chance of meeting a few boys I know.
>
> You have no idea how hard it is for a chaplain to do anything for these poor fellows who come in wounded. Doctors and Nurses are buzzing around and you are made to feel you are only barely tolerated. Besides to clear them away at a critical moment might mean taking from a chap a chance of life.

On 18 October he seemed in great good humour when writing:

> Life is flowing along very smoothly. This evening I had Confessions from 6.30 - 7.30. Not a soul turned up.
>
> I met among some Australian patients a fellow called Casey. He was born in Leap. His zeal for the Empire leaves a good deal to be desired.

But on 22 October he was home-sick: 'No *Weekly Examiner* yet. I wish I had a little Cork news. Mud all over the place. Were it not for my two pairs of artillery boots I'd be lost.'

On 28 October the Cardinal duly arrived and Tom formed part of the welcoming party:

> Yesterday all the chaplains of the area met Cardinal Bourne at the convent in whose grounds poor W. Redmond lies buried. I hope when I knelt down to say my prayers at his grave I wasn't misunderstood.

On 10 November he tells his mother that he has had a letter from Jer, his brother. Jer is also in the British Army but has not yet succeeded in getting overseas:

> I had a letter from Jer this morning. How sad his journey to the Front is being continually postponed. If he doesn't come soon he is likely to miss the fighting. It looks as if the war will be over soon.

He was on his way to hear Confessions but he was not very hopeful: 'If I have luck, I may have one. It won't be more and it won't be less.'

He wrote to Lucy for her birthday and sent a present: 'I'd send more but I am afraid if I did so, you would be admonished to spend it on something useful.'

He had been to Bethune to visit his cousin, Sister Laurence. He travelled by train:

> The French trains are the limit. The Schull Express is a flier compared to them.
>
> Bethune is less than four miles from the Front. The Town-Hall clock can be seen from the German trenches. When it goes wrong the Germans regulate it with gun fire.
>
> The nuns were wonderfully decent to me but somewhat overpowering. They all insisted on kissing me. Two goes each, one for each cheek.

He was thinking of leave when he wrote on 24 November:

> My three months are up on the 18th December and who knows what a grateful country may do.
>
> The Belgians are at a discount out here at present, both with English and French. The village Curé can't understand what any sensible people see in them to fight for.

On 14 December he writes to say he has a new address: 'Ist Battalion Royal Dublin Fusiliers will find me.'

On Christmas night he was very lonely: he wrote to his mother:

> This is my first Christmas night away from home and I am feeling it. There is great talk of peace here. It seems the Kaiser's forthcoming note is likely to be dealt with more ceremoniously than his other efforts.
>
> I am on Midnight Mass tonight. I shall say it for you and for your intentions. My battalion is in the line at present. The poor lads are in shell holes. There is no room for me as I am away down here miles away. You can't get near them in daylight as the Germans are not supposed to know where they are.

He kept the good news for the last: 'I have just been transferred to the Munsters and Connaughts which means I am off in a half hour to a place miles down the line.'

The Munster Fusiliers And The Calm Before The Storm

Insofar as man can be happy near the front line in war, Duggan was happy in the company of the Connaught Rangers and the Munster Fusiliers for the first few months of 1918, the final year of the war.

He had got his long-awaited leave early in the New Year and when he returned from home in Ballyheeda towards the end of January things were as quiet as ever. His journey back was by slow stages as he told his mother on 23 January:

> Got to Boulogne yesterday, at 5 o'clock. Left it at 9 and arrived in Amiens at 2 a.m. Had a stroll in the moonlight (not by choice but I got lost on the way) and then went to the Officers Rest House. All beds full but I slept very comfortably in the rug which I was lucky enough to forget to post at Folkstone. Said Mass this morning in Amiens Cathedral and now (12 a.m.) I am half-way back to the Division.

He arrived in due course and wrote again on 26 January: 'Going strong à la Johnny Walker. Back to same place and as quiet as ever....a very comfortable billet.'

On 1 February he wrote: 'I am afraid my letters have been very irregular lately. I promise amendment....I am in the front line at present. It is horribly quiet.'

Writing on 4th February, he had the same story to tell:

> Another day gone and I haven't written. The peace and quiet here is 'almost' distressingly monotonous – only 'almost' because needless to say I am only too delighted. We are moving soon away down the line.

He wrote to Jer a few days later:

> I am now attached to the 1st Munsters. The 2nd are now joined to the Div. and the two battalions are side by side here.
>
> Where do you expect to be sent? It would be nice to have you here but make a bid for Salonika if you can at all manage it.
>
> I have just now arranged a hurling match between the 1st and 2nds. It is to come off in about a fortnight.

> Kane, the C.O., is a rather original kind of ass. He confided in me yesterday that he was not at all pleased with Fr. Gleeson who wasn't 'a fighting parson'. Also he promised to give me points for sermons. Taken all in all, a most fascinating study.

On 10 February he mentioned that he had sent his mother some books; among them was Canon Sheehan's *The Graves of Kilmorna*, the great Fenian story. He gives a very amusing account of his domestic arrangements. Apparently by then he had acquired the services of a batman called David and he is loud in his praise:

> My dug-out is running into all manner of luxuries. We have now reached the stage of a steel boot-scraper and a bath. Needless to say I carefully avoid the scraper but I use the bath twice a week. The bath is a tub which David obtained. When it gets dark and the enemies of the human race can't see us we light a fire. Then in two petrol cans we heat water and everything is ready. D. retires and I proceed to scald and otherwise harass passers-by. Then I don clean clothes and in return retire while D. launders my dirty linen.
>
> The boy is invaluable. I always sub-consciously think of him as Jeeves. He is terribly superstitious. I had considerable difficulty the other day in assuring him that no harm would come to him even if he did look at a priest's bare feet.

He wrote again on the following day:

> Jeeves increases daily in virtue. The only thing is he is becoming terribly ambitious. He has been ironing my shirts and handkerchiefs for quite a while and now wants to get to work on the alb. I haven't had the cruelty – or possibly the moral courage to refuse him so I compromised. I told him I would have to get blue and starch first. I am hoping that will deter him but though the nearest shop is 25 miles away I shall not be a bit surprised if he has some tomorrow.
>
> He belongs to the Connaughts but I shall try to take him with me to the Munsters. I change over tomorrow.

Writing to Lucy soon after he had a funny story:

> I was down the line today. Coming back I met a youth from Blackpool who confided in me he had walked 4 miles (he meant 2)

> for a 'bat' and 'clane shirt' and that it was not 'wort' it. From what I know of him I doubt it.
>
> Jeeves' latest exploit. During the week I have lost two pipes. He has just turned up with a second-hand Kapp and Peterson. Where he may have procured it I shudder to think but it is smoking well.

Writing on 13 February, Tom is in high good humour:

> Less than ever happening. I had cabbage yesterday which was got in 'no-man's land'.
>
> Jeeves continues to progress in virtue. He has now gone in for table decorations. I am now confronted with two vases of flowers. He is sharing my billet with me at present. He sleeps on the floor and I, I am ashamed to confess, on the bed.

Writing to his mother on 17 February he told her that he was hoping to meet Dr. Scannell, another Cork chaplain who is working not very far away. He says: 'I was surprised to hear Jer was at Tilbury Docks. That looks as if his commission were in the Dublins.'

On 18 February he assured his mother that he was happy: 'Still going strong. Nothing doing. I am enjoying life thoroughly at present. Hope to move away down the line very soon. What is Son's address? I would like to write to him.'

He had news to report on 21 February:

> Sorrow of sorrows. I have lost Jeeves. He had to remain with the Connaughts.
>
> I have a new servant, a youth named Danny Kenny from Shandon St. My eyes are red from weeping for Jeeves. If he had remained with me I should be the most hen-pecked man in Europe but it would be well worth it.
>
> The Munsters had a famous raid the other night. I have a souvenir for you – a German flash lamp. One of the escorts of an unfortunate prisoner gave it to me. It was most amusing to hear them marching to the starting-off point whistling *The Rising of the Moon*.

A few days later he reported that life is still very uneventful: 'My new man though not a Jeeves is doing A.1. Jeeves is now ministering to the new chaplain of the Connaughts.'

News was scare on 24 February:

> I am writing once more to assure you there is nothing to be said. I am living (and very comfortably) 50 feet below the ground at present.
>
> They are sending for shamrocks already here. A number of females called the Irish Womens' Association are only too glad to get something to fuss over.
>
> I saw in the *Times* that Jer has been gazetted as from the 30th ult. Hope he will go to Salonika. If he comes out here there is an even chance that I will be his chaplain.
>
> I was very sorry to hear that war-bread had disagreed with you. I wish you could have some of the stuff we get. It is still pure white.

Tom's sister, Lucy, had started a camogie team in Ballinhassig and he teases her about it:

> I am sure your mother, grounded in the Model School in loyalty and respectability, will hesitate to allow you identify yourself with the disgruntled malcontents who misrepresent our old and historic parish.

On 4 March, all was quiet on the Western Front:

> Nothing happening. We move out today for a rest. The poor men want it though I have been very comfortable here.
>
> I spent today and yesterday learning how to ride a horse. Am doing well. The brute ran away with me today.

He wrote a long letter on 8 March:

> After forty-two days in the line we are having a very easy time now. While in the line I always slept in my trousers and pyjama jacket. It worked wonderfully. My under-clothing of course had lost much of its virgin whiteness. However, Danny – my new boy – has a grand bleach out at present.
>
> I am afraid that Son has been painting the town. I hope that he will lose his commission. His stay at Moorpark has served its purpose and he would be safer out here as a full private.
>
> I am having riding lessons at present. I can just stick on now.

> I was sorry to hear of poor Redmond's death – sorry and glad because his political life was over in any case and he has made the most dignified possible exit (R.I.P.).

In a note to Lucy he confided that his riding lessons were not going very well: 'My nose is all swollen today – one side of it sticking over the edge of my face. That unfortunate horse bumped his face into mine.'

On 9 March the Munsters were still resting:

> The weather here is glorious. I have spent all yesterday and today hurling. Where we are at present you'd never dream there was a war on. We are having Benediction this evening. Needless to say I am in good voice.
>
> Don't worry your head about Son. When his money is spent (which it probably is by this) he will be alright.

He wrote two important letters on 19 March. To his mother he concentrated on Jer's welfare and spoke about the very ominous calm on the Western Front:

> Any more about Son lately? The chances are that he will be let off with a reprimand. I hope sincerely they will deprive him of his commission because it has served its purpose and as a full private he would be exposed to far less temptation than as an officer.
>
> With Ned I am inclined to pity him and only to blame him in a very secondary way. He is quite incapable of causing all this worry and trouble out of pure malice. What he wants is a wife. If he got a proper martinet I can see him the most law-abiding (and hen-pecked) man in Europe.
>
> Nothing doing here. There are all kinds of rumours of offensives, counter offensives but nothing ever happens. I am still in that little village from which I started for home the last time. However, the place is so quiet now that we no longer sleep in a cellar. In some ways I miss it. Especially the dirt ....
>
> I ought to be at home for my birthday with any luck – the first time for I don't know how many years.
>
> I am enclosing a cheque. My account mounts up very fast as I have no expenses. If I kept it I should only fritter it away. Would you or Lucy take it as a present. As far as I know I have nearly as much more.

> I had nearly forgotten to thank you ever so much for the shamrock. It arrived just in time – the evening of the 16th. I never saw so fine a bunch. I had a square yard of it on my cap. It was green and fresh. Dom* sent me some. It arrived on the eve of the 17th and was all shrivelled.

In his letter to Lucy he gave a hilarious account of the St. Patrick's Day celebrations:

> We celebrated St. Patrick's Day in great style. We meant to have an open-air Mass but when we arrived at the place selected there were four German sausages (observation balloons) gazing down at us so we decamped another half-mile to a hut. The boys sang 'Hail Glorious St. Patrick' till they were black in the face. Of course I had to tell them that St. P. (as might be expected from a man of discernment) held the men of Munster in a special esteem. As a matter of fact I believe he boycotted them.
>
> After dinner we had a hurling match (which I refereed). Most of the spectators were from Cork city. You'd think you were at the Athletic Grounds to hear the shouting 'Go on, Tarry', 'Go on, Busty'. The warriors referred to are known in their official capacity as Sergeant O'Donoghue (from de Marsh, Fader) and Sergeant Busteed (from de sout side.).
>
> After the match they consumed 20 barrels of beer and weren't a bit the worse for it. It is only the light French ale and has no effect on them. I went down to their concert about 9 o'clock. I made for the biggest knot of men. That was where the beer-barrel was. About twenty yards away there was a much smaller crowd. That was the stage where someone was singing of:
>
> The men who knew no fears,
the Munster Fusiliers.
>
> I was talking to one of them the other day. He was temporarily in bad humour about something: 'If I was once back in Cork, Fader, with Bull's cap off me, the divil himself wouldn't drag me out again.' They always refer to the Empire as 'Bull'. It is great to hear them when both artilleries are bombarding, 'Go on, Jerry', 'Go on, Bull', 'One up for Bull', etc. etc.

* 'Dom' was Sister Dominic of the South Presentation Convent.

The final letter from the Western Front was written on the following day, 18 March. In view of what was about to happen, it is full of dramatic irony:

> I sent to J. Beckett to forward to me 6 hurleys. So far I have not heard from him. Don't be a bit worried about me. This will add years to my life. And as far as danger goes I am as safe here as 2, Morningside.*
>
> You don't give me a bit of B'hassig news. Did anyone succeed even in getting arrested? How is the Sinn Féin club going?

The next communication to reach Ballinhassig was in the form of a telegram from the War Office, London, dated 8 April, 1918 to 'Cassidy, Ballinhassig, Co. Cork. [Fr. Cassidy was the Duggans' local priest.] Regret Capt. Rev. T.F. Duggan reported missing March twenty second. No details known. Secy. War Office.'

One can imagine his poor mother's feelings. But the next day there was a second telegram addressed to 'Duggan, Ballinhassig, Cork' with somewhat better news: 'Thomas Francis Duggan Munster Fus. Prisoner War unwounded. Camp unknown. Signed 'Prisoners, South Kensington'.

And so Duggan and the Munster Fusiliers parted company. They had got on famously together. He would miss them sorely over the next six months.

Prisoner of War

In the Spring of 1918, the Germans concluded realistically that if they were to win the war they had no alternative but to risk everything on a massive pre-emptive stroke against England and France before unlimited American resources could be brought into play. They had no new revolutionary military tactic such as the Allies had discovered in the form of the self-propelling tank, a very destructive and demoralising new weapon; the Germans had to rely on the old methods, a pulverising preliminary bombardment followed by wave after wave of infantry attacks to infiltrate and overcome a demoralised enemy.

And so at 4.40 a.m. on the morning of 21 March, the 'Big Push' began, a mere four days after the Munster Fusiliers had celebrated St. Patrick's Day so memorably. The attack began, in a dense fog, the most frightful artillery bombardment of the whole war. A historian has described the bombardment as 'the most concentrated artillery bombardment the world had ever known':

> Nearly six thousand German guns opened fire almost simultaneously along the forty mile front between the Sensee river and the Oise.

* His mother's address in Cork.

> Tons of steel and high explosive fell with shattering force upon the forward positions and the Battle Zone. As the men crouched deafened and dazed in their trenches or staggered drunkenly towards control points, the ground rocked and heaved under them, the surrounding fog coiled and twisted, then sweetened suddenly with the sinister taint of lethal and lachrymatory gas. Shocked, cursing with anger, yet sick with fear, those who survived the first few seconds pulled on their gas masks and listened despite themselves for the sound of their own deaths rushing near.
>
> It was all done systematically, accurately and inexorably.....At 9.40 a.m., the German infantry rose to their feet and stormed forward. Aided by the fog, they passed quickly through the forward positions, evading the known isolated posts and redoubts. Behind them the second and third attack waves mopped up – sometimes by merely directing dazed and bleeding prisoners to the rear, sometimes completing the havoc of the guns with bayonet and rifle butt.*

Basil Liddell Harte, the military historian, sums up the early phase of the offensive:

> By nightfall a German flood had inundated the British front; a week later it had reached a depth of nearly forty miles, and was almost lapping the outskirts of Amiens; and in the ensuing weeks the Allied cause itself was almost submerged.†

But the Germans failed to maintain their all-conquering opening impetus; the offensive gradually lost momentum, giving time to the demoralised British and French to regroup. Germany never recovered.

But how had Tom Duggan fared on that fateful morning? He never claimed to have played a hero's part; he frankly admitted that he was terrified out of his wits. He admitted also that afterwards his nerves were never quite the same. Those who lived in the same house thirty years later remember how a sudden noise such as a door banging would startle him even then, and how as President of Farranferris he so arranged that the room above his bedroom was always left vacant.

He wrote his own personal account of his experiences on the opening days of the offensive, at the request of the War Office:

* Pitt, Barrie, *The Last Act.*

† Harte, Liddell, *History of the First World War.*

> At the beginning of the German offensive, I was R.C. Chaplain to the First Royal Munster Fusiliers. When the bombardment opened I took up as Battle position (appointed for me by Senior Div. Chaplain) the Regt. Aid Post. Worked all day on March 21st. On the morning of the 22nd had warning Germans were coming. Might (chances against) have escaped but Aid Post was full of wounded – a large portion of them delirious from lack of water. German advance party entered about 8.30 a.m. Ordered out of Regt. Aid Post by larger party about 12.30 p.m. By all treated with extreme courtesy and consideration.

In the prison-diary which he kept very faithfully, Duggan gives a more detailed account of those grim days:

> 21 March, 1918. Bombardment opened at 4.45 a.m. Nearly killed by 5.09. Worked at Aid Post in St. Emile all day. My only memory of that evening is that everyone I knew especially in the Connaughts was either brought in badly wounded or I heard they were killed.
>
> 22 March. Captured once at 9 a.m. but Germans driven back. Captured again at 1 p.m. In meantime almost murdered by our own artillery. Taken to Ronnsoy through fields with easy-going German escort. Anointed many. One (Evangelist) wanted me to pray with him. Turned him over to Scanlen* sorry.... In meantime I had a look at the wounded, and pitiful they looked in the evening light.
>
> We started off again, got to La Bassée. Had to wait for escort. Got Doc's sheepskin and was fast asleep when escort came. Had to help carry a badly wounded German.
>
> At a make-shift C.C.S. met a German chaplain. He was very kind but could do little. Secured a stretcher and managed to get my head inside tent. Too cold to sleep. Dozed till morning. Saw German chaplain gazing at me very pityingly once. Got near fire in the morning and slept decently for an hour.

So began Duggan's long, harrowing, and hungry journey into captivity. It subsequently transpired that their final destination was the city of Mainz in the South of Germany at the junction of the rivers Rhine and Mainz. It seems very odd that with so many far more weighty matters in mind the Germans should have gone to so much trouble to transport their captives to a prison of war camp

* Scanlen was a Church of England Chaplain.

many hundreds of miles away. It is probably an example of the German habit of following regulations to the letter.

It took them a full month to reach Mainz, first on foot and then by frightfully slow German trains. Duggan remembered some of the highlights of the journey. Palm Sunday was 'a nice Spring day with a soft breeze blowing'. On Easter Sunday morning he 'read Book of Common Prayer for morning prayers .....Our jailers fed sumptuously if not aesthetically'.

On April 1 they reached Strasbourg, 'looked a very fine town, well laid out. Had a distant view of the Cathedral which looked small'. They went on to Karlshrue near the Rhine where they spent a week in a prison-camp. The food there was tolerable and they were well-treated.

After this they passed through some of the most beautiful country in Europe along the Rhine and Neckar valleys but of course they were not in the mood to enjoy scenery though Duggan did notice the beauty of Heidelberg, 'beautifully situated town'.

They finally arrived in Mainz where his prison life began in earnest. In his prison-diary which still survives, tattered and dog-eared, he poured out his soul. For one as hyper-active as Duggan, always in over-drive, it must have been a shattering experience. He had been very happy with the Munsters. Most of the rank and file came from Cork city, especially the North Side. He was able to identify fully with them, at work, at play, and at prayer. He loved their light-hearted approach to life and their cavalier attitude towards the war.

Now he was 'cribbed, cabin'd and confined' in a miserable row of huts. The distinction between officers and men was very strict in the German army which meant that he was completely separated from 'other ranks' and was now restricted to the company of a few officers, mostly doctors and chaplains. Most of the latter were Protestants and there was a small chapel which he shared with them.

Through the kindness of the local German priests he managed to assemble a Mass kit and the volumes of the Breviary. The German Camp Adjutant was a fervent Catholic and very helpful. After a while Duggan was able to celebrate Mass daily. Nevertheless his field of pastoral activity as a priest was very limited and to make up for this he tried to deepen and broaden his own spiritual life. The local priests brought in some theological books in Latin, relics of their Seminary days but rather heavy going for one in Duggan's situation. But he gradually found his interest reawakening in volumes like the *Summa Theologica* of St. Thomas Aquinas.

He was well treated in comparison with some prisoners of the past. He was not treated as an animal or as a slave as his grandfather had been in Portland and Freemantle. He had a fair amount of freedom within his own section of the prison camp, unlike Oscar Wilde in Reading jail, looking:

> With such wistful eye
> Upon that little tent of blue
> Which prisoners call the sky.*

The violence which Duggan experienced was not physical cruelty; it was rather violence of the spirit, the unceasing monotony and boredom, the lack of purpose, the inability to carry out a priest's work through lack of a flock to care for. It was a case of the good shepherd being deprived of his sheep.

He had never been one to worry about creature comforts; by no stretch of the imagination could he ever have been classified among *bon viveurs*. He had always been more or less indifferent to food, but in his diary, especially in the first few months of captivity he gives the impression that food had become something of an obsession; he constantly complained of hunger and its attendant weakness. The prisoners, therefore, must have been pretty close to starvation level.

Of course it was not altogether the Germans' fault. The 'Big Push' had failed, there was no further hope of a break-through. Morale was at a very low ebb. The hope of ultimate victory which had buoyed them up over the years was gone. Now with defeat and famine staring them in the face the Germans could hardly have been expected to provide the kind of food for their prisoners which they themselves did not enjoy.

As time went on, Duggan became more resigned to his lot, especially when food parcels containing mostly canned meat and vegetables began to arrive. To get an idea of his feelings at the time it may be helpful to quote some extracts from his prison diary:

> 19 April, 1918:
> Have spent first day in Mainz. Sad change as regards food after Karlsruhe. Hungry now but after a long, lingering look at my bread I have decided to fast.... Worked a bit at German today. Wonder will revival be like my Gaelic ones.
>
> Hope to be able to say Mass every morning next week. The C. of E's may prove embarrassing yet. The oratory is obviously Catholic and I do not like to allow them to pontificate there.

* 'The Ballad of Reading Jail', by Oscar Wilde, in the *Works of Oscar Wilde.*

I must make a determined effort to get back some degree of spirituality. I used to think that I once had some but the world has entered the holy place. Above all I must watch food and the snatching thereof. Too hungry to go to bed, I'm sick of German and in no hurry with the Office.

22 April:
Had a fairly substantial lunch but dinner very poor. Have encroached on reserve ration but am still (9.50 p.m.) as hungry as a wolf. Had a bath today and had clothes fumigated. Wanted it. Wish I could get a change.

26 April:
I don't want to meditate on food. Twenty minutes after dinner and feel hungry. German study very unsatisfactory. I do not quite know what is wrong.

29 April:
I felt in rotten form all day. So bad that I was not even hungry.

Thinking of asking Benby* to try and transfer me to privates' camp. Won't, I suppose, succeed. I wonder is the energizing motive zeal or patriotism or desire to be out of the ordinary, or chances of better food. Who shall say? Probably all enter in.

30 April:
Did no German. Ashamed. Tin of corned beef came in. Was generous though I doubt motive. Have arranged interview with Adjutant tomorrow re: May devotions .....Meal unsatisfactory. Am hungry.

1 May:
Did a little Theology. Interviewed Benby. No chance of getting to another camp as I seem to be more or less officially recognised here. Darned socks and pyjamas, and watered flowers in chapel during afternoon. German priest brought in a large bundle of theological material. Wish he had catered for body half as well as for soul and mind. Supper same as last night. It only made me hungry.

2 May:
Washed my shirt and forgot to bring it in off line. Didn't improve it much. Did a little theology in the morning and less German in the evening. Feeling very hungry.

* Benby was the German camp adjutant, a strong Catholic.

3 May:
Concert this afternoon. Bored me stiff. Good supper, exceeded ration, still hungry. Possibly only imagination. Inclined to think it is.

4 May:
Must look for a book giving a presentation of Germany's case.

5 May:
Steeped my under-pants today. Will wash it in the morning. Washed my shirt and under-shirt on Thursday and Saturday. Latter especially not a success.

Had hymns at Mass today, heard confessions and gave Communion; a short Benediction after Mass.

Waited an hour and a half for supper. Hardly worth it – only two potatoes (with their jackets on) and a sardine. After dinner came down to light fire. Stuffed too much shavings in: couldn't make them catch at first. Then they blazed out and singed eye-brows and hair.

Supper a poor thing. Feeling beautifully hungry. That is the only effect food seems to have. Before a meal one is weak, after it, hungry.

6 May:
Out in the open all the evening. Weather delightful. Still a mistake. Developed enormous appetite and dinner did very little to satisfy it.

7 May:
Was perfectly miserable all day with hunger ....Too weak to do German.

8 May:
Nearest thing to a birthday present was a rather full supper; feeling, if not satisfied, that I have had probably enough.

10 May:
Felt out of sorts all day. Got a pipe of English tobacco. Consoled me for indifferent supper.

Sunday, 12 May:
Said the 9 o'clock Mass. Did not preach. So badly prepared that I argued (I still think wisely) that they would be better without it.
Lunch almost a full meal. Hungry as a wolf for supper which wasn't bad.

13 May:
Did nothing all day. Feeling seedy. Laziness pure and simple.

14 May:
Comparatively speaking, a useful day. Read in turn Schopenhauer, German and a little Theology. Supper indifferent except for excellent hors d'oeuvre, basis of which was fish.

16 May:
For over a fortnight past, I have had a rash on my face. German priest called. Gave me a bit of bread and sardines. More appreciated I am afraid than promise of requested books.

20 May:
Reading my theologies for the past hour. Did not learn much.

24 May:
On very short rations for bread .... In cooking it yesterday to drive mildew out I scalded my fingers – two of them blistered.

28 May:
I had my first letter from home today. All well at home.

31 May:
Got a book containing two plays by G.B. Shaw in the library, one on marriage .... Wish the man would meditate a little on the fundamentals of Christian teaching. There may be more in them than he suspects.
Harks back *ad nauseam* to fact that a woman of spirit and honour cannot be expected to become a mother when the privilege has to be purchased at the price of becoming a wife. Can't see anything in that.

6 June:
Feast of Corpus Christi. Fr. Farning, the local priest, sent up monstrance, thurible and incense. We had Mass at 10 o'clock with the Blessed Sacrament exposed. How I wished I could have sung it. Benediction after Mass and at 4 o'clock. Meant to stay the whole day in the chapel. Did not spend a half hour all told.

3 June:
Never so hungry in all my life before. Yet should be satisfied as we had dried veg. and beans.

Preached twice. At Mass, to announce that we proposed to start a Sodality. Again in evening on John, chapter six. Sermon bad enough to make any man doubt the Real Presence.

Reading a good deal. Finished Shaw. Nothing worthy of note has stuck in my mind from his essay on censorship.

Sent all my clothes last evening to be fumigated. Had dinner in our rooms. No suppers at present. No parcels and fierce appetite.

8 June:
What a longing I have to get back once more to B'hassig. We had the first meeting of our Sodality last night. I addressed them and did it wonderfully badly. Daly spoke well. [He was another Catholic chaplain.]

9 June:
Gave £66 to distribute among needy orderlies. Am afraid I should have gone to work less ambitiously. It will not give them £2 each.
Mass this morning at 9. No sermon....I think Daly is right that no sermon is better than a bad one.

11 June:
There is an orderly here who speaks Irish. I wonder should I have a try at it. I do not quite know how my work is doing with the orderlies. I am certainly not an ideal chaplain for them but I must do my best.

12 June:
Called the orderlies together last night and appealed long and loud to them. Very few more than the usual number turned up for Mass.

16 June:
Passed last couple of days in a very unsatisfactory manner. Reading too much, and, I am afraid, eating too much. Reading trash again such as Kipling's short stories.

17 June:
Bath and finished letter for home..... St. Thomas is duller, drier and more unprofitable than ever.

25 June:
Rounded up 11 orderlies on Sunday. Preached on frequent Communion. Not very convincingly.

Have read in quick succession Wilde's *Dorian Gray* and *A Woman of no Importance.* Liked former very much. Good portion is, I imagine, autobiographical. Has left me with very soft spot for the author. Cannot understand outcry against it. Seems to me to be highly edifying – the pros and cons for a life of vice eloquently set forth and the cons convincingly winning.

Reading Pendennis. Prolix but charming.

Eyes are curiously painful and bad.

18 July:

Have just spent half an hour in the chapel. Resolutions:

1. Visit of $^1/_2$ hour daily to the chapel; 2. Be resigned; 3. Make most of your time.

19 July:

The Irish Women sending me more parcels than I want.....I read somewhere that when a beggar complained to Louis XIV that he was hungry, all Louis said was, 'happy devil'.

It is only now I am beginning to appreciate Louis' side of the story.

11 August:

Daly and myself finally decided yesterday to give a three day Retreat.

25 August:

German going passably well. Began to attend classes about three weeks ago.

Had a letter from home. The poor mater seems very cut up....I wonder which she would like better, my staying here in prison in Germany, away but safe, or at the front, in danger but going home occasionally.

16 September:

I should like to be transferred to a men's camp. An officers' no use because no Catholics. Any real Irishmen who have ever taken part in war have done so as hewers of wood and drawers of water.

1 October:

Everyone here bucked with the war news. Am afraid not quite in sympathy with the brethren about that. As a detached sportsman, one feels sorry to see a country which has put up such a fine fight against such odds verge on a breakdown.

16 October:

A number of officers – don't quite know how many – tried to get away last night. We are locked up.

This is the final entry in the diary. Among his papers, however, is a very interesting account written by Duggan about an effort made by the Germans to seduce him from carrying out his contract with the British Army:

> Speaking of sapping allegiance, a small effort was made on myself. About July, 1918, an Intelligence Officer from Frankfurt came to see me. [Frankfurt was Corps HQS]. He pointed out that Germany was obviously winning the war, but that owing to the obstinacy of Lloyd George and the *Daily Mail* that fact was not generally understood. Remember this was July, 1918. He wanted me to point out the desirability of peace by negotiation, and he guaranteed to get everything I said into the *Manchester Guardian* and the *Daily News.*
>
> I had to point out to him, of course, that, whatever about allegiance, I had a positive and unexpired contract with England. He argued long, and then he summed me up, uncharitably, one hopes:
>
> 'To meet an Irish patriot, a long distance I have come. An Irish patriot, I have not met. An Irish humbug, I have met. Good morning.'

Duggan's prison days were coming to an end. A few days before the war ended, the following brief note was added to his Army file:

> Repatriated and returned to United Kingdom 1 - XI - 18.

It was farewell to arms – at least for a while.

THE WEARING OF THE GREEN

SECRETARY TO BISHOP DANIEL COHOLAN

As Tom Duggan trudged up the steep hill to the Bishop's quarters in Farranferris following his demobilisation from the British Army in July 1919, he had not the slightest inkling of what lay in store for him. One can imagine his surprise, when, having welcomed him effusively, Bishop Coholan announced that he was appointing him as his residential-secretary.

He left the Bishop's presence with his mind in a whirl. Ordinarily the secretaryship was a very prestigious appointment for a young priest and, as such, should have been very welcome news to Tom Duggan. But these were not normal times: they were strange and stirring times in Ireland. Since his return he had fully briefed himself on the political situation and had renewed his contacts with the militant wing of the Sinn Féin movement.

Bishop Daniel had also taken a keen interest in the changing political situation. He had welcomed the victory of Sinn Féin in the historic general election for the British House of Commons on 14 December 1918. When the elected members of Sinn Féin who were not in prison assembled in the Mansion House on 21 January 1919, and proclaimed themselves the lawful government of the country under the name of Dáil Éireann, he had no difficulty as a democrat in recognising the legitimacy to their claim. But when they claimed that the mandate to govern which they had received implied recognition of the Irish Republic proclaimed in Easter Week, 1916, and when they formally renewed this declaration, the Bishop disagreed. In his view the declaration of a republic as the chosen form of government was a matter for the people as a whole, and needed a much firmer foundation than an assumed mandate by a minority of the elected members of parliament. For the Dáil to declare a republic was *ultra vires*, he believed: in doing so they went beyond their constitutional rights.

In declaring the Republic, the members of Dáil Éireann pledged 'to make this declaration effective by every means at their command'. To the militant wing of the movement 'every means' included force of arms, and their view prevailed. In fact, on the very day Dáil Éireann met for the first time, the first shots in the War of Independence were fired at Soloheadbeg in Tipperary. From that day forward the physical force movement grew in strength especially in Cork.

All this raised a serious moral issue for Bishop Coholan. An ardent nationalist at heart, a distinguished theologian, a man of great firmness of mind and strength of character, he was on record as having stated at a lecture in Cork on 22 October 1918:

> In judging the liceity of such actions, international protest and moral success and not merely material victory must be taken into account. Martyrdom for the freedom of Ireland is a glorious death.
>
> Men like Pearse, MacDonagh and others had not the slightest delusion about a military success. I take it they knew they had no chance. But I take it they knew they were doing a great service to Ireland, if, by shedding their blood, they drew the attention of the world to the misgovernment of Ireland.

This could hardly be interpreted other than as an authoritative post-factum justification of the sacrificial aspect of the 1916 Rising. It seemed logical, therefore to assume that, *a fortiori*, the armed struggle beginning in 1919 had even greater moral justification and consequently would have the moral support of the Bishop of Cork. Tom Duggan knew otherwise. He knew the Bishop's mind too well to believe that in spite of those patriotic sentiments he could ever adopt such a simplistic approach as to give *carte blanche* to any revolutionary armed struggle. Only so far as the revolutionaries acted within the bounds of the moral law would they have the Bishop's support.

In the local elections of January, 1920, the tide of popular approval swung even more decisively towards Sinn Féin. Tomás MacCurtain was elected as the first republican Lord Mayor of Cork, and the Corporation transferred its allegiance to Dáil Éireann. Again Bishop Coholan fully recognised the municipal authority of the Lord Mayor and Corporation and of the Republican courts.

A month later, in February 1920, the Bishop issued a famous Lenten pastoral letter* which contained a detailed exposition of his views on the current political situation. Duggan must have been highly pleased with the opening passages which amounted to a ringing affirmation of Dáil Éireann's right to govern:

> The people of this country have chosen as their Parliamentary representatives, and to municipal positions, advocates of the policy and claim of Ireland to choose her own form of government by the free self-determination of her people. The people should support their representatives by moral and financial aid.

* The official version of the pastoral is in the diocesan archives.

Duggan must also have been pleased with the Bishop's outright condemnation of coercion as practised by the British regime in Ireland:

> And now, as during the Land Agitation, we are subjected to a regime of the extremest coercion...The executive government seems to have no other purpose than repression. It has created lawlessness by its repression, and having created the lawlessness it declares that self-government cannot be thought of until law and order are re-established. This mode of government has no sanction in the moral law; and historians will say of it, as they now say of the coercion government of the Penal Days and of the Land Agitation, that it was an unlawful mode of government.

So far so good but it was in regard to the crucial question of what form resistance should take against this unlawful mode of government that the Bishop and Duggan were at variance. According to the Bishop, it should only be by passive resistance:

> If an unjust aggression comes from a private individual it is lawful to resist it. Theoretically, too, if an unlawful aggression comes from the agents of a coercion government it is lawful to resist it, for neither governments nor their agents have a right to commit an act of unlawful aggression on the individual citizen.
>
> And whatever may be said theoretically and in the abstract about the lawfulness of opposition to the agents of coercion when their oppression is unlawful, I say to you to submit without violence and without harm to the police or soldiers, to the annoyances, the injuries, the losses of the moment....I say to you again, bear this period of persecution patiently; it cannot last long. Though resistance to unlawful aggression may be lawful theoretically and in the abstract, it may be wrong in practice.

His repeated use of the words 'theoretically' and 'in the abstract' meant that the Bishop was reserving the right of dissociating himself from the methods being used in practice by the revolutionary movement. But the young men flocking to take up arms were unaware of all these fine distinctions: to them it was enough that their bishop had condemned the British as oppressors to make them think that he was with them all the way. It would make it all the harder when they would discover that his support was conditional.

Duggan had no such reservations about the use of force. Less scrupulous than the Bishop, he believed that extreme ills justified physical retaliation. He failed to see how any form of passive resistance could be effective.

The Bishop soon found himself at odds with the methods being used by the I.R.A. The practice of launching attacks on barracks and personnel of the Royal Irish Constabulary was the first aspect of the armed struggle to incur his disapproval.

The R.I.C. men were in an unenviable position. The great majority being Irish and Catholics, at least in the South of Ireland, they were the agents of the Crown for maintaining law and order. Up to this they had been accepted by the people but suddenly in 1920 they found that the whole fabric of British administration in Ireland was under attack by the I.R.A. with at least the tacit support of the public at large. The R.I.C. were left standing in the middle, their lives were at stake. While other categories of people could sit on the fence they had to decide, and the wrong decision could mean death for themselves and ruin for their families. Bishop Coholan felt keenly for these men in the dilemma in which they found themselves. He was not the sort of man to keep silent in such a situation.

The scarcity of arms and ammunition was the chief handicap under which the I.R.A. suffered. R.I.C. barracks with their well-stocked supplies of arms were an obvious target. Bishop Coholan believed that lack of arms in itself did not justify attacks on police barracks or individual policemen. Following some such attacks he condemned them out of hand in a sermon in the Cathedral on 15 March 1920:

> I venture to say there is hardly one in Cork who was not horrified on reading that Mr. MacDonagh, District Inspector had been shot, and hot-foot on the shooting of Mr. MacDonagh came the announcement of the murder of Constable Scully of Glanmire, a most inoffensive man, now mourned by a wife and children..... I have never met Mr. MacDonagh but I am very sorry for him and I shall avail myself of the earliest opportunity to visit him in hospital.*

He went on to make a moving plea on behalf of the R.I.C.:

> I have always got this testimony of the police on the whole, that they are a respectable and upright body of men, maintaining a high moral standard, edifying in their Church life, discharging faithfully their duties as guardians of the peace and of social order. The police as a civil force are necessary for the maintenance of public order; they

* *The Cork Evening Echo*, March 16, 1920.

> would be necessary no matter what form of government we had. A campaign against the police, even though not meant to be so, is really a campaign against public order....
>
> The men who raid police barracks would be glad, I am sure, if they could seize or shatter a police barrack without loss of life. But men cannot fire into barracks, or use bombs and grenades, without the greatest danger of human life. Let there be no mistake about it, dear brethren, whether an attack is made on an individual policeman, or on a barrack, to the danger of human life, the act involves the malice of murder.

Within days of delivering this sermon Bishop Coholan found himself faced with an acid test of his courage and of his fidelity to principle. On the evening of 19 March 1920, a policeman was shot on Pope's Quay. Later that night Lord Mayor Tomás MacCurtain was brutally murdered in the presence of his wife in their home in Blackpool. All the circumstances pointed to R.I.C. involvement; the coroner's jury found the agents of the Crown were guilty of wilful murder. The inhuman circumstances of the murder of a very popular Lord Mayor caused an outcry of unparalled proportions. Following on his policy of showing every respect to those duly elected to civic office Bishop Coholan celebrated the funeral rites of the dead Lord Mayor even though he was well aware that as well as being Lord Mayor the dead man was also O.C. of the 1st Cork Brigade of the I.R.A. But he steadfastly refused to join in the witch-hunt against the police. In a letter to *The Cork Examiner* on 28 March he wrote:

> And if the worst should happen, if it were proved that the Lord Mayor was murdered by members of the R.I. Constabulary, or if a serious doubt remained about it, I would ask the public to be just to the general body of men in the R.I. Constabulary. A murder, a very deliberately planned murder, might be committed by a group of any organisation; and it would not be fair to punish the whole organisation for the crime. There should be no thought of retaliation. This could only mean that two sections of Irishmen would begin mutually murdering each other, while the enemy of their common country gloated over the disorder.

Later he proposed a solution to help the R.I.C. in their dilemma:

> I respectfully submit that it might be a question – a moral question for the general body of Bishops. The question is this: should the

> Bishops tell the police that they are not bound in conscience to perform the many acts of coercion which are goading the public beyond restraint; that when the mode of government has no sanction in the moral order, its execution has no sanction in the moral law. Nothing should be left undone to re-establish confidence and to restore friendly relations between the people and the police.

He was a voice crying in the wilderness. It was expecting too much of a divided body of bishops, and so a suggestion which might have eased tensions all round was not acted upon and Bishop Coholan was left standing alone.

Duggan felt sorry for the Bishop, torn as he was between his detestation of the excesses of British rule in Ireland and his abhorrence of the crime of murder in any circumstances. On his part the Bishop began to have doubts as to where his secretary stood in the delicate political mine-field of the time. Stories were coming to his ears about his close contacts with the I.R.A. Duggan seemed to him to be always on the move: he found him nervous and hard to pin down. It is not known whether any particular incident triggered off the break between the two men. It was probably rather a number of straws in the wind. At all events, early in August the Bishop decided to dispense with Duggan's services. He had lasted barely a year as Bishop's secretary.

The Bishop then appointed him as chaplain to the Bon Secours Home and directed him to study for a Higher Diploma in Education at U.C.C. They parted amicably but the close relationship of earlier times was never afterwards restored. A certain coolness developed which cast a cloud over their future relationship.

The Hunger Strikes

Within weeks of Tom Duggan vacating his post as secretary to the Bishop, a number of untried prisoners in Cork Jail commenced a hunger strike in protest against their continuing imprisonment without trial. A few days later, on 12 August 1920, Lord Mayor Terence MacSwiney was arrested and decided to join in the hunger strike. To avoid public demonstrations he was transferred to Brixton prison in London.

The hunger strike in Cork Jail gave Tom Duggan his first real opportunity of becoming personally involved in the national struggle. The jail was situated only a few hundred yards from the Mercy Hospital on one side and from the Bon Secours Home, where Tom was now chaplain, on the other. The strikers refused all food and all offers of medical assistance from the prison doctors. Duggan became a regular visitor to the jail. His army experience with the wounded and his familiarity with soldiers preparing for death made him the ideal person to establish a good *rapport* with the prisoners. He became especially friendly with Michael Fitzgerald, the leader of the strikers.

In his booklet on Michael Fitzgerald, Tomás O Riordáin pays Duggan this tribute:

> Early in October, Rev. Fr. Duggan took on the duties of second and assistant chaplain to Cork Jail. During the long hunger strike his kindness and devotion in ministering to the spiritual and temporal needs of those suffering for Ireland's cause is ever to be appreciated.

In a letter to the author, Tomás O Riordáin wrote: 'During my enquiries among the survivors of that period and those closely associated with the hunger strike I found that the name of Fr. Duggan was held in reverence.'

The Sisters of Mercy from the nearby hospital lived up to their name; they were admitted on humanitarian grounds to the prison and went to endless pains to provide nursing care for the prisoners. The Bon Secours Sisters also became involved, no doubt with the active encouragement of their chaplain.

During the hunger-strikes, Bishop Coholan showed a deep sense of compassion for the prisoners. On 25 August he visited Lord Mayor MacSwiney in Brixton. The Bishop was refused an interview by the Home Secretary, Edward Shortt, unless his visit was 'to discuss the question of what could be done to induce the Lord Mayor to take food'. Nothing daunted, the Bishop penned a fiery letter to *The Times*:

> The decision of the cabinet to allow the Lord Mayor of Cork to die in prison is greatly to be deplored. This decision and the whole Government administration in Ireland are vividly reminiscent of the Balfourian administration in the days of the land agitation. Now, as then, the orders of the day are, 'Don't hesitate to shoot'. 'Put them under lock and key': 'Humiliate your political opponents when you have them in jail; let the fellows die in jail.'
>
> To add a personal touch, let me add that I have visited the Lord Mayor of Cork in prison. To put it mildly, I was scrupulously careful against saying anything that would confirm him in his resolution to continue the hunger strike. He said to me, 'Your Lordship, my conscience is quite at ease about the course I am taking. I made a

> general confession this morning. I receive Holy Communion every morning. I might never again be so well prepared for death. I gladly make this sacrifice. They are trying to break the spirit of our people. My death will be an example and an appeal to our young men to make every sacrifice for Ireland'.
>
> May I ask you, sir, is it just to prolong the suffering of such a noble specimen of our humanity? I hope you will continue to use your powerful influence for the immediate release of the Lord Mayor of Cork.

In fairness to *The Times*, they made this comment:

> The case which Dr. Coholan makes in favour of the release of the Lord Mayor of Cork is well argued. We have more than once stated the opinion that if the Lord Mayor is permitted to die an irreparable injury may be done to all present hope of an Irish settlement.*

On Monday, 13 September, the Bishop visited Cork Jail and saw all the hunger-strikers. He was specially moved by the condition of a young Limerick boy of nineteen who was semi-conscious.

Mick Fitzgerald was the first fatality; when he died on 19 October, Tom Duggan was among those who knelt at his bedside. Fitzgerald was aged thirty and his hunger strike had lasted sixty-seven days.

According to *The Cork Examiner* his death had a profound effect on the others:

> Owing to Joseph Murphy's serious condition he was the only one of the prisoners Father Fitzgerald did not inform of the death that had occurred. He is by far the worst case. He gave grounds for grave alarm throughout the day. He collapsed at one o'clock, and the assistant prison chaplain, Fr. Duggan, attended him.

Joe Murphy's ordeal ended on Monday night, 25 October; he died aged 24, after seventy six-days on hunger strike. *The Freeman's Journal* reported:

> He died while Father Fitzgerald, the prison chaplain, was reciting the Rosary and the Prayers for the Dying in his cell. His father, mother,

* Idem, August 30, 1920. According to *The Freeman's Journal*, (August 30, 1920), during the visit to London which lasted several days, Bishop Coholan, visited the Lord Mayor a second time and found him much weaker.

> sisters and some other relatives were present at his bedside. Fr. Duggan, the assistant chaplain, was also at the dying man's bedside.

Joe Murphy's remains were removed to the Lough Church. Father Edward Fitzgerald and Father Tom Duggan walked in front of the hearse in the funeral procession.

On 25 October, the same day as Joe Murphy's death, Terence MacSwiney died in Brixton. Bishop Coholan celebrated his funeral Mass in the Cathedral and presided at the obsequies at St. Finnbarr's cemetery.

Perhaps the most memorable tribute paid to him took the form of a letter from Bishop Coholan to *The Cork Examiner*:

> I ask the favour of a little space to welcome home to the city he laboured for so zealously the hallowed remains of Lord Mayor Terence MacSwiney.
>
> For the moment it might appear that he has died in defeat. That might be conceded if there were questions merely of the individual, but it is not true when the issue of the Nation is considered.
>
> Was Lord Edward Fitzgerald's death in vain? Was Robert Emmet's death in vain? Did Pearse and the other martyrs in the cause of the Irish Freedom die in vain?
>
> We are the weaker Nation in the combat. Sometimes we tire of the conflict. Anyhow, special questions such as the questions of the land, of local government, of housing, of education, for a time engage our attention. But periodically the memory of the martyr's death will remind a young generation of the fundamental question of the Freedom of Ireland.
>
> Terence MacSwiney takes his place among the martyrs in the sacred cause of the Freedom of Ireland. We bow in respect before his heroic sacrifice. We pray that God may have mercy on his soul.

After the deaths of Joe Murphy and Terence MacSwiney the remaining prisoners continued their fast. But pressure began to build up to persuade them that further sacrifice of life would add nothing to the magnitude of the moral victory already won. On November 10, for instance, *The Cork Examiner* published the following announcement:

> We are authorised to say that His Lordship, the Most Rev. Dr. Coholan visited the prisoners in Cork Gaol some days ago and endeavoured to induce them to give up the hunger strike.

On 12 November, *The Cork Examiner* published the following letter from Bishop Coholan:

> The continuance of the agony of these brave men is a shock to the conscience and moral sense of the public.
>
> Everyone admired the heroic sacrifice of the late Lord Mayor. His death has drawn the attention and the sympathy of the world to the cause of Ireland, and one can say that the nation has got value for his life.
>
> But if the hunger strike in Cork Gaol is not called off these self-sacrificing men will pass away one after another without impressing the world any more than it has been impressed already. The continuance of the Hunger Strike will only lead to a waste of human life.
>
> The morale of the nation can be maintained without the useless sacrifice of valuable lives. In war the useless waste of troops is avoided. This Hunger Strike should be ended at once, and every effort should be made to nurse these brave men back to health.

However, it was a most striking letter written to Arthur Griffith, acting President of the Irish Republic, by Fr. Tim O'Leary, C.C., St. Finnbarr's South, that proved decisive:

> All the Sinn Féin priests of this diocese, and all the laity to whom I have spoken – and I have spoken to very many – look on the further continuance of the hunger strike as a sort of atrocity. Let me state the case as it presents itself to us:
>
> 1. Now that the Lord Mayor, Michael Fitzgerald and Joe Murphy have made the supreme sacrifice, we think the principle for which they died has been sufficiently vindicated, and that it is needless cruelty and a waste of valuable lives to prolong the agony further. The eyes of the world were fixed on the Lord Mayor; the sacrifice of his humbler brethren will be comparatively unnoticed. We in Cork have sufficient evidence of this.
> 2. It may be said that Dáil Éireann has no responsibility for the strike and that it is not the duty of the Executive to call it off. The public are perfectly aware that these soldiers of the Irish Republic will obey orders, and will not absolve your Government from a share in the responsibility for the death of these brave men. If you look at them dying in such horrible agony, the public will call on you to

> show the reason why they should be permitted to suffer so, and, as I think, no sufficient reason can be shown, it may be well to leave with the English usurper the monopoly of callousness and brutality.
>
> 3. It may be further said that it will give scope for scoffing and jeering to our foes and that it will look badly in the eyes of the world. We can afford to despise the scoffs and jibes of Englishmen. We know them for what they are worth. No decent person will imagine there is a hauling down of the flag, and the whole incident will pass almost unnoticed as far as the world is concerned.
> 4. I say with all seriousness, and as representing the views of my brother-priests, that the conscience of the people is being revolted, and that the continued torture and the death of these men may do irreparable harm to the prestige of the Irish Government. I am convinced that a plebiscite would result in an almost unanimous verdict for calling off the strikes. Minutes may be of the utmost importance at this crisis, and we shall all be ever grateful for an immediate reply.*

The letter was unanswerable; it was an appeal from the heart from within the ranks of the Sinn Féin movement itself and could not be ignored. Fr. O'Leary received the following letter by return from President Griffith:

> I have received your letter and I concur in your conviction that our countrymen in Cork Jail have already sufficiently demonstrated by their sufferings their fidelity to the cause of Ireland.
>
> Terence MacSwiney, Michael Fitzgerald and Joseph Murphy laid down their lives that the world might understand that those whom England advertises as criminals are Irishmen whose patriotism is proof against torture and death. Their heroic sacrifice achieved the full result. The sacrifice which their nine comrades in Cork are equally prepared to make could not further emphasise it.
>
> As the hunger strike in every case is the voluntary action of prisoners themselves and has never been dictated to or ordered from outside, I cannot order it to cease, but express to my gallant countrymen in Cork Prison my conviction that the sacrifices already

* *The Cork Examiner*, November 15, 1920.

> made have achieved their object, and my earnest wish that they will re-build their strength and live for Ireland.

President Griffith also sent a message to the Lord Mayor asking him to convey these sentiments officially to the strikers. As a result, the strike was called off and through the efforts of the prison doctors, and the nursing Sisters the strikers were nursed back to health.

The Cork Examiner in a leading article commended Fr. O'Leary:

> It is evident from the relief with which the ending of the strike was received that Father O'Leary's views expressed the opinion of the vast majority of the people both clergy and laity, and the people owe Father O'Leary a debt of gratitude for his action in connection with the matter.

Fr. O'Leary was reluctant to take the credit. He told a priest-friend, 'Don't thank me. Thank Duggan and Kiely as well. We all had a hand in it'.

There is another aspect of Tom Duggan's involvement in the hunger strikes which reflects less credit on his conduct as a priest. It emerges from a fragment of autobiography which is extant:

> In August, 1920, I ceased to be residential secretary to the Bishop. I was appointed to the Bon Secours Hospital, which is adjacent to the jail. Occasionally I had to do duty in the jail for the official chaplain. I was coming out on one such occasion and a man asked me how were the hunger strikers. In loquacious detail I told him, and, to my astonishment, next morning I saw the caption of the old *Freeman's Journal* (dying but not yet dead) – 'Exclusive Interview with Assistant Chaplain'. *The Cork Examiner* needless to say, was not going to be outdone in politeness. The Warders of the jail joined in; henceforth I signed, not the Visitors' Book but the Officials' Book. The irregularity of my appointment gave me a freedom of manoeuvre, which I am afraid I availed of 100%.
>
> There was the affair of blowing up the jail walls. What I chiefly remember is that I was made a beast of burden for the preparations. I went in one day with: (a) a wooden mallet to percuss warders; (b) a knuckle-duster with dagger – youth and instinct for melodrama; (c) two slabs of gun cotton. Gun cotton worn as a chest protector gives an indescribable feeling of levitation. I can still remember it after thirty years.

> There was an inner wall which was to have been blown out and a parallel wall in U.C.C. to have been blown in. The gun cotton was available, gelignite was not. Afterwards I had to bring out the gun cotton unused.

There is no possible justification for this action of Duggan. He was taking advantage of his position as a priest to become directly involved in acts of violence which might have caused deaths and injuries. But judging from the extract given above, even after thirty years he does not seem to have entertained any feelings of remorse whatsoever. The tone of the letter suggests a school-boy prank rather than a highly dangerous military operation.

In his book *Guerilla Days in Ireland*, General Tom Barry recalls this episode:

> In April, 1921, I had discussed the defences of Cork prison with a very good friend of the I.R.A. who had entrée to them. He was Reverend T.F. Duggan (now Very Reverend Canon Duggan, President, St. Finnbarr's Seminary, Farranferris, Cork) and he was prepared to take any risks to save the lives of Irish soldiers condemned to die.
>
> Fr. Duggan had been a military chaplain in World War I and had a good grasp of technical military matters. Not being suspected by the British of I.R.A. sympathies he had many opportunities of making a study of the gaol defences, and his information only confirmed the view of Cork I Brigade of the impossibility of rescuing the prisoners, although Fr. Duggan personally thought it could be effected.

By this time it was clear that Bishop Coholan and his former secretary held very divergent views about the morality of the I.R.A. campaign. The further Duggan was being admitted into the inner counsels of the I.R.A., the more the Bishop was finding their methods reprehensible.

The Excommunication

Just a month after the death of Terence MacSwiney, Tom Barry's Flying Column carried out the first major stroke of the War of Independence in the South. At Kilmichael in hilly terrain a few miles from Dunmanway two lorry-loads of Auxiliaries were attacked and almost wiped out: sixteen Auxiliaries were killed and three of the I.R.A.

As compared with the massive slaughters of recent times Kilmichael may seem a very small engagement but at the time it created a major sensation at home and abroad and gave renewed confidence to I.R.A. columns.

But one place where the news brought no joy was in the Bishop's quarters at Farranferris. He had never liked the idea of ambushes as a method of warfare and now the most deadly attack so far had taken place in his own native parish and among his own people. As news came through of widespread burnings, searches and intimidation as a reprisal for the ambush he was strengthened in his view that ambushes were morally wrong and counter-productive. The knowledge that some of his priests took a very different view was an added source of anguish, especially the news that Tom Barry who had collapsed with a heart complaint soon after Kilmichael, and was a patient in the Mercy Hospital was receiving frequent visits from Tom Duggan. But the Bishop held his peace and waited apprehensively for worse to come.

He had not long to wait. On Saturday evening, 10 December 1920, a lorry-load of Auxiliaries on their way from Victoria Barracks to the city centre was ambushed at Dillon's Cross: several were wounded and one died later in hospital. Reprisal was swift. The houses around Dillon's Cross were burned to the ground and later on in the night, St. Patrick's Street, the centre street of the city, was devastated by fire. The City Hall was burned to the ground.

From the terrace of Farranferris, Bishop Coholan had a grandstand view of the burning city. What he saw appalled him. It was a night of terror and destruction, unprecedented for centuries. The thought of the aftermath, the loss to the city in terms of business and commerce, the massive unemployment, dismayed him. Another atrocity took place in the small hours of the morning in Dublin Hill in the northern side of the city. Two youths, the Delaney brothers, were pulled out of their beds by agents of the Crown and shot in cold blood. One died instantly; while the other lay dying, his sister was prevented from calling a priest.

In the course of the night Bishop Coholan composed a statement to be read out in the Cathedral on the following (Sunday) morning. The rough hand-written draft of his statement was an almost indecipherable scrawl in contrast to his usually meticulously clear writing, a clear indication of the emotion under which he wrote. *The Cork Examiner* published the statement verbatim:

> Yesterday at the close of the Solemn Mass at the Cathedral, offered for the members and benefactors of the Sick Poor Society, His Lordship, the Bishop, Most Rev. Dr. Coholan, referred to the ambush at Dillon's Cross and the subsequent burning of the principal shops in Patrick Street on Saturday night. The Bishop said:

'Murder is murder and arson is arson whether committed by the agents of the Government or by members of the Volunteer organisation; and it is the duty of a Bishop to denounce murder and arson and all crime from whatever source they come. And today, in the presence of the destruction of the city, I ask you to consider reasonably the subject of the murders, of the arsons, of the kidnapping and ambushes with which unfortunately we have got only too familiar.

It was a safe exploit to murder a policeman from behind a screen; and until reprisals began there was no danger to the general community. But, leaving aside the moral aspect of the question for the moment, what has the country gained politically by the murder of policemen? Some Republicans spoke of such and such districts of their country being delivered from British sway when policemen were murdered and barracks burned. It was a narrow view, and who will now mention any district that has been delivered from British rule by the murder of the old R.I.C. men and the burning of the barracks? No, the killing of the R.I.C. men was murder and the burning of barracks was simply the destruction of Irish property.

'I may say that reprisals began here with the murder of Lord Mayor MacCurtain; and now it is like a devil's competition between some members of the Republican Army and the agents of the Crown in feats of murder and arson.

'Recently ambushes have taken place with serious loss of life and I would say this about the ambushes, leaving out for the moment the moral aspect: the ambushers come to a place from no one knows where, and when their work is done they depart, no one knows to what destination. There is not much risk to the ambushers personally. But by this time boys or men taking part in ambushes must know that by their criminal acts they are exposing perhaps a whole countryside, perhaps a town or city, to the danger of terrible reprisals.... That is not very valiant. And then, over and above all, there is the moral aspect of these ambushes. Let there be no doubt about it, there is no doubt about it, these ambushes are murderous, and every life taken in an ambush is a murder. Oh! there is even a danger of becoming familiar with murder, or simply considering a successful ambush as a nice exploit brought off, of thinking no more of shooting a policeman than of shooting game or a wild animal. I am afraid some of our young men have got wrong views from people who should know better...

'As a result of the ambush last night at Dillon's Cross, the city has suffered, I think, as much damage as Dublin suffered during the rebellion of 1916. The city is nearly a ruin, and the ruin followed on the murderous ambush at Dillon's Cross...

'If any section of the Volunteer Organisation refuse to hear the Church's teaching about murder, there is no remedy but the extreme remedy of excommunication. And I certainly will issue such a decree.'

True to his word, the Bishop issued the decree in the same issue of *The Cork Examiner*:

DECREE OF THE BISHOP OF CORK IN REFERENCE TO AMBUSHES, KIDNAPPING AND MURDER

Besides the guilt involved in these acts by reason of their opposition to the law of God, anyone who shall, within this Diocese of Cork, organise or take part in an ambush or in kidnapping, or otherwise shall be guilty of murder, or attempt at murder, shall incur by the very fact the censure of excommunication.

Daniel, Bishop of Cork
Patrick Canon Sexton (witness)
Farranferris, Cork.

The days that followed brought further sorrow to the Bishop. A special meeting of the Cork Corporation heard angry denouncement of the Bishop's decree. One member stated that the burning should have given cause for the greatest resentment from one in the Bishop's position but he had not uttered a single word of protest. Another councillor added that, 'He stands now only where his people always stood – in the wrong'.

On Wednesday 15 December came further tragedy. Canon Magner, parish priest of Dunmanway, was shot dead on the roadside near Dunmanway by the cadet in charge of a party of Auxiliaries. Such widespread horror and condemnation followed that Dublin Castle took the very unusual course of admitting the murder:

> At 1 p.m. yesterday about thirty auxiliary police left Dunmanway in two motor lorries, with a cadet in charge, to go to Cork to attend the funeral of one of their number who was recently shot dead in Cork. About one mile from Dunmanway, on the road to Bandon, they met the Rev. Canon Magner, aged 73 years, parish priest, Dunmanway, and Timothy Crowley, a farmer's son.
>
> The cadet in charge stopped the lorries, walked over to Timothy Crowley, asked him for a permit, and shot him dead with his revolver. The cadet then turned to Canon Magner, who was close by, and shot him dead also. A resident magistrate, Mr. Brady, was present at the time, and he narrowly escaped a similar fate.*

Bishop Coholan addressed the following letter to *The Cork Examiner*:

> This is the latest move in what I call a devil's competition in crime which is taking place in our midst. I was apprehensive of some such terrible tragedy since the Kilmichael ambush. The ambush took place on the Macroom-Dunmanway road, and I had reason to fear a priest's life would be taken in reprisal. Whether that be the explanation of Canon Magner's murder or not, the ambush involved the murder of fifteen Englishmen, the death of three of the ambushing party, several deaths since, and it has not brought us nearer to be a Republic.

On the following Sunday the Bishop addressed a pastoral letter to his people to be read at all Masses. It is a somewhat fuller and more carefully-phrased version of his Sunday sermon already quoted.† That he had not yet fully regained his usual composure is shown by the fact that he added a second letter which bitterly denounced the Corporation and in particular Professor O'Rahilly 'their lay theologian' as he styled him. A dignified written protest was made by O'Rahilly in *The Cork Examiner* challenging the theological validity of the Bishop's decree and its implication that 'a lay theologian' is a contradiction in terms. There was no response from Bishop Coholan.

In spite of a leading article in the London *Times* which attempted to goad the other Irish bishops into following Bishop Coholan's lead, no other bishop took any action. The ordinary members of the laity were shocked by the severity of

* *The Cork Examiner*, December 16, 1920.

† *The Irish Independent* received a copy of the letter published on December 28, 1920.

the decree though they were vague about what an excommunication involved since such a censure had not been applied within living memory. [Actually in Church law an excommunication is a penalty by which a person guilty of a particular crime is removed from communion with the Church and is deprived of the ordinary rights and privileges of members of the Church, such as the reception of the Sacraments.]

The priests of the diocese were faced with an unwelcome crisis of conscience. They were divided in their response to the Bishop's letter. Some, probably the majority, read out the Pastoral letter and considered themselves bound by its contents and consequently refused absolution to those who confessed their involvement in ambushes etc. Others refrained from reading the letter. Amongst these, it is alleged, was Canon Jeremiah Coholan, parish priest of Bandon and a brother of the Bishop. As might have been expected, Tom Duggan was amongst those who disagreed with the Bishop on theological grounds and ignored his imposition of the censure of excommunication. Many years later, some old I.R.A. men were still wending their way up to Farranferris to their confessor, Fr. Duggan.

General Tom Barry was a patient in the Mercy Hospital when the excommunication was imposed. He speaks about it in his book *Guerilla Days In Ireland*:

> It was while I was in hospital that the Bishop of Cork issued his decree saying that anyone taking part in an ambush was guilty of murder and would incur the censure of excommunication. Let nobody minimise the gravity of such a decree in a Catholic country. Every Volunteer in the West Cork Brigade was a Catholic, and, with few exceptions, deeply religious. Dr. Coholan's decree applied to territory including a large part of our Brigade Area, as it extended from the City to Bantry. My own reaction was one of anger. Everyone knew that if the I.R.A. laid down their arms as requested by the Bishop at least 200 members in Cork city and county would be killed off within a week by the British forces. Yet Dr. Coholan did not even extract a promise from the British Commanding Officer that there would be no executions or murders if the fight for independence stopped. For days I brooded over the decree, knowing full well how deeply religious the I.R.A. were. However, in the event, every active service man in our Brigade continued the fight, most priests continued to administer the Sacraments and the I.R.A. practised their religion as before.

Liam Deasy in his book, *Towards Ireland Free*, bears out Barry's words. He tells of an experience a few weeks after the decree was promulgated. In those days it was an occasion of risk for I.R.A. soldiers to be seen going to Mass as often during Mass churches were surrounded and congregations searched on their way out:

> On New Year's Eve, Tom Barry and I were near Enniskeane, and we thought it would be reasonably safe to assist at Mass in the local church on the following morning....The celebrant of the Mass was none other than Father O'Connell, the parish priest of Enniskeane, who had officiated at the burial of my brother Pat and his two fallen comrades a month earlier. After the Gospel he preached a most encouraging sermon.
>
> While distributing Holy Communion, Father O'Connell recognised both Tom Barry and me at the rails, as we were both well known to him...As we left the church afterwards, the sacristan approached us in the porch, and told us that the parish priest requested us to come to the presbytery for breakfast. We were very pleased to accept this invitation and joined him at his hospitable table.
>
> We made a point of thanking the good priest for his courageous sermon; indeed we thought it really heroic considering that Father O'Connell's neighbouring parish priest, Canon Magner, had been murdered by the Auxiliaries just two weeks previously. Father O'Connell turned the conversation to the progress of the war and showed the keenest interest in every detail of our activity. He was most complimentary in his references to our contribution to the national effort, and encouraged us to persevere in the patriotic task to which we were committed. A few hours slipped by unnoticed, and as midday approached we were suddenly interrupted in our discussion.... the house in which we had spent the night had been surrounded by a party of Auxiliaries just ten minutes after we left to attend Mass.
>
> There were ten tenders of Auxiliaries in the district during the remainder of the day....so we remained with our kind host all day in the presbytery, and did not venture to leave until the scouts reported that the enemy had withdrawn...

> Father O'Connell never made any secret about his disapproval of the pastoral of Dr. Coholan, Bishop of Cork, condemning our activities, and in this he shared the feelings shown privately by many other priests in the diocese.

It was surely an extraordinary situation. On the one hand, Bishop Coholan regarded the I.R.A. who participated in ambushes as murderers, and on the other, one of his parish priests harbouring two of the most wanted men in all Ireland; Liam Deasy, commanding officer of the Third Cork Brigade, the most feared brigade in the country, and Tom Barry, officer commanding the Flying Column of that brigade, responsible for the Kilmichael ambush and several other daring exploits.

It goes to show that far from there being unanimity in regard to the Bishop's excommunication order, every priest and every lay person became his own theologian and interpreted the Bishop's decree as best he could in the light of his own conscience.

The Morality Of The War Of Independence

It may seem strange that two such competent theologians as Bishop Coholan and Fr. Tom Duggan could arrive at such diverse conclusions about the morality of the War of Independence. It has to be understood, however, that the application of general abstract principles governing the use of force to attain political ends can be extremely difficult in a concrete situation.

Their very different backgrounds exercised considerable influence in forming the theological conclusions of the two men. Theologically speaking, Bishop Coholan had been brought up in an anti-revolutionary mentality. Ever since the French Revolution, Catholic theologians had cast a very cold eye on the use of violence for any purpose. The later revolutions of 1848 and the violence associated with the *Risorgimento* in Italy which brought the clash of arms to the *Eternal City* itself reinforced this prejudice. Revolutionaries like Garibaldi aroused little sympathy among moral theologians.

The example of Pope Pius IX, himself a victim of violence, and particularly the teaching of Pope Leo XIII lent powerful support to this attitude. Leo abhorred violence. Even in the area of social justice, possibly as a reaction against socialist teaching, he looked for improvement to be brought about in the treatment of the workers not as a result of agitation and violence from below but from a more enlightened attitude on the part of employers. *A fortiori* in the political sphere he would have gone so far as to regard the use of revolutionary violence in any circumstances as immoral.

Pope Leo's fundamental principle was that all authority comes from God. As a corollary, obedience to political rulers is a form of submission to the authority of God because God exercises his sovereignty through human agents. This ultimately led him to believe that questions about just means do not arise. Even to attempt to overthrow a regime by non-violent means is not morally allowable.

In a recent authoritative study Fr. Breifne Walker sums up the important part played by Leo XIII in forming the Catholic theology of his time in regard to the use of force to obtain political objectives:

> The papacy of Pope Leo XIII was a very important point of conflict between a classical Christian conception of order and radical secularising movements which profoundly affected western Europe society after the French Revolution – nationalism, socialism and republicanism. In addition Pope Leo XIII was deeply engaged by the problems of order and authority and what he believed to be the lurking theme of revolutionary violence. His authoritative statements, along with his theological perspective, have had considerable influence on the later tradition of Catholic thought about politics, and the specific question of armed resistance against the State.
>
> Embedded in his social teaching there is a view of history which hinges around the authority of the Church and the Roman papacy. This in turn determined his understanding of the new social and political forces which were changing people's habitual ways of thinking and feeling. In Pope Leo's view the bloodshed, revolutions and wars of his own time were the outcome of a process which began with the Reformation in the sixteenth century. This paved the way for the collapse of respect for authority, and the exaltation of the power of reason striving to be independent of divine revelation.*

To challenge violently existing political and social orders was equivalent in Leo's mind to challenging to some degree the divine arrangement of society. This led him to conclude that the mere fact that rulers abuse their powers gives subjects no right to rebel:

* Breifne Walker, C.S.S.P., The Irish Theological Quarterly volume 57 (1991-I). Article entitled 'Official Roman Catholic Teaching on Revolutionary Armed Force'.

> Should it, however, happen at any time that in the public exercise of authority rulers act rashly and arbitrarily, the teaching of the Catholic Church does not allow subjects to rise against them without further warranty, lest peace and order become more and more disturbed, and society run the risk of greater detriment. And when things have come to such a pass as to hold out no further hope, she teaches that a remedy is to be sought in the virtue of Christian patience and in urgent prayer to God.*

This seems to be quite unrealistic. Leo seems to be thinking in terms of a Christian utopia rather than dealing with the harsh facts of life. Nevertheless as a result of his teaching, late nineteenth century theology was coloured by an anti-revolutionary bias and, in particular cases, to support the status quo or at least not to challenge it by violent means.

Bishop Coholan was a child and heir of this process. As with Leo, stability in society was for him a fundamental principle.

But he set limits in his deference towards Leo's teaching. He permitted the use of passive resistance and went so far as to tolerate the use of violent resistance provided that certain conditions relating to a just war were fulfilled. If the status quo needed to be challenged it ought to be done by peaceful means, by passive resistance as he had passionately declared in his pastoral letter of 1920. Before lending any moral support to armed insurgents he would need to be satisfied that the conditions traditionally laid down by moral theologians were being observed.

The theology of the just war had developed considerably when Tom Duggan returned from World War I. The rights of small nations, e.g. Belgium, against the encroachments of more powerful neighbours had come to the forefront. Such powerful figures as Cardinal Mercier had given increased stature and status to small nations and created a more liberal and open approach to the use of force against unjustifiable aggression. Tom Duggan was well aware of this, and from what he had seen of the realities of modern warfare it was likely that he would adopt a less strict approach in judging the morality of actions taken against unjust aggressors.

Neither of the two, strictly speaking, were professional moral theologians. But Bishop Coholan had the greater responsibility as the moral guide of his flock to

* Donal Corr, *Option for the Poor*. The quotation is from Leo's encyclical 'Quod Apostolici Muneris'.

apply moral principles correctly and not to overstep his powers in making his opinions mandatory on all.

On the fundamental issues involved in the Irish revolution, Bishop Coholan and Duggan were in broad agreement. They both accepted the legitimacy of Dáil Éireann as the lawful government. They both permitted the use of violence as a last resort to win international sympathy and thereby moral victory for their cause. Bishop Coholan had made his attitude clear in his post-factum justification of the Easter Rising though later he seemed to withdraw somewhat from that position.

Agreement on the basics did not extend to the morality of the I.R.A. struggle and how the fighting men stood in relation to the conditions laid down for a just war. Tom Duggan had no difficulty in supporting the I.R.A. guerrilla campaign. Bishop Coholan never explicitly condemned guerrilla warfare as such but he did so implicitly in the Irish context by declaring that the pillars on which it rested, namely ambushing, killing policemen, arson and kidnappings were contrary to the moral law.

Bishop Coholan based his views and subsequent condemnation on the following grounds:

1. The ineffectiveness of the campaign, the lack of any possibity of ultimate success.
2. The serious lack of proportionality between the few successes gained and the harm caused by reprisals.
3. The means being employed were outside the limits of the moral law.

As regards the first, with hindsight, it seems fair to say that the Bishop's views on the ineffectiveness of the struggle were largely based on a mistaken notion of the aims of the I.R.A. Guerrilla warfare as practised in Ireland was a new form of warfare with which the Bishop was unfamiliar: the objective of the I.R.A. was not to win pitched battles or conquer territory but by constant harassment of the enemy, to destroy his morale by psychological pressure and so eventually force him to withdraw. Therefore when Bishop Coholan asked sarcastically, who will now mention any district that has been delivered from British rule, he was missing the point.

Seán O'Faoláin, who was an interested observer at the time, gives the true picture:

> The only men to whom the Troubles gave no least respite were our regular fighters or guerrillas, few in number, who carried the full strain of the fight, day in and day out, on their backs, whether in risky ambushes in city streets or in the open countryside. For these men every day was intense, exhausting and relentless: they could never slacken. They had to be few because they had so few arms. One of the most able and active of the guerrilla leaders in West Cork, Tom Barry, records in his published memoirs, *Guerilla Days In Ireland,* that in his entire brigade area, in that spring of 1920, all he could muster against some three thousand war-hardened British military and police, Auxiliaries and Black and Tans, was thirty-five rifles and twenty revolvers or automatics, with about thirty rounds for each rifle and twenty rounds for each small arm. There never was an Irish Republican Army constantly in the field. The fight was carried on by those tremendously gallant few, darting here and there for an ambush, folding back into their 'normal' lives, until they could get another crack at the enemy. They could not, it must be said, have done anything without the silence, patience, and loyal help of the whole people.*

Dr. Charles Townshend, *The British Campaign in Ireland 1919-1921* agrees with this assessment:

> Guerrillas do not have to stand their ground in defense of strategic points or lines; they can and must operate only at the time and the place to suit them. For the I.R.A., with a few thousand poorly-armed men, any idea of fighting 'by the book' was absurd. The conventions of war, which now seemed akin to civilized morality to the well-matched European states, meant certain destruction to Irish rebels, whose prime concern was not to act with honour but to survive.
> The I.R.A. of 1920 was to find that by matching its operations to its needs it could survive for long enough to achieve a psychological victory out of military stalemate.[1]

* O'Faoláin, Seán, *Vive Moi!*

Nigel Hamilton in his widely-acclaimed biography of Field-Marshal Bernard Montgomery of Alamein gives a strong testimony to the effectiveness of the I.R.A. campaign. At a time when the War of Independence was at its height, on 5 January 1921, Montgomery arrived in Cork as Brigade-Major of the 17th Infantry Brigade. Hamilton describes his activities:

> Organising themselves on similar lines (and uniforms) as the British Army, the I.R.A. had invented a new form of guerrilla tactics: the use of Flying Columns that could move in specially-trained units across large areas, calling upon local units to help in ambushes, concealment, re-supply and intelligence. This was to become a model for guerrilla warfare the world over – and it certainly proved impossible for the cumbersome British formations to counter....
>
> Bernard, as Brigade-Major, became responsible for a number of large-scale manoeuvres or 'drives' in which several brigades co-operated in traversing the countryside and flushing out rebels. Meticulously planned and executed, these drives nevertheless failed to locate, let alone destroy, the I.R.A. columns and were eventually discontinued... Montgomery was increasingly realistic about the long-term chances of success. Unlike General Strickland and even Major Percival, the most ruthless of the British Intelligence officers of the Brigade, Bernard came to see evacuation as the only feasible solution of the Irish problem.

Hamilton sums up:

> It was Bernard Montgomery's misfortune to be cast into the Irish fray at the very worst moment, when insurrection, far from being contained by the massive increase of British troops stationed in the country, had escalated to the point of war.

Writing to Percival in 1922 Montgomery himself corroborates this view:

> I consider that Lloyd George was really right [in initiating peace negotiations] in what he did; if we had gone on we could probably have squashed the rebellion as a temporary measure, but it would have broken out again like an ulcer the moment we had removed the troops; I think the rebels would probably have refused battle, and hidden away their arms, etc. until we had gone.[2]

It looks, therefore, judging by these very authoritative British Army assessments, that Bishop Coholan seriously underestimated the effectiveness of the I.R.A. campaign and was wrong to use this as an argument for condemning and excommunicating I.R.A. soldiers.

As regards his second argument, that there was a lack of proportionality between the few successes gained e.g. at Kilmichael and the harm caused by reprisals e.g. the burning of Patrick Street in Cork, he was equally wrong. Reprisals are a two-edged weapon: the action of the British agents in burning Patrick Street did little to deter the I.R.A. or the civilian population at home but it did much to diminish British prestige abroad. In fact, within a few months of the burning in Cork the British abandoned their policy of reprisals. Again Nigel Hamilton is a witness:

> The policy of Official Reprisals, instituted when martial law was declared in December 1920, had backfired, since the I.R.A. merely burned the houses of loyalists in retaliation. By early June 1921 the British Government banned reprisals.

This leads on to the Bishop's third argument, namely, that the means being employed by the I.R.A. were outside the limits of the moral law.

In denouncing the various aspects of guerrilla warfare and particularly ambushes, Bishop Coholan stood alone among theologians of his time. The use of guerrilla tactics by an oppressed people unable to engage in conventional warfare was not condemned by Bishop Coholan's brother-bishops or by higher Church authority.

The history of warfare since World War I shows that for a people under oppression but unable to engage in a conventional war guerrilla warfare has become so common that it might be regarded as the norm. During World War II underground movements used guerrilla tactics continually to ambush the enemy forces or to sabotage their production of essential war equipment and supplies. Even after the massacre of over three hundred civilians in Rome as a reprisal for a bomb-throwing incident which caused the death of a dozen German soldiers there was no suggestion that the ambush was immoral. If, as seems likely, humanity will be forced to outlaw nuclear warfare and to curb the activities of perpetrators of mass civilian slaughter such as that carried out by 'Bomber' Harris at Dresden and by the Americans at Nagasaki and Hiroshima, and more recently in Korea and in the Gulf War, the likelihood is that guerrilla warfare will become more and more the norm. A distinguished authority on just warfare makes this point very strongly:

> 'Modern war' is not nuclear war. Instead, the possibility of nuclear war has made the world safe for insurgency. The balance of terror, which some foolishly thought would compel peace, produces instead a multiplication of wars. The military strength of the nation-state, which we thought made it impossible ever again to have a successful revolution, has led instead to an era of revolutionary wars...
>
> Thus, at the heart of the great strength of the modern state there is weakness (as Mao Tse Tung, Ho Chi Minh, General Nguyen Giap and Che Guevara discerned). And in the weakness of the present guerrilla there is strength; better to strike and run away, and live to fight another day; and if there are enough of those who would endure long enough they may bring down a whole nation without ever winning a conventional battle. This will remain the military situation for decades to come.
>
> Therefore the type of warfare that deserves to be called truly 'modern' is 'insurgency warfare'. There can be no doubt that the most urgent, practical, military and political question during our lifetime is: How is it possible, if indeed it is possible, to mount an *effective* counter-insurgency war, and to deliver such retribution upon it that future insurgency will be deterred?*

A soldier of great experience of the different forms of modern warfare came to the same conclusion. In his autobiography, *Memoirs d'Espoir*, General Charles de Gaulle recounts how in the course of a visit to Paris, President John F. Kennedy sought his advice about the advisability of engaging in war in Vietnam:

> Instead of giving him the approval he wanted, I told the President that he was taking the wrong road.
>
> 'You will find, I told him, that intervention in this area will be an endless entanglement. Once a nation has been aroused, no foreign power, however strong, can impose its will upon it....
>
> I predict that you will sink step by step into a bottomless military and political quagmire, however much you spend in men and money.

Of course the fact that guerrilla warfare has become the norm does not mean that it is always morally acceptable. In a particular case it still has to fulfil the

* Ramsey, Paul, *The Just War.*

conditions laid down for a just war. The present I.R.A. campaign in the North of Ireland and South American movements such as the so-called 'Shining Path' in Peru are morally indefensible. The cold-blooded practice of placing bombs in busy shopping areas or leaving explosive devices in parked cars thereby endangering the lives of innocent civilians is an affront to civilisation. People like 'Bomber' Harris would probably deny that in war-time there is any such thing as 'innocent civilians' but this view would be repudiated by all right-thinking people. On the other hand when employed within the perimeters of the moral law as a last resort by an oppressed people guerrilla warfare cannot be faulted on moral grounds.

It would appear, therefore, as if Bishop Coholan was wrong in arguing that the immorality of the methods used by the I.R.A. was one of the reasons why the guerrilla campaign was deserving of censure, even the ultimate spiritual sanction of excommunication.

By way of extenuation it may be said that in condemning the I.R.A. campaign he was still thinking in terms of conventional warfare and did not realise that the I.R.A. leaders had evolved a new concept of warfare which was best suited towards achieving their aims.

No assessment of Bishop Coholan's attitude towards the War of Independence is complete without reference to his excommunication decree which applied to a large number of those actively engaged in the struggle in his area. It was an action which aroused very bitter feeling in some quarters. A contemporary called Seamas Ó Maoileoin in his book *B'Fhiu An Braon Fola* goes so far as to attribute to Michael Collins the saying: 'There is neither sense nor reason in shooting ignorant uneducated idiots as spies and letting people like the Bishop of Cork get away with it.'

With all due respect to the author it would need more than his uncorroborated statement to accept that this was Michael Collins' attitude. On the other hand there can be no doubt that the Bishop's action aroused intense hostility.

It is a painful subject. Here one is dealing with a patently sincere and honourable man, acting from the highest motives, namely, respect for human life and property, a man whose main concern was the welfare of his people.

Yet he was wrong in two ways. Firstly he was wrong politically and tactically because his decree was foreseeably ineffective, ignored by those directly affected and greatly resented by the majority of his flock. It was, however, welcomed in some quarters. *The Cork Examiner*, for instance, referred to it in its editorial as 'an overwhelming indictment':

> The Pastoral Letter read in all the Churches of the Diocese of Cork yesterday was, apart from the moral lessons it teaches, and the sound and practical and healthy doctrines it enunciates, and the wholesome advice it contains, is an able and analytical document, fearlessly conceived, and judicially stated.

By and large, however, its effect was the opposite to that intended by the Bishop in that it alienated many from the Church and turned some into irreconcilables.

Secondly, Bishop Coholan was wrong because he overstepped the mark as pastor and moral guide of his people in imposing his private judgement under pain of excommunication on those with whose methods he did not agree.

His judgement was based on his own personal interpretation of a universal principle applied to a particular situation. Any such practical application involves making a judgement about which reasonably well-informed people may differ. In this case the silence of the Church in general and of the Irish bishops in particular is an indication that they did not share Bishop Coholan's views.

It seems that he failed to take the role of individual conscience into account and seems to have excluded or denied the right of people to arrive at a conscientious personal decision after having taken his advice as well as other relevant factors into consideration.

In fairness to the Bishop it should be pointed out that the emphasis on the primacy of informed individual conscience is the result of recent theological investigation which provides new insights into this complicated subject, insights which were not available to Bishop Coholan or to other theologians of his time. The modern consensus is that diocesan bishops have the right to guide and advise their people on contentious moral issues but not to make their views binding on all and certainly not under pain of excommunication.

It would appear, therefore, as if Tom Duggan was right when he informed I.R.A. soldiers that in his opinion the Bishop's decree was not binding in conscience.

There is no doubt that Bishop Coholan was a man of highest principle and that he was prepared to accept the consequences – as indeed he did for long years and in isolation. Fr. Tom Duggan had the advantage over him in that he espoused the popular viewpoint and people who do so find themselves popular too. Principle did not matter quite as much to Duggan as it did to Bishop Coholan. Perhaps it might justly be said that in comparing the two one might conclude that Duggan was a fearless man with unlimited physical courage but that in the more difficult area of moral courage he would have to give way to Bishop Coholan.

It is pleasing to have proof that Duggan made full allowance for the conflict which took place in Bishop Coholan's mind between his strong nationalist views and his firm theological convictions, and that he felt a great sympathy towards him in the situation in which he found himself. In what amounts to an apologia for the Bishop's actions he left the following assessment in his most carefully preserved papers:

> Back in 1919, I was appointed resident secretary to the Bishop of Cork, Most Rev. Dr. Coholan. The vacillations in the utterances of Daniel of Cork are a matter of history. I should like to make an effort not to reconcile them (they cannot be reconciled) but to attempt to throw light on the conflict in his being.
>
> And first of all a story. The Battle of Kilmichael was fought on a dirty November afternoon in 1920. There was some mix up about the Black and Tan surrender, and, as we know, the thing ended in carnage. Tom Barry himself told me this. His men were cooling down...and the horror was growing on them. At that critical moment an old man, in his clean Sunday flannel jacket, drove twelve cows down the road...He lifted his hat and with the solemnity of an Old Testament prophet he intoned, 'Jesus Christ be praised! I have lived to see this day'. A vision of the mills of God grinding out retribution. Daniel of Cork was born within a couple of miles of the scene of the ambush, and Daniel's outlook was little different from that of the old man.
>
> It is note-worthy, the fiercest fighting men at Kilmichael were of the Bishop's own blood and stock. If Daniel had not been sicklied o'er by the pale cast of (theological) thought he could have been an I.R.A. man, as ardently patriotic as any (and more ruthless than most).
>
> His difficulty was the pronouncements of the Irish Church. He sought but failed to find a mandate for armed resistance. And not finding it, the theologian had, first intermittent and then final, victory over the Kilmichael farmer's son.
>
> Even after the excommunication (Dec. 1920), we did not despair of him. I remember well, in May, 1921, four ardent young clerics (one of them now a bishop) were estimating the chances of securing a declaration of recognition of the Republic from the Irish Hierarchy. One and all of us put Daniel on the list of our supporters.

The Drift Towards Civil War

Excommunication or no excommunication, the war went on unabated. The I.R.A. continued to enjoy the wholehearted support of the people in the Cork area, the 'splendid people' as Tom Barry called them. Barry knew well that successful guerrilla warfare cannot be waged without the active support of the people as another great guerrilla fighter, Mao Tse Tung discovered some decades later: 'It is only undisciplined troops who make the people their enemies and who, like fish out of its native element, cannot live.'*

On 19 March, 1921, Barry's Flying Column won their last major engagement when they routed a vastly more numerous British force at Crossbarry. The British by then were only too well aware of the disadvantages inherent in fighting a guerrilla enemy: 'The guerrilla fights the War of the Flea and his military enemy suffers the dog's disadvantage: Too much to defend, and too small, ubiquitous and too agile an enemy to come to grips with.'†

Consequently by the June of 1921 the British were in a quandary: repression had failed and it had become a choice between a massive escalation of force or of calling a truce. They chose the latter and de Valera was invited to send a delegation to London for talks.

The Truce came into force on 11 July 1921. It came as a complete surprise to the I.R.A. command in the South. Its immediate result was a relaxation of discipline for most of the I.R.A. formations. The feeling of euphoria and the illusion of victory were strong in the cities and towns. It was as if 'The Boys' had already won and that The Republic was only a stone's throw away. Even Barry admits to feeling a great sense of relief:

> Gradually it dawned on me that the forcing of the enemy to offer such terms was a signal victory in itself; that days of fear were ended, at least for a time, and that we could return to normal life and thought, away from the hates, the callousness and the ruthless killings of war. The respite might only be brief but one could not dwell on that. The sun blazed from God's Heavens during those cloudless days of the longest and most brilliant Summer in living memory, as if to remind man that the world held brighter things than the darkness of war. At peace and relaxed, we rejoiced with our own people, who had been so good to us in the troubled past.

* Quoted in Paul Ramsey's, *The Just War.*

† Taylor, Robert, *The War of the Flea*, quoted in Paul Ramsey's, *The Just War.*

Some of the leaders were more worried. Liam Deasy, O.C. of the Third Cork Brigade, was more apprehensive:

> The feeling seemed to be that this was the end of an epoch and that things would never be the same again. Even in retrospect after more than fifty years, I well remember that my personal feeling was one of disappointment and I must admit that I foresaw defeat and trouble ahead.

At headquarters in Dublin, Michael Collins had no illusions: 'Once a truce is agreed and we come out into the open, it is extermination for us if the truce should fail...We shall be like rabbits coming out from their holes'.*

The trouble was that truce meant compromise as the politicians well knew but were not prepared to say openly. After the Treaty had been signed Arthur Griffith admitted it: 'To say that we went to get a Republic and nothing else is false.' De Valera knew that some form of association with Britain was inevitable; this was implied by his acceptance of Lloyd George's invitation 'to ascertain how the association with the community of nations known as the British empire may best be reconciled with Irish national aspirations'. But in the long months of the Truce de Valera held his peace.

Collins came nearest to telling the truth to the I.R.A. leaders of the South. The occasion was before an important I.R.B. meeting in Cork in November, 1921, when he gave the first inklings of compromise in a private conversation with key I.R.A. leaders. One of them, Florence O'Donoghue describes the incident:

> Collins gave in very general terms the first indication that any of these officers had heard that some modification of the full Republican demand might have to be made in the London negotiations if a settlement was to be reached, but he did not make any reference to this aspect of the matter when speaking at the meeting.†

Liam Deasy gives a fuller account but with the difference that he blames Liam Lynch for Collins' silence at the subsequent meeting:

> I recalled a meeting of the I.R.B. in Parnell Place, Cork, in the previous November. It was a large gathering including practically

* Coogan, Tim Pat, *Michael Collins.*

† Donoghue, Florence, *No Other Law.*

> every centre in Munster... Before going into the meeting Michael Collins had a private talk with Liam Lynch, Florrie O'Donoghue and myself. Collins said privately but quite definitely that there would have to be some compromise in the current negotiations in London. There was no question of getting all the demands they were making. Lynch asked Collins not to repeat this at the meeting or else it would 'blow up'. Collins made no reply and we went into the meeting.
>
> Thinking back on the meeting I wondered if Lynch was wrong in stopping Collins from issuing a warning that a Republic was not on the cards. I thought he was and felt it would have been better if Collins had ignored Lynch and put his cards on the table rather than encouraging his audience in the hope that the promised land was round the corner. At that meeting he was among friends, tried and true, and I felt they should have been put fully in the picture.

A great deal of subsequent misunderstanding might have been avoided if not only Collins but de Valera and the other principals had done as Deasy says. As it was, different people were left with different expectations with tragic results for all when the 'blow up' came after the Treaty rather than before.

During that long hot summer of 1921 the shadows of discord among the I.R.A. began to grow. The unity which had been maintained during the war began to show signs of strain. Ominous cracks appeared and new alliances began to form. There were many straws in the wind. For instance, some weeks before Tom Barry's marriage to Leslie Price, Leslie sensed a change of atmosphere when one of her brothers in Dublin sent her word to make her wedding list as representative as possible in the apparent hope that in the friendly atmosphere of a family wedding misunderstandings among friends might be smoothed over and unity restored.

When the wedding took place on 22 August 1921, most of the bright stars in the I.R.A. galaxy were present. The wedding photograph in which Fr. Tom Duggan is prominent, and which always hung in a place of honour in his study, is surely among the most historic photographs of the period: it was the last occasion for many of those present to sit down together in peace. Many years later Tom Duggan told one of his curates that during the reception Michael Collins had taken him aside and said, 'Father Tom, I'm afraid there's going to be trouble'. His fears were well grounded: a year later almost to the very day, he met his death at Béalnabláth.

The Truce which had appeared to promise so much proved instead a harbinger of disaster. The Treaty was signed on 6 December 1921, by Collins and Griffith among others on the Irish side. A month later it was ratified by the Dáil by 64 votes to 57, a Provisional Government was set up but Eamonn de Valera and his followers repudiated the Treaty and refused to recognise the Provisional Government.

The Provisional Government began to recruit for a national army while the majority of the old I.R.A. men declared against the Treaty. Units of the old Dublin Brigade seized the Four Courts as an armed headquarters but the Provisional Government refused to be provoked into retaliation, largely, it is believed through the influence of Michael Collins who abhorred the very thought of civil war.

In subsequent efforts to avoid war, Collins concluded an election pact with de Valera with the intention of making it possible to form a coalition government after the general election which was due. But eventually he was forced by pressure from the Cabinet and from the British to repudiate the pact which he did at a mass meeting in Cork a few days before the election.

The election results strengthened the hands of the Provisional Government though not to the expected extent. Claiming now a mandate from the people, the Government ordered the national army to attack the Four Courts on 28 June 1922. As the first shells began to pound against the walls of the Four Courts, the Civil War had begun. It was only bringing into the open a conflict that had already begun in men's minds.

1 Dr. Charles Townsend, in page 66 of his new book *The British Campaign in Ireland 1919-1921* agrees with this assessment:
'Guerillas do not have to stand their ground in defence of strategic points or lines; they can and must operate only at the time and place to suit them. For the I.R.A. with a few thousand poorly armed men, any idea of fighting 'by the book' was absurd. The conventions of war, which now seemed akin to civilised morality to the well-matched European states, meant certain destruction to Irish rebels, whose prime concern was not to act with honour but to survive. The I.R.A. of 1920 was to find that by matching its operations to its needs it could survive for long enough to achieve a psychological victory out of military stalemate.'

2 On the Irish side, General Tom Barry expresses the same opinion in somewhat more callous language:
'We had no illusions about our weakness or the enemy's strength, and knew well the heavy price that Ireland would have to pay before the dawn of freedom ended the long night of terror, devastation and death. Many, many other volunteers would join their dead comrades, but we would go on and on killing those old-age enemies of our race, until they had enough and departed from the shores of our island.' (*Guerilla Days in Ireland*, page 223).

BLESSED ARE THE PEACEMAKERS

(MATTHEW 5.9)

CIVIL WAR RAGES

It soon became clear that the anti-Treaty forces (the 'Irregulars' as they were derisively called by their opponents in the Free State Army) were not going to win. Their occupation of the Four Courts might have made sense as a gesture of defiance, a symbolic stand on behalf of the Republic but as a military operation it was doomed to failure unless help arrived quickly for the beleaguered garrison. As the Free State army was still numerically small, a resolute thrust from the South might have transformed the military situation in the early days but like the pikemen of '98 the Four Courts garrison waited in vain for reinforcements. Like the Wexford men they might have lamented, 'Mo léan ar an Mhumain nár eirigh.' On the fourth day of the siege fire swept through the Four Courts and there was no option for the garrison but to surrender. The survivors were led off to captivity including Liam Mellows and Rory O'Connor, the guiding spirits.

Fighting continued in O'Connell Street for a further few days. Cathal Brugha, a legendary figure in the War of Independence, refused to surrender and fell mortally wounded as he charged a Free State Army barricade in the street. Unfortunately it was the shape of things to come.

Thenceforth, the anti-Treaty forces were fighting a losing war. The trouble was that though they enjoyed numerical superiority at the start, they lacked any sort of over-all strategy or plan of campaign. Liam Deasy paints a grim picture of their unpreparedness in his book *Brother against Brother*.[1]

> We had no real military policy. No discussions ever took place on the strategy and tactics we should adopt in the event of the Provisional Government forcing us to fight a civil war... At best, the Four Courts could only be considered as a protest in arms with failure as the inevitable end. It had become clearly evident to me that we were not prepared for this war which should have ended with the fall of the Four Courts.

Tom Barry was equally pessimistic. He had been captured as he tried to join the garrison in the Four Courts. Somehow a Free State Army uniform found its way into Mountjoy. Barry takes up the story:

> In Free State uniform one of us stood a great chance of getting out of Mountjoy. We discussed who would make the attempt and the others were unanimous that it should be me. I wanted Mellows out as it was my view that the military war was lost already and he could be more useful politically.

Incidentally Barry's attempt to escape was foiled and he was forced to spend the early months of the Civil War in prison.

The military situation continued to deteriorate for the opponents of the Treaty. Though they numbered in their ranks many of the famous guerrilla leaders of the War of Independence such as Barry and Deasy, Liam Lynch and Sean Moylan, Dan Breen and Dinny Lacey, they were hampered by lack of arms and ammunition and a chronic shortage of financial resources. They also lacked another vital element, the support of the people: many 'safe houses' in Black and Tan days were no longer prepared to open their doors to men 'on the run'.

All the advantages lay with the Government. They enjoyed the full support of all the resources of the State. The newspapers were with them and the Hierarchy. Their initial numerical inferiority was soon more than offset by the formation of a regularly paid and well-armed large national army. The benevolent attitude of the British was another decisive factor.

Within weeks the anti-Treaty forces were incapable of waging open and offensive warfare. The territory under their control gradually shrank and soon, for practical purposes, it was reduced to the area south of a line drawn from Limerick to Waterford, the so-called 'Munster Republic'. Following some landings of troops by sea in Cork and Kerry even this line could not be held and slowly at first and then very quickly it began to crumble. Limerick, Waterford and Clonmel fell in turn, and on the tenth of August, Cork city was captured. On the following day Fermoy, the last town to be held by the Republicans, was abandoned by General Liam Lynch.

Thenceforth the Republicans were virtually an army without territory or barracks. It was back to the old days of guerrilla tactics. But the glamour was gone. In the Cork area the remnants retreated west and gathered in the remote but beautiful countryside around Ballyvourney and Coolea, deep in West Cork. This rugged terrain with its little homesteads scattered among the hills, and a few small villages, one of the last strongholds of the Gaelic tongue, became now the unlikely last outpost of those who still believed in the lost Republican military cause. Here, backed only by what de Valera called 'their allies, the hills', they saw their dreams turn to ashes as the Government troops captured every town and village. As far as making war was concerned, the Republicans were now reduced to making occasional small-scale attacks on Free State units, perpetrating acts of sabotage on roads and bridges and railways, burning houses and public buildings – a pathetic make-believe kind of warfare.

In late August, 1922, two weeks after the capture of Cork, Michael Collins, as commander in chief of the Free State Army, made a tour of inspection of the conquered South. Whether he also meant his journey to be in the nature of a peace mission has never been definitely established but the available evidence would seem to suggest so. On his return journey to Cork after a sentimental reunion with old friends in the towns of West Cork, he was ambushed at Béalnabláth near Crookstown and shot dead.

His passing led to increased bitterness. The inability and failure of the Free State Army to round up the scattered remnants of the Republican forces led to frustration and acrimony among the leaders of the Government, particularly between General Richard Mulcahy, Collins' successor as commander in chief, and Kevin O'Higgins, the Minister for Home Affairs. With a view to demoralising the enemy, the Government adopted a policy of extreme repression, going as far as executing prisoners in retaliation for acts of war waged by their comrades outside. Four Republican leaders Liam Mellows, Rory O'Connor, Dick Barrett and Joe McElvey, one from each province, were executed on the morning of 8 December 1922. Military courts were set up and in all seventy-seven executions took place.

The position of the Republican fighters became increasingly desperate. Those in captivity greatly outnumbered those on active service. By February 1923, only the obstinate determination of Liam Lynch and a few others prevented a general laying down of arms.

Tom Duggan's Attitude

How had Tom Duggan reacted to the Treaty? His immediate and spontaneous reaction had been positive. Like Michael Collins, he viewed it as a means to an end, a stepping-stone towards the Republic which was not attainable in the existing circumstances. But he soon discovered that this view was not shared by the Republican leaders in Cork, including many of his closest associates. To a certain extent he could identify with their feelings. They had borne the heat of the day and its burdens during the War of Independence but during the Truce they had found themselves ignored, out on a limb politically speaking. Even a moderate like Florence O'Donoghue was worried:

> The Truce wrought changes which penetrated even to the very foundations of the national movement. After the eleventh of July nothing was or ever could have been the same no matter how the Truce ended. The most obvious change was that the Army's role of leadership in the struggle was ended and the responsibility for pressing the national demand for Sovereign Independence was translated to the field of diplomacy.

It soon became clear that there existed a hard core of doctrinaire Republicans who were determined to remain faithful to their oath of allegiance to the Republic, come what may: the mystique of the Republic dominated and overshadowed all their thinking. In the course of a pastoral letter Bishop Coholan tried to allay their fears of breaking their solemn oath by telling them that the oath was invalid from the beginning[2] – one cannot swear allegiance to an aspiration, an oath to a non-existent republic could not be binding in conscience. He was wasting his time: such fine distinctions passed over the heads of the Republicans.

Intellectually, Tom Duggan did not agree with the extremists. He preferred the more pragmatic approach of Michael Collins. But in his view the rights and wrongs of the Treaty was not the paramount question of the moment. The reality which overshadowed everything else was that these men were preparing to resist the Treaty by force. Civil War loomed very closely: somehow it had to be averted.

Duggan was opposed to civil war for several reasons:

> Firstly, in the abstract he abhorred the very concept of civil war which he regarded as a primitive and uncivilised way of settling differences between people of the same race. From his knowledge of history he was aware that civil war leads to the commission of atrocities by both sides which would never be even contemplated against a common enemy. He knew that civil war leaves deep and lasting scars which are almost impossible to eradicate.
>
> Secondly, the Irish Hierarchy[3] had condemned the Republican cause on moral grounds and excommunicated those who were involved and Bishop Coholan[4] described priests who defied this order as 'cheap-john sort of confessors'. It was one thing for a priest to adopt a different theological view-point to that of his Bishop during the War of Independence when he was alone in his

condemnation but the unanimous condemnation of the Hierarchy made it very difficult even for a priest of strong republican convictions to dissent publicly.

Thirdly, a majority of the people in the June general election had signalled their approval of the Treaty. The Government could claim a mandate from the people and as a democrat Duggan felt that this view had to be respected.

Fourthly, as a realist and as a man with some experience of military matters he regarded the struggle being waged by the Republicans as a useless sacrifice of lives without any prospect of even a moral victory. Too many had died already: it was time for common sense to prevail.

In view of these compelling arguments he decided to adopt the role of peacemaker. While there was still hope of a negotiated peace in the early months of the war he tried to influence the leaders on both sides towards peace but according as the struggle became more and more a lost cause for the Republicans he concentrated all his efforts on getting them to desist from the struggle.

To help achieve his aim Duggan made common cause with a group called the 'Neutral I.R.A.' who although anti-Treaty were anti-Civil War as well and included in its ranks such respected figures as Sean O'Hegarty and Florence O'Donoghue, O.C. and adjutant respectively of the old Cork I Brigade. O'Donoghue describes their motivation:

> The body consisted exclusively of men who had pre-Truce service, and who had not taken an active part on either side in the civil war... The only purpose of its existence was to make peace; it sprang up spontaneously in every area in response to an appeal for this purpose. The opinions of its members for or against the Treaty was immaterial, but there is no doubt that the sympathies of the great majority were with the Republicans.

As the Civil War grew in bitterness, Duggan's political outlook began to change. Following the death of Collins and the emergence of Kevin O'Higgins as the strong man in the Government, Duggan began to have grave misgivings about the political outlook and intentions of the Government. He had never doubted the genuineness of Michael Collins's republicanism and had accepted his assurance that the Treaty was only a stepping-stone towards the Republic. But by the end of 1922 he had come to the conclusion that for most of the members of the Government the Treaty was an end in itself. The repressive policy of the Government and particularly the execution of prisoners revolted him. Gradually he found himself, politically speaking, moving towards the Republican party.

Much later in life he described his attitude at the time in pragmatic terms by saying that he felt it was better to be wrong with the right people than to be right with the wrong people. In other words, that, though the Republicans had erred grievously in taking up arms nevertheless, they represented for him the best long-term hope for the future.

Early Peace Moves

The Civil War had scarcely begun when peace moves were afoot to bring it to an end. Cork city had been a depressed area since the burning of the city centre in December 1920. Trade and commerce had languished and unemployment was rife. Economically speaking, being capital of the 'Munster Republic' was a doubtful privilege. The 'Merchant Princes', for centuries a powerful force in the public life of the city, decided that something would have to be done to remedy the situation. They decided to call a meeting under the aegis of the Cork Harbour Board for 17 July 1922, 'to discuss the best means of ending the present disastrous conflict'. Those present at the meeting formed themselves into a body to be known as The People's Rights Association and passed resolutions to be forwarded to General Michael Collins and General Liam Lynch, the leaders of the opposing sides.

The resolutions demanded an immediate meeting of the newly elected Dail 'as the only authority now recognised by both sets of belligerents' and 'pending the meeting of the Dail we call upon the Government in Dublin and G.H.Q., Clonmel, to cease fire'.

The wording of the resolutions was an indication of the political immaturity of its sponsors and could not but be regarded as deeply offensive to the Provisional Government. The use of phrases such as 'both sets of belligerents' seemed to place the two armies on an equal footing and to overlook the fact that one was the properly constituted army of a lawfully elected government.

When the communication from Cork reached Collins he was deeply hurt. His reply was cold and dismissive:

> The representatives who gathered together must know that this is a fight to the finish for the rights of the people's representatives to govern. It is a fight for the people. Even now it is a simple matter to

> end hostilities if those who are opposing the people will but turn aside from their resistance and give the people the chance they deserve.*

Liam Lynch's reply was equally unhelpful: 'I wish to inform you that when the Provisional Government cease their attack on us, defensive action on our part can cease.'[5]

Failing to read the signs that nothing further could be done at the time to bring about a change in these entrenched attitudes the People's Rights Association decided to communicate further with Collins and Lynch. Collins was asked two questions:

> 1. Do you agree for such a cessation of hostilities as General Liam Lynch intimates he is prepared to accept?
> 2. Do you agree to call forthwith a meeting of the Dail and to allow the Sovereign Assembly of the people to decide on the necessity or policy of a bitter and prolonged war?

It was at this point that Tom Duggan's aid was sought to act as an intermediary along with Tom Dowdall, a prominent Cork businessman: apparently Duggan was chosen because of his known links with both Michael Collins and Liam Lynch. The request placed him in an awkward position. On the one hand, he did not like to refuse any request that might help the cause of peace but at the same time he felt the appeal was being made by the wrong people at the wrong time and was bound to end in failure. Eventually he agreed to act and a meeting with Collins was arranged to take place in Dublin.

The Collins they met was not at all the friendly smiling extrovert that Duggan had known since 1916. He was grim and unfriendly and informed them coldly that they had come to the wrong man: he was simply a soldier carrying out the orders of his government from which he had been seconded. He refused to discuss the matter further but indicated that as a matter of courtesy he would send a formal written reply to the question asked. The written reply clearly signalled that Collins wanted nothing further to do with the People's Rights Association:

> Your memorandum dated 1 August addressed to me has been delivered to me by Mr. T. Dowdall who was accompanied by Fr. Duggan.

* *The Cork Examiner*, August 1922.

> With reference to the reply from Liam Lynch, described by you as Chief of Staff, Fermoy, with reference also to the two categorical questions you ask me:
>
> This is a time when above all things there should be clear thinking on the part of the public representatives. The Government is sending you an official answer as presumably your communication was meant to be addressed to them.
>
> So far as the Army is concerned I am merely obeying the orders of my Government. The Government has made it fully clear that its desire is to secure obedience to proper authority. When an expression of such obedience comes from the irregular leaders, I take it there will be no longer any need for hostilities.

Duggan also interviewed Liam Lynch at this point. He told Ernie O'Malley:

> I was sent by Tom Dowdall before the Republicans left Cork to see Lynch in Fermoy. I suggested that there should be a peace settlement but Lynch said: 'I am working on behalf of the Republic and there I'll stay.' He was the most un-cooperative of the whole lot.*

It was Duggan's last meeting with Collins: within three weeks the 'Big Fellow' was dead. In spite of that unsatisfactory meeting in Dublin, Duggan remained firm in his belief that with Collins' death the cause of peace lost its strongest advocate.

Duggan realised what he had suspected all along, that any highly-publicised peace move by outside bodies or individuals at this stage was doomed to failure. The split was in the Sinn Féin movement and it could only be healed from within. He saw his future task as a peacemaker, as a go-between, as one trying to set up informal meetings between former comrades-in-arms, now on opposing sides.

Following the death of Collins there was a certain hardening of attitude on the part of the Provisional Government. This was less evident in Cork than elsewhere, possibly because the commanding officers of the Free State army there, Generals Tom Ennis and Emmet Dalton and others, belonged to the old Michael Collins circle and shared their leader's antipathy towards the Civil War. A series of meetings took place between them and Tom Barry and Liam Deasy on the Republican side. The first, set up by Fr. Dan McCarthy, acting on behalf of his friend Tom Duggan, took place on 23 October 1922, near Crookstown. The final

* Ernie O'Malley papers.

meeting took place in the home of the O'Connell family at Ballinguilley near Ballincollig. In his interview with Ernie O'Malley, Duggan described this meeting:

> Deasy, Tom Barry and Hyde met Ennis in O'Connell's near Ballincollig. I was the guide. Ennis and the others had an *aide de camp* who fell asleep. They met at 7 in the night-time and the meeting continued until 4 in the morning.*

The Free State officers present, judging by Barry's subsequent report to the Republican executive, were prepared to go a long way towards meeting Republican demands. This may be seen as evidence of the growing disillusionment of the Collins faithful with the atmosphere prevailing at government headquarters in Dublin. This was the impression of Connie Neenan, at the time a prominent figure on the anti-Treaty side in Cork:

> In my opinion, for what it is worth, we would never have had an execution had Collins lived. Emmet Dalton was a case in point. I knew Emmet and Charlie, all of the Dublin crowd. In his resignation statement, Dalton said, 'I cannot stand for the execution of any Irishman'. There you have the authentic Collins type speaking out through Dalton. But who succeeded him? People who hated us and murdered indiscriminately.†

Judging by Barry's account the terms agreed on at the final meeting at Ballincollig included the disbandment of both armies and the formation of a new Volunteer Army under an agreed Executive and no Minister of Defence. But both sets of headquarters repudiated the proposed agreement and the Civil War dragged on.

Possibly as a result of this series of meetings a better atmosphere prevailed between the two high commands in Cork. It is noteworthy that as compared to Kerry, for instance, Cork was comparatively free of atrocities and excesses.

Tom Duggan succeeded in maintaining a good personal relationship with the Free State Army authorities, particularly with General Tom Ennis. It is interesting to read in this regard what Calton Younger in a book entitled *Ireland's Civil War* relates: 'Dinny Cronin told me of an occasion when General Tom Ennis accompanied Canon Duggan to Gouganebarra with a proposal. Cronin was ready to run when he saw Ennis's uniform.'

* Ibid.

† Eoin, Mac, *Survivors.*

It is interesting but highly unlikely. Dinny Cronin was a man gifted with a lively imagination. It is stretching credulity to believe that a Free State general would walk in unannounced to a Republican stronghold even in the company of Tom Duggan.

Whatever about the situation in Cork, the Government continued its repressive policy generally. The vigorous protests of Archbishop Byrne of Dublin who questioned the morality of the executions went unheeded. The year 1922 ended on a sad and bitter note.

Liam Deasy's Surrender

Liam Deasy, the current assistant chief of staff of the Republican forces, was found with arms, taken prisoner and sentenced to execution on 18 January 1923. For some time before his capture he had been seriously considering making an appeal to the Republican executive to lay down arms. He asked his captors for permission to communicate with his comrades. Permission was granted provided he signed a letter of surrender in the following terms:

> I have undertaken for the future of Ireland to accept and aid in an immediate and unconditional surrender of all arms and men as required by General Mulcahy.
>
> In pursuance of this undertaking I am asked to appeal for a similar undertaking from the following: E. de Valera, P. Rutledge, A. Stack, M. Colivet, Domhnal O'Callaghan, Liam Lynch, Con Moloney, T. Derrig, F. Aiken, F. Barrett, T. Barry, S. MacSwiney, Seamas Robinson, Humphrey Murphy, Seamus O'Donovan, Frank Carty, and for the immediate and unconditional surrender of themselves after issue by them of an order for this surrender on the part of all those associated with them, together with their arms and equipment.

Deasy agreed whereupon his sentence of execution was revoked and he was allowed to write a confidential letter to each of the men named. He was also asked to nominate a courier who would deliver the letters.

Deasy's confidential letter took the form of an apologia for his action, the conclusion of which was as follows:

> I realise the effect this action of mine will have against our forces continuing, but my comrades when they view the whole outlook nationally will see the absolute urgency of bringing the present chapter to a close: if we conserve our forces the spirit of Ireland is

> saved. Our advance may be greatly impeded for a time but the freedom we desire will be achieved by, we all hope, our united efforts again.
>
> Your reply to the attached is expected by 6th February, or as soon after as you have had an opportunity of considering carefully the whole matter. This note is absolutely confidential and is being handed enclosed and sealed by me to a courier appointed by me.

In his book *Brother against Brother* Deasy reveals the identity of his courier:

> I was also asked to nominate a friend who would act as courier for me and undertake to deliver each of the sixteen letters to the anti-Treaty Executive. Because of the delicate nature of this mission I suggested Fr. Tom Duggan who was then a secretary to the Bishop of Cork and well known because of his efforts for peace since the start of the Civil War.
>
> I had no hesitation in entrusting this delicate mission to him. Fr. Duggan arrived and was most enthusiastic in his efforts to be helpful. Thanks to his generous co-operation all the letters were delivered to the addresses without delay. Fr. Duggan returned to Arbour Hill a few times bringing answers from some members of the Executive including Liam Lynch.
>
> All of these gave an unqualified NO to my suggestion which did not entirely surprise me. In fact it was what I had anticipated because the idea of ending the conflict would not have appeared so drastic if I were advocating it from a position other than as a prisoner.

The summons to Dublin came as a complete surprise to Tom Duggan. The first he heard about it was a message he received from General Emmet Dalton, G.O.C. of the Free State troops in Cork, enclosing a telegram from the Adjutant General in Dublin which he (Dalton) had just received, dated 8.20 p.m. 29 January 1923 which read: 'Send Father Duggan, Victoria Cross, Cork, to report to Dublin G.H.Q. at once. Important that he should travel tonight.'

When Duggan arrived in Dublin he was given a safe-conduct signed by Gearóid O'Sullivan, Adjutant General. It stated:

> Rev. Fr. Duggan who bears this note travels with my permission and is to receive every facility from officers and men of the army.

> The officer or n.c.o. who inspects this permit will report the number of same to his G.O.C.
>
> This permit holds until midnight on Monday fifth prox.

Duggan received a corresponding safe-conduct from General Tom Barry: 'Bearer Rev. T. Duggan is travelling on important army business. He is not to be interfered with and he will be facilitated in every way possible by all officers and men.'

And so Tom Duggan was on centre-stage at national level. The immediate response to Deasy's appeal was negative. Duggan himself received the following reply from Liam Lynch, dated February 1st, 1923 and addressed to Rev. Fr. T. O'Dubaghain, Hibernian Hotel, Dublin:

> A Chara Urramaigh,
>
> To acknowledge your letter, with accompanying communication from Liam Deasy, D. C/S. Same has been painfully noted. The Republican Government will give its answer in due course to the latest terror of the enemy.
>
> The proposal of the enemy is that of mad men and would not get a second thought from us. We would not even under such circumstances discuss peace with him. Unless enemy has completely lost his Irish outlook he would not ask such terms. At any time, on our side, we would not press such terms on the enemy, as it would put the nation as a whole in such a position that it would never recover.
>
> Even if our last volunteer is to be wiped out we will not accept being British subjects. This being so we cannot be asked to do the impossible.
>
> Even in his barbarous and un-Irish methods enemy seem to forget that it was practically our forces alone who drove the common enemy to discuss peace with us. It is indeed sad to see leaders with such records in the last war being so unnecessarily sacrificed. Our ideals now are only as in the last war and no enemy will change them nomatter what method he may employ.
>
> We fully realise that no matter how long this war lasts victory will be on our side. We are fully alive to our resources at home and abroad and all these in time will be brought to play on the situation. There is no one more anxious for peace than we who are in such

close touch with the consequences of this war. The war is getting more savage every day owing to the unchecked policy of enemy in carrying out executions. Every week of war in future will be worse than any month of the past.

Certain people, perhaps trying to be neutral, have done considerable damage to the general situation. These curious people seem to concentrate all their energies on our forces.

I am writing in the hope of finding you at your hotel. I presume you got all documents delivered to our people through the one source.

I would like to be assured by you that outside of documents which D/C.S. signed the enemy did not see other confidential documents.

I would like to know how these were typed.

I fully realise your position in this painful duty and furthermore have in mind your services to the REPUBLIC in the last war against the common enemy.

Mise le meas mór
Liam Lynch, CHIEF OF STAFF.

To Deasy, Lynch wrote as follows:

To acknowledge receipt of your personal and private letter, with your circulated correspondence of 30-1-23.

As to your views that we could become British subjects for even a temporary period, you should have realised that our forces would fight to the death rather than accept this. We have lost patience with the enemy in their execution policy. If any further executions take place we will have to meet them with very drastic measures. You do not seem to realise the numerous enemy difficulties, as you only refer to ours, besides they must accept responsibility for everything that has happened and will happen.

As requested by you F. O'Donoghue arrived here and tried to obtain an interview with me. I did not arrange this but informed him as to the only lines on which to obtain peace.

I assure you I will do my utmost to obtain a cessation of hostilities but this must be within very definite lines.

> I hope that your life will be spared and that we shall soon meet again in a free and happy Ireland. Though you marked your covering letter as being strictly confidential we only take the enemy at his face value.

Reading through the letters one wonders in what sort of dream world Lynch was living at the time. But the man's absolute sincerity shines through. Considering that Deasy's defection must have come as a crushing blow his letter is remarkably free from personal bitterness or recrimination. Indeed there is a certain nobility in his replies that seems to have been inherent in his character.

As might be expected, Deasy's call produced very varied reactions. On the government side, there was jubilation and an offer of an armistice to all Republicans prepared to follow Deasy's lead. On the Republican side it was an occasion for closing ranks among members of the Executive. The general feeling was one of shock and surprise: it was summed up in a letter from Sean Moylan, then working for the cause in the United States, to Liam Lynch:

> Deasy's attitude knocked me silly. I thought he'd be the last man to cave in. It wasn't a question of being able to win with us. It was that we were right, that we couldn't surrender, being right. It wasn't cowardice on his part, I know.

As time went on, many began to have second thoughts, and hidden misgivings began to surface. This was particularly true of Tom Barry. The rank and file Republicans were dumbfounded. Deasy was a national figure who had commanded the famous Third Cork Brigade of the I.R.A. in the War of Independence. As news of his action sank in, it led to a general reappraisal of attitudes and a growing consensus about the futility of continuing the struggle. It could be said that Deasy's action signalled the beginning of the end for the Republicans.

The next few months were among the most dangerous and eventful in Tom Duggan's life. His involvement with Deasy had brought him into the closest contact with those at the very centre of national affairs.

He was aware of the danger in which he stood, knowing that there was still a very determined hard core of Republicans who refused even to listen to any talk of surrender and who looked on any would-be peacemakers as traitors to the cause. Even Tom Duggan was not immune. In case he did not realise where he stood, it was brought home to him very forcibly in a letter he received from a high-up Republican source:

Headquarters Cork I Brigade I.R.A.

To Fr. Duggan,

Re yours of yesterday's date, I want you to understand that I will not allow you to interfere in any way with the military situation in my area.

In future you will not communicate with me on the question of peace. I have definitely made up my mind, and I will have nothing to do with you or anybody else except through G.H.Q., I.R.A.

You will be running a grave risk in travelling through the 3rd, 7th and 8th Battalion areas of Cork I from now on.

It was a chilling warning: its peremptory tone was calculated to instil fear but Duggan was a brave man and he ignored the threat though the 8th Battalion area included the Ballyvourney district where the headquarters of the southern I.R.A. was located and which in many ways had become the eye of the storm. He continued to visit that area again and again in his peacemaking efforts. In fact his life during the next few months was one of almost continuous motion. He carried with him permits from both sides for the use of his motor-cycle but now the distance became too great for that form of transport and he was forced to hire a car from Messrs. Johnson and Perrott of Cork. The subsequent statement of accounts, paid personally by Duggan, gives some idea of the extent of his journeying. Often the governing factor in his itineraries was the whereabouts of General Liam Lynch with whom the ultimate power of decision largely lay. The extreme limits of his circuit were Dublin and Ballyvourney and included such strategic points as Cahir, Ballyporeen, the Glen of Aherlow, Araglin, Kilworth and Thurles – in fact anywhere he could find the key figures, most of whom were now hunted and 'on the run', their main problem now being simply to survive.

He was welcomed generally by the Republicans wherever he went. The Free State authorities were more guarded in their approach and gave only limited support to his peacemaking efforts as can be gathered from the following communication of General Mulcahy:

G.H.Q. Portabello, 21-2-23

To all Officers and Men:

This is to demand safe-conduct for the Rev. T.F. Duggan and two companions in their journeyings up to 12 noon on Wednesday, 28

February. They shall be offered any necessary assistance without any unnecessary association with them.

Risteard Ua Maolcata
General.

The two anonymous companions were Tom Barry and Tom Crofts who had taken over Deasy's role as O.C. First Southern Division. By this time both men were actively co-operating with Duggan's peace efforts.

Barry and Crofts tried to impress on Liam Lynch the absolute need of calling a meeting of the National Executive of the army to discuss the crisis. They found themselves up against a stone wall: Lynch would not listen. Instead he issued a proclamation to all ranks. While admitting that a 'supreme crisis' had arrived he claimed that they were in a stronger position than ever and warned against the danger of premature peace initiatives: 'The situation can only be destroyed by ill-considered and precipitate actions of individuals.'

But the situation was rapidly moving out of his control. Back in Ballyvourney, Barry and Crofts reported on their fruitless journey to Dublin to a meeting of the divisional council of the First Southern Division at Cronin's in Gouganebarra on the next day. Barry's demand for a meeting of the National Executive met with almost unanimous support.

Ordering Tod Andrews to join him as adjutant, Lynch left Dublin for the South on 13 February 1923. He told Andrews that the purpose of his journey was to 'pull the South together'. It was only a dream and he never returned to Dublin. For a Chief of Staff who still harboured hopes of victory, the long journey to Ballyvourney should have dispelled such illusions. His ability to close his eyes to the evidence of the almost complete disintegration of their fighting units caused Andrews to conclude that 'he had developed a mental block which prevented him from believing that we could be beaten'.*

They travelled by all sorts of make-shift transport, sometimes by car, by pony and trap and once, crossing a river near Newcastle, they were nearly drowned, but mostly they travelled by foot, avoiding built-up areas, travelling mostly by night, more like fugitives on the run than a Chief of Staff and his adjutant.

Lynch finally arrived at Leaca Bán on 26 February only to find out next day at a meeting of the officers of the First Southern Division at Jamie Moynihan's in Coolea that they wanted only one thing – to end the nightmare struggle which was leading nowhere. A firm call was made for a meeting of the National

* Andrews, C.S., *Dublin Made Me.*

Executive of the Republican army. Lynch hesitated, pointing out the danger inherent in bringing all the members of the National Executive together. Eventually he agreed on 3 March to convene the meeting and the date was fixed for Thursday, 15 March in the Second Southern Division area.

Everything now depended on the outcome of the Republican Army Executive meeting. In such a situation Duggan was never willing simply to allow matters to take their course. At heart he was an intriguer, and believed in a little judicious lobbying of members beforehand. He thought it unlikely in this instance that the Executive would agree to lay down arms unless some honourable peace formula could be devised to be placed before them. He resolved to produce such a formula and with this in mind he consulted some trusted friends in the movement and eventually they agreed on the following formula:

> To end the present deplorable state of affairs in Ireland, we, the undersigned, appeal to officers and men of the I.R.A. to accept in the interests of the future of Ireland the following proposals for peace:
> 1. The immediate cessation of hostilities by calling off all activities and operations of the I.R.A.
> 2. The dumping of all arms and ammunition by the Republican forces, under the charge of Battalion Commandants to be responsible that the arms will not be used against the Free State Government or Forces.
> 3. Subsequent to a General Election, the arms and munitions to be handed over to the elected government of the country.

The next problem was to find, for respectability sake, someone of high standing to sign the document. Archbishop John Harty of Cashel was suggested and when approached by Duggan agreed to sign along with Canon Ryan, Administrator, Thurles, Fr. Tim O'Leary, C.C., St. Finbarrs South, Fr. Michael Kiely, C.C., St. Peter's and Paul's, Frank Daly, Chairman, Cork Harbour Board, T.P. Dowdall and Dr. Tadhg O'Donovan.

Duggan's next move was to request General Tom Barry to arrange for copies of the peace proposals to be forwarded to each member of the Army Executive. His covering letter to Barry was as follows:

> A cara dílis,
>
> I have been directed to forward to you attached for circulation and adoption by the I.R.A. as a basis for peace.

The signatures attached were collected at very short notice.

In a day or two I hope to let you have the signatures of other representative Irishmen.

Would you please transmit copies of these proposals to the various members of the I.R.A. Executive.

Mise do chara,
T. O Dughagain, sagart.

Barry's reply came the same day:

A Chara and a Athair,

I have received you letter of March 4 enclosing copy of proposals for peace signed by His Grace, Most Rev. J. Harty, Archbishop of Cashel.

I note your request that I circulate these proposals for consideration amongst the members of the I.R.A. Executive Council. I will readily do so.

I await your further communications.

Mise le meas mór,
Tom Barry, Comdt. General,
Irish Republican Army.

Florence O'Donoghue makes it clear in his book *No Other Law* that Duggan was responsible for this peace proposal:

> The moving spirit in this effort was Father Tom Duggan, now Very Rev. Canon Duggan, President of St. Finbarr's College, Farranferris, Cork. He had been associated with nearly every peace effort from the start of the civil war, and had been indefatigable in striving to find an acceptable solution. After the issue of Dr. Harty's proposals he continued to urge on both sides the desirability of peace.

A few days later Barry again wrote to Duggan:

> The terms of peace that we discussed are attached. I think that they are now in the form you suggested. They meet my view on the matter only because of circumstances. I have already promised you to urge their acceptance by my fellow-members in the Executive.

Barry did more. Along with a copy of the proposals which he sent to each member of the Army Executive he enclosed a resumé of his own personal views, concluding with a strong recommendation urging acceptance of the proposals. The resumé is in handwritten form in Duggan's papers and though unsigned it bears all the signs of Tom Barry's handiwork. Possibly he and Duggan had worked together in preparing the final version.

He began with a cold analysis of the military situation. The Republicans had only 8,000 men on active service as compared with 13,000 in prison. They had no finance, not even to buy cigarettes for the men; in some areas there was no longer any arrangement for the supply of clothes and boots; they were living on their friends and these were becoming fewer and fewer.

In contrast, the Free State forces were a modern army, outnumbering the Republicans by six or eight to one; they were paid regularly, possessed armoured cars, aeroplanes and munitions.

Their own organisation was very bad and non-existent in many counties:

> There are not 20 active men in many of these areas. Most of our divisions do not equal in strength an enemy Battalion, except perhaps the first Southern. Intelligence is very bad owing to the people not co-operating with us to any appreciable extent. You are aware how essential in guerrilla warfare good intelligence is!

He went on to the political situation:

> Finally as regards the political situation, the Free State is functioning as a normal Government accepted by the people as such, and those opposing it are regarded as guilty of national sabotage. The Republican Government is only a name and there has been no attempt to set up a network of administration.

What was his conclusion?:

> I can anticipate a dragging on of our activities for a period of not more than two months before we are finally forced to accept their terms. After hearing the views of many officers I am convinced – in short – that we are losing and about to be beaten.
>
> Realising the sacrifices that will be made if the war which is now hopeless is allowed to drag on for a couple of months, the impending execution of some of our best officers and men, in enemy custody.... the losses other than lives the country will suffer, I am

> urging on you a stopping of the war. I believe that you are not justified in carrying on once you decide as I have decided some time after I received Liam Deasy's document.
>
> We would not be justified morally, neither would it be justice to our Army inside or outside jails, and I contend that it certainly would not be in the interests of Ireland or her Independence to carry on with the hope of success gone.

What did Barry want the Army Executive to do?:

> I suggest to you that the attached peace terms basis is simply an alteration in Republican policy. It entails (a) The calling off of the war. (b) The dumping of arms. (c) The recognition of the principle that must be accepted sooner or later viz: that all arms in the country must be controlled by the Government as soon as a properly elected Government can be elected.
>
> The acceptance of this basis of peace does not entail any negotiation whatever with the enemy, nor compromise our principles. It is the altering of our policy and methods without reference to the enemy, although we recognise that there are certain conditions to follow as a natural sequence, such as the stopping of Executions, Arrests, Raids for arms, Release of prisoners etc.
>
> We have to choose between accepting this or carrying on for a short time until we are wiped out without attaining our objective. I urge on you very earnestly the acceptance of this alteration in policy in the interests of our freedom, our army and our country.

Having made sure that the peace proposals were in the hands of each member of the Republican Executive, Duggan next tried to intervene personally with the leaders. O'Donoghue relates:

> On 15 March he [Duggan] saw Liam and many of the officers of the 1st Southern Division in the area between Ballingeary and Ballyvourney. Two days later he travelled to Dublin with Frank Daly and Sean O'Hegarty, where he interviewed Archbishop Byrne and Mr. W.T. Cosgrave, the head of the Free State Government.

Tod Andrews in his book *Dublin Made Me*, confirms this account and provides some colourful details:

> From the beginning of the civil war, Father Tom, who was liked and trusted by everyone, tried to heal the split in the I.R.A. He was now making his last effort. He had seen Liam Lynch who made it clear that he was not willing to compromise in any way. Barry was more flexible. In a strongly worded letter, which I saw, Liam ordered him to discontinue further involvement in peace talks.

Andrews goes on to describe the final meeting between Duggan and Lynch – it was more like a parley between enemies than a friendly exchange of views between friends:

> The local pacificators got busy. A meeting between Liam on the one hand, with, on the other, Tom Barry and Father Duggan was arranged to be held in Ballingeary. Liam, Con and I duly went to Ballingeary to find that Father Duggan and Tom Barry accompanied by several men I did not know, had already arrived and were grouped on the opposite side of the street. The scene resembled one from a Western film when rival groups of ranchers come into some cowtown to shoot out their differences.
>
> No progress was made at the conference between Father Duggan and Liam Lynch.

Some days later, Lynch wrote to Tom Derrig, the new Adjutant-General, following the capture of Con Maloney: 'The new move by Fr. Duggan with Bishops etc. is worrying especially when one of our senior officers gives a hand in the game. All this humbug will have to be cleared up.'*

The peace proposals put forward received wide publicity in the national press, putting added pressure on the I.R.A. leaders. Hopes were high that peace was at last in sight. Both sides were expected to refrain from provocative activity.

On 12 March 1923, *The Cork Examiner* reported:

> Since the publication on Thursday last in *The Cork Examiner* of the proposals put forward by His Grace the Archbishop of Cashel and other prominent clerical and lay gentlemen in Munster to end the present deplorable state of affairs in Ireland, the feeling in favour of peace has grown with extraordinary rapidity. Reports from various

* Quoted in part in Michael Hutchinson's *Green against Green*. See also O'Malley papers (P. 17a/24).

> districts show that the proposals have been received very cordially, and people on both sides seem to realise at last that a halt must be called to the headlong race to ruin to which the country has been driven.

Any hopes of a gesture of reconciliation from the government were dashed by a report in the same issue of *The Cork Examiner* of a press conference given by Kevin O'Higgins, Minister for Home Affairs in the course of which he categorically rejected any possibility of the Government becoming involved in peace talks:

> There can be no truce on the basis of the proposals which the Archbishop of Cashel and others have address to Mr. Barry. There must be a complete and unqualified acceptance of the right of people to decide all issues arising in the politics of the country, and, as a corollary to that, weapons of war must be placed in the effective custody and control of the people's representatives.
>
> There can be no quibbling. We are not going back to the position that existed between January and June of last year. We will not betray democracy to the petrol can.....This Government will not be threatened or cajoled into departing from it. This is not going to be a draw with a re-play in the Autumn.

Some days later he was even more blunt in a speech in the Dáil:

> Of course, the challenge is fizzling out in the sordid and squalid way one would expect. There is very little ennobling in it, and there are very few redeeming features in it, and very few outstanding acts of personal courage or gallantry, if we except one in the first week in Dublin.

Nevertheless an atmosphere of peace had been created and both sides eased off, particularly the Republicans. Duggan, however, complained to Tom Barry that in some cases the Republicans were not observing the unofficial cease-fire. Barry was hurt and indignant:

> I am in receipt of your communication re. the burning or the attempted burning of Mrs. Powell's house and the increased activities in Kerry.

> You are doubtless aware that since the peace-basis proposals have been formulated that our forces have been on the defensive practically throughout the whole country and particularly in the area of the Southern Command comprising Cork, Kerry, Waterford, Tipperary, Limerick, Clare, Leix, Offaly, Wexford, Wicklow and parts of Galway. You must have recognised this and I do not think that you can point out three instances of offensive action by our troops in the Southern Command area for the past month. Every one of our actions are defensive. They are frequent but this is due to increased military pressure by Free State Forces who are not 'easing off' as we have done. I need not state to you that there would not have been any relaxing on our part either were it not that we believe that peace is impending and we certainly do not want to sacrifice one other man's life on either side in view of this.

Barry went on to describe atrocities committed by Free State troops in Kerry and concluded:

> To sum up, I deprecate offensive action by our forces at this period and I think you will agree that on the whole we have succeeded in stopping offensive operations. Even after the massacre in Kerry not one reprisal has taken place. During all this time the Free State forces have done the opposite and their actions have not been conducive to a peace atmosphere, but in spite of this I still believe that within a week our final decision will be made and that that decision will be for peace.

Following the O'Higgins statement it was clear that there was no hope of any sort of honourable peace for the Republicans and the only way that the Civil War could end was by their unconditional surrender. There was nothing further Tom Duggan could do – short of breaking into the Executive meeting.

The Bitter End

The crucial meeting of I.R.A. chiefs began on 24 March 1923 and lasted several days. It was held in a remote area in hilly country near the Tipperary-Waterford border. Even there the participants were not left undisturbed. Rumours of a Free State army presence forced them to adjourn the conference and reconvene in the Nire Valley in County Waterford.

Tom Duggan was not far away. His car hire bill for the period reads as follows:

> 19 March: Hire from Thurles to Dublin and around Dublin.
> (The residence of Archbishop Harty was in Thurles).
> 20 March: Dublin to Cork.
> 24 March: Cork to Cahir and back.
> 28 March: Cork to Cahir and back.
> 29 March: Cork to Cappaquin and back via Mitchelstown.
> 31 March: Cork to Ballyvourney, around to various places and return to Cork.

The conference was made up of the eleven members of the I.R.A. National Executive still at liberty, and for the first time de Valera was invited to a meeting of the Army Executive but in a non-voting capacity. Finally Tom Barry's motion was put to the meeting: 'That in the opinion of the Executive, further armed resistance and operations against the F.S. Government will not further the cause of independence of the country.'*

The voting was inconclusive, five for, six against. In view of the clear division of opinion it was agreed to meet again at Araglin on 10 April.

Liam Lynch had been right on one point – the grave risk of bringing together so many wanted leaders, so many hunted men. Word of the meeting spread and inevitably reached the ears of the Free State army authorities. A huge comb-out of the district began. The group from the Southern Divisions made their escape and made their way back to Ballyvourney. Meda Ryan mentions in her book *The Tom Barry Story* that 'a few days later Barry met Fr. Duggan and again he told him that he was hopeful that some form of compromise could be achieved'.

The net was closing around Liam Lynch. With a few companions he moved in the direction of Araglin. By Good Friday they were at Kilcash, the subject of a famous old Gaelic lament. They decided to rest over Easter at a favourite hiding-place near Mullinahone, in Kickham country. But Lynch grew impatient and persuaded them to resume their journey to Araglin. A few days later they found themselves surrounded by Free State troops converging from different directions. It was 10 April 1923 when Lynch, Frank Aiken and Sean Hyde, Duggan's old neighbour in Ballyheeda made a dash for safety up the slopes of the Knockmealdowns. Lynch was fatally wounded and ordered his two companions to make good their escape.

* Hutchinson, Michael, *Green Against Green.*

Lynch was taken down the mountain-side by Free State troops, borne on an improvised stretcher. Some hours later this very gallant but stubborn man died in hospital in Clonmel. He told the doctor who attended him that he wanted to be buried near Fitzgerald at Kilcrumper near Fermoy.

In its report on his funeral which his Republican comrades could not attend *The Cork Examiner* noted that: 'One of Mr. de Valera's children, and Mrs. MacCurtain, Miss Annie MacSwiney and Rev. T.F. Duggan, of Cork, were also present. It was the nearest thing there was to an I.R.A. presence at the funeral.'

Lynch's death heralded the end of the struggle. The war dragged on for a few weeks with a few forlorn attempts at peace-making by de Valera. Hostilities finally ceased on 24 May 1923, when Frank Aiken, Lynch's successor as Chief of Staff, ordered all ranks to cease fire and to dump arms. De Valera issued an emotional proclamation:

> Soldiers of the Republic, Legion of the Rearguard!
>
> The Republic can no longer be defended successfully by your arms..... Military victory must be allowed to rest for the moment with those who have destroyed the Republic. Other means must be sought to safeguard the nation's rights.
>
> Seven years of intense effort have exhausted our people....A little time and you will see them recover and rally to the standard. When they are ready, you will be, and your place will be again as of old with the vanguard.*

Normally a war ends with an armistice and a treaty signed by representatives of both sides. This was not so in the Irish civil war. There was no armistice, no peace settlement, no amnesty. Thousands of prisoners remained in prison camps whilst thousands of others lived in a sort of limbo, on the run, with no prospect of employment or of picking up the threads of their normal living. No attempt was made to heal the scars or to think of the future damage likely to be caused to the spirit of the nation.

There was nothing to be proud of in the final chapter of the Irish civil war, unlike, for instance, the close of the American civil war when both sides exhibited a certain chivalrous appreciation of the fact that the common good of their country took precedence over party pettiness.

Bruce Catton in the third volume of his monumental history of the American Civil War *Never Call Retreat* describes the closing stages:

* McCardle, Dorothy, *The Irish Republic.*

> The President, Abraham Lincoln, wanted an easy peace with no hangings and no reprisals: a real peace in which the shattered country could grow together again... He hoped to see the disarmed Confederate soldiers going back to their homes, picking up the threads of life as peaceful citizens of a reunited nation....
>
> Lee sent Grant a flag-of-truce message saying he was ready to talk surrender.
>
> The two men met that day in a house at Appomattox Courthouse, a few miles from the station. But before he went to this meeting Lee quietly spoke a few words that were both a judgement on the past and an omen for the future. To him, as he prepared to meet Grant, came a trusted lieutenant who urged him not to surrender but simply to tell his army to disperse, each man taking to the hills with rifle in his hand: let the Yankees handle guerrilla warfare for a while and see what they could make of that. Lee replied that he would have none of it. It would create a state of things in the South from which it would take years to recover, Federal cavalry would harry the length and breadth of the land for no one knew how long, and he himself was 'too old to go bushwhacking'.
>
> The unquenchable guerrilla warfare this officer had been hinting at was perhaps the one thing that would have ruined America forever. It was precisely what Federal soldiers like Grant and Sherman dreaded most – the long, slow-burning, formless uprising that goes on and on after the field armies have been broken up, with desperate men using violence to provoke more violence, harassing the victor and their own people with a sullen fury no dragoons can quite put down. The Civil War was not going to end that way (although it was natural to suppose that it might, because civil wars often do end so) and the conquered South was not going to become another Ireland or Poland, with generation after generation learning hatred and the arts of back-alley fighting. General Lee ruled it out, not only because he was General Lee but because he had never seen the war as the kind of struggle that could go on that way.

When Lee and Grant finally met, it was Grant's turn to be magnanimous and he rose to the challenge nobly and chivalrously:

> It was not grim old Unconditional Surrender with whom Lee sat down to talk terms. Instead it was a sensitive man who angrily

> stopped his own soldiers when they began firing salutes in loud celebration of victory, reminding them that the late members of the Army of North Virginia were their fellow citizens now, and calling on them to send rations into the Confederate camp. His terms were generous: Lee's soldiers were to lay down their arms, accept paroles, and then go to their homes, the officers keeping their side-arms, the men taking their horses so that they could do the spring ploughing. Beaten men were not to be paraded through Northern cities and then held in prison camps while the government made up its mind how it might punish men taken in rebellion.

Because of what happened when he and Grant at last met, Lee, when he left Appomattox – a paroled soldier without an army – rode straight into legend, and he took his people with him.

Sad reading indeed when we contrast it with the sullen animosity which remained as the tragic legacy of the Irish Civil War.

Perhaps even more tragic is the failure of the modern I.R.A. to read the lessons of History.

1 Deasy's assessment finds support in Eoin Neeson's, *The Irish Civil War*, page 219: 'The Anti - Treatyites never appear to have asked themselves the question: What if Civil War does come? They had no shadow cabinet in preparation; there was no Republican war loan raised. The war was fought on the anti-Treaty side for five months on the sole authority of the Army Executive, with little money and with no Government authority behind it.'

2 Bishop Daniel Coholan in pastoral letter of 25 September, 1922:
'The Dail oath was not an oath to work for the establishment of an Irish republic: it was an oath of fidelity to the Republic as already existing ... Now a promise of fidelity even confirmed by oath, to a non existant form of government is an invalid promise.'

3 Pastoral letter of the Irish Hierarchy, quoted in national newspapers of 11 October, 1922:
'All those who in contravention of this teaching participate in such crimes are guilty of grievous sin and may not be absolved in confession nor admitted to Holy Communion if they persist in such evil courses. It is said that there are priests who approve of this irregular insurrection. If there are any such they are false to their sacred office and are guilty of grievous scandal and will not be allowed to retain the faculties they hold from us.'

4 Pastoral letter of Bishop Daniel Coholan, 25 September, 1922:
'Republicans themselves I am sure would regard the priests who gave absolution to republicans as a cheap-john sort of confessor, and as a priest who does not give edification.'

5 In fairness to Liam Lynch it must be stated that the second part of his reply was more conciliatory: 'If the second Dail, which is the Government of the republic, or any other elected Assembly, carry on such Government, I see no difficulty as to allegiance of army.'

FARRANFERRIS AND THE BON SECOURS

During the troubled years from 1920 to 1923 Tom took his academic commitments lightly. He was supposed to be studying for his Higher Diploma in Education and taking classes in Farranferris. In addition he had signed on at U.C.C. of his own volition for a master's degree involving a thesis in agricultural economics. But the pressure of outside events in the political sphere was more than he could resist: as a result he quite often became an absentee scholar, an absentee teacher and an absentee chaplain. Occasionally he felt a twinge of remorse but salved his conscience with the reflection that he was engaged in work of national importance.

Already a close friendship had sprung up between him and another eccentric genius, Professor Alfred O'Rahilly of University College, Cork. For alleged political misconduct, O'Rahilly had been interned on Beare Island where he fretted and fumed, only to be told by Duggan in a letter written on 7 July 1921, 'On the whole you are comparatively lucky. I have spent ten months writing 20 pages of trash on Agricultural Economics. I have got to write 60 and I am pumped dry. Friend, weep with me.'

One can imagine O'Rahilly's reaction: it was not the sort of letter a sensitive man would write to a dedicated academic interned on a small island and deprived of access to libraries but then Duggan could be very obtuse about hurting other people's feelings.

On the other hand Mrs. O'Rahilly spoke highly of his solicitude for their welfare in her letters to her husband, but she was not blind to Tom's little peculiarities as, for example, when she wrote in October 1921:

> That Duggan man came in this morning for the loan of your hood for a conferring of degrees in the College, but, God forgive me, I pretended I did not know where it was. I knew we would never see it again.

When Alfred asked Tom to borrow a certain issue of the *Irish Theological Quarterly* from the College library he sent the wrong quarter and Mrs. O'Rahilly commented: 'The poor man would do anything for you but he has no head.'

Eventually he completed his thesis but he was not under any illusions about its worth. He wrote to O'Rahilly:

> If you remember I contracted this year to write an M.A. thesis. I spent the first ten months telling my unfortunate neighbours how hard my

> fate was to have to study when the world was so full of interest. I did manage to work a little latterly and twenty-four hours after the scheduled last day I prevailed on Swain to accept my contribution to economic thought, viz., a hundred pages of third rate journalism.
>
> I am marking time now waiting for the (written) subsidiary examination, mildly interested in doctrine of 'maximum satisfaction' and similar rubbish. Smiddy is in Dublin but expected back today so I shall get finished tomorrow.

One gathers the impression that Tom was already a well-known figure on campus and on familiar terms with those who mattered in the University. He retained his link with University College, Cork, until he left for Peru in the final months of his life. Even in Peru he did not forget it and in one of his last letters home he inquired as to who had replaced him on the Governing Body of which he had been an active member for a long number of years.

Reading through his M.A. thesis which bears the rather sweeping title, *Irish Rural Economics*, one is forced to agree with his own disparaging assessment: it is far from being vintage Duggan.

In his opinion the Irish rural economic picture had changed little since Goldsmith's time: 'The bold peasantry' were still on the bottom of the heap and counted for little – they were helots in their own land, a situation not at all in keeping with the spirit of 'the new Ireland that we hope to see arise from our present period of national travail'.*

He believed that the current exclusive concentration on economic values was detrimental to the true welfare of rural dwellers on small farms and a clear violation of the principles of social and distributive justice. The small farmer, and even more so, the agricultural labourers were the chief victims of a discriminatory system wholly geared towards serving British interests. Contrasting the position of the small farmer in Goleen with the rancher in Meath, the two extremes of the rural economic picture of the time, he concluded that in economic terms the more fertile the land the fewer human beings it supported. This led to the conclusion that in the eyes of those who governed the country the bullock was more important than the man whereas in Duggan's eyes the principles of good economics and good sociology should go hand in hand.

It was easy to indict the system but not so easy to suggest remedies. His solution (which was not very original) was a pooling of resources among small farmers, a co-operative system under which small farmers of an area came

* Duggan, Thomas F. *Irish Rural Economics.*

together to share the costs of more modern machinery and more efficient means of production, so creating a system of joint ownership which would work to the benefit of all. He advocated also that agricultural labourers should be given some stake in the farm: this would give them an enhanced dignity and an incentive to work harder. Perhaps he failed to see the snag in his solution, more machinery would eventually lead to fewer workers.

The thesis may not offer a very profound economic analysis but it shows that Duggan's concern was always for the small and marginalised people. It shows also that he suffered from the common delusion of the time that once the Irish people secured control over their own destinies, exploitation and discrimination would cease.

With a diploma in Education and an M.A. degree in October 1921, Tom was now fully equipped academically for secondary teaching but he was far from being ready psychologically. During the years of the national struggle he had acquired a degree of prominence and influence very rare for a young priest. In political circles he was among the best known priests in the country. When civil war broke out he found it impossible to stay aloof and during the period up to May 1923, he was constantly on the move, and for weeks on end his only connection with Farranferris was his name on the staff register. In this conflict of interests, Farranferris was definitely the loser. Naturally his frequent absences from class-duty entailed a great deal of co-operation from his fellow-staff members who had to take over his classes and especially from Canon Sexton, the President. It says a good deal too for the genuine patriotism of Bishop Coholan that he was prepared to turn a blind eye on the frequent absences of one of his seminary priests, apparently in the hope that Tom's efforts might help towards bringing peace to the country.

After the end of the Civil War in May 1923, it was high time for Tom to take up his teaching duties seriously; he could no longer justify his absences as being in the national interest. Consequently at the start of the school year 1923-1924 he began his full-time teaching career. He did so with a heavy heart, because he felt he was not temperamentally suited for the work. Though teaching was in his blood (his father and mother and grandfather had all been teachers), he did not want to teach. Possibly with the more flexible time-table of a university lecturer or professor he might have been happier, but taking class in a secondary school hour after hour, day after day, year in – year out, was a prospect which filled him with dismay. He did not even have the consolation of being able to exercise a worthwhile influence on the students' spiritual or character formation. Since he commuted daily from his home on the College Road, his influence was confined to the class-room which in pastoral terms put him at a great disadvantage compared to the residential members of the staff. To some extent at least he felt that he was wasting his time as a priest.

But there was nothing he could do except to settle in to his task with the best grace possible. For one who had been so much in the limelight it was a situation which called for a great deal of humility and self-subordination, qualities which he did not possess to any marked degree. On the other hand, he could hardly have expected any sort of preferential treatment especially in view of his lowly place on the diocesan seniority list.

His routine, then, for long years to come, was to celebrate an early Mass in the Bon Secours hospital, take Holy Communion to the patients and visit those critically ill, then make his way to Farranferris on his motor-cycle for the beginning of class at 9.00 a.m. After class ended at 3.15 p.m. he dined in the refectory and then returned to the little stretch on the College Road which took in his mother's house, the Bon Secours Hospital and University College, Cork. This was his real home, his little kingdom where he was relaxed and happy.

He settled in as best he could in Farranferris. While it could never be said that he enjoyed his years there as a commuting teacher he gradually became reconciled to his lot and found a certain degree of fulfilment.

It would seem that at first he entertained the hope that a short experience in charge of a class would show up his inadequacies as a teacher. Writing to Leslie Bean de Barra (General Tom Barry's wife) in May 1924 he mentioned his disappointment:

> In your all-embracing charity I would ask you to condole with me. By means of the Easter exams. I intended to prove to the Very Revd, the President of Farranferris, that neither nature nor grace intended me to be a teacher. But would you believe it, every wretched little brute in my class passed the Exam. Net result, a renewed lease of misery for yours humbly, humbly and unfortunately.*

Lest readers might form a wrong impression from his use of the phrase 'wretched little brutes' it should be explained that this was a favourite expression of his, indicating affection rather than contempt!

Just about the time that Tom began to take his teaching duties seriously, there was a change at the top in the Seminary, Canon Sexton making way for Dr. Joseph Scannell. Scannell's background was very different to Tom's. A city boy,

* Original in Canon Micheál Ó Dálaigh's possession.

educated at the Irish College in Rome and Louvain he was ordained after a brilliant theological course in 1903 and taught as a residential member of the staff until the outbreak of the Great War in 1914 when he became a military chaplain with the British Army. For much of the war he was a chaplain with the Irish Guards, an élite unit of the British Army with very little in common with more proletarian regiments such as the Munster Fusiliers.

A polished gentleman, he looked splendid in uniform and prided himself on his military bearing. Politically he and Duggan were poles apart, Duggan never forgetting his Irishness and remaining a country boy at heart whereas Scannell was very much a city man and, unlike many of his staff, not involved in the Irish-Ireland movement.

Predictably they found themselves on opposite sides in the Civil War. Following the capture of Cork by Free State troops in August 1922, Bishop Coholan appointed Scannell as the first official chaplain to the Free State Army in the south. At a time when Duggan was deeply involved in trying to convince the I.R.A. leaders to make peace, Scannell was telling the Free State troops in Cork: 'I will give you all the help and assistance I can, remembering and I hope you will remember, that I am now your priest and you are my men.' It did not help to endear the I.R.A. to Scannell that the army transport in which he was travelling collided with a barricade set up by the I.R.A. and as a result his arm was permanently injured.

In view of all this it might have been expected that a personality clash would reveal itself when Scannell became Duggan's superior officer in Farranferris. Perhaps their army training had helped them both to conceal any feeling of dislike they might harbour towards one another. Anyhow the expected conflict never materialised. Both were big men in different ways with a healthy respect for each other. There seems to have been a tacit agreement between these two old soldiers not to introduce politics. For all the years that Scannell was president they never crossed swords and worked harmoniously together, Scannell a very hard-working president and Duggan a loyal staff member. Of course this good working arrangement did not prevent either of them from making caustic remarks about the other. Strangely enough, although he lacked Duggan's nimble wit, it was Scannell's remarks which lived on in staff-room folklore, two memorable remarks in particular 'Tom would sell his soul for the turn of a phrase,' and 'Poor Tom! Spends his life helping lame dogs over stiles and toppling over himself.' Cruel perhaps but with a grain of truth. On the other hand it would take a very lame dog indeed to approach Scannell so perhaps Duggan had the last laugh. Nothing infuriated Tom more than to be told that Joe Scannell had referred to him as 'Poor Tom'.

Next to the President in seniority was Fr. Denis Murphy. A former honours student at Maynooth he made little effort to continue his studies afterwards. He had few scholarly interests. A good Latin scholar, he knew his Virgil and Horace well. He loved their evocations of rural happiness and especially Horace's descriptions of his Sabine farm.

He was a good teacher when he put his mind to it but wasted time in class listening to the students' tittle-tattle. Duggan consistently underestimated and denigrated him. He considered him a lightweight and referred to him disparagingly as 'Little Dinny'. Perhaps he was too hard on him, but even in class Dinny poked fun at Tom and naturally it went back to him. Their incompatibility was evident and made it all the harder for Duggan to bear when later on he was forced to stand by and watch Dinny carrying off the 'plums' in terms of diocesan promotion.

Fr. Denis Deasy was another very colourful member on the staff. He was frequently at odds with authority especially with Scannell but it was said that Bishop Coholan had a soft spot for him and turned a blind eye to his little peccadilloes. As far as he could, Duggan tried to keep him out of trouble. Deasy's relationship with authority was uneasy especially in the case of Joe Scannell who perhaps lacked Duggan's broad humanity and sense of compassion.

Later arrivals on the staff included Fr. Michael Roche, Fr. Jim Kelly and Fr. Michael Nagle, all of whom became close and cherished friends, devoted to Tom in their very different ways. With this trio, Tom had a most happy relationship both during their time together in Farranferris and in later life.

An tAthair Tadhg Ó Murchú arrived on the staff after his ordination in 1935 and he certainly added a little touch of colour. Joe Scannell was inclined to look down on him but in Duggan he always had a ready champion. They became great friends. Tadhg was an only child and was delicate in his young days but in his small frame he carried a great heart. Visitors found it hard to find a place to sit down in his quarters as nearly every available space was cluttered with books. It was a mark of the great esteem in which he was held by students that more of them came back to visit him than any other member of the staff.

Immediately on arrival he launched an Irish language campaign among staff and students. It was a courageous course to adopt seeing that the President, to put it mildly, did not share his enthusiasm for the language. As might be expected, Duggan took him under his wing and shielded him from ridicule. Duggan's own knowledge of Irish was minimal but this did not prevent him from saying the Rosary in Irish for the students when his turn came around, more as a gesture of solidarity than from any close acquaintanceship with the correct Irish version of the prayers.

At the time, Farranferris was a small college with less than a hundred residential students and a scattering of 'day boys'. The administrative system could hardly have been simpler. It would not be a great exaggeration to apply to the President Louis XIV's dictum: *L'état c'est moi.* The President had no secretarial assistance whatever and he did not enjoy the assistance of a board of management or staff meetings.

Educationally speaking, however, Farranferris enjoyed one great advantage: there was a very favourable pupil-teacher ratio which allowed for greater individual attention than was usual at the time and much more so than in the modern context. The residential staff were at the core of the system, pastorally speaking, and their influence on students was considerable.

Perhaps Duggan under-estimated his own influence. Letters he received from past pupils seem to suggest so and in particular a 'thank you' note received from Garda Commissioner, Dan Costigan:

> I received a number of messages of congratulations but yours gave me special satisfaction and pleasure. It is no easy task for a civil servant to change over to a job like this, and it has done me good to have got a message of approval from the priest who not only taught me Greek and Mathematics, but helped to instil in me whatever little character I possess.

At first he taught Greek and Latin as well as Mathematics but he gradually confined himself to the latter. Though he had done little in the way of formal third-level Mathematics he had a natural bent for the subject. True to his strong individualism, he did not follow orthodox teaching methods or use any text-book systematically. The class never knew what to expect. Each day was an end in itself and had little connection with the work done on the day before or the day after. There was a certain hit-and-miss element in his teaching; admittedly it was not examination orientated and yet his pupils usually acquitted themselves well in the public examinations.

In a submission to the Council of Education set up to review the educational system he defended his methods:

> Having handled (more or less continuously) the Farranferris intake for the past thirty years I could know at once a boy who had been well grounded in Mathematics or the reverse. I could know, for instance, the product of a teacher who over-emphasised the unimportant, and, generally speaking, who lost sight of the wood for the individual trees. What I would not be able to do is to draw up a detailed programme for them, still less turn out what might be regarded as a suitable text-book.
>
> I find the question of a text book of precious little moment – the question of teacher is all-important. As a head-master my emphasis is almost entirely on getting an inspiring teacher, the book he uses matters not at all.

Maintaining discipline came easily to him: possibly his army experience helped in this regard. It was a foolhardy student indeed who took liberties in his class. The pupils quickly realised that it was in their own interest at least to feign interest: any deviation or lack of concentration brought swift retribution. To yawn in his class was the ultimate crime, far worse than copying or other minor misdemeanours. On one occasion a pupil who had exceptional talent at waggling his ears decided to take a chance in Duggan's class when his back was turned. Duggan, noticing what was going on with the help of his spectacles, swung round and caught the culprit red-handed, so to speak. 'Young man,' he said 'Please refrain. Any donkey can do better.'

Dr. Jim Good summed him up as a good teacher but unpredictable: 'A student who got all his sums wrong might be praised for trying while one who got them all right might get a "clout" for writing a single letter carelessly. One did not relax in his class or take any chances.'

His pet aversion was pretentiousness: he was continually on the look out for what he called 'pretentious idiots': they quickly discovered that 'pride comes before a fall'.

He was an easy target for good mimics. His speech was slightly artificial and he had a peculiar habit of pausing suddenly in his remarks, putting a hand to his head and pursing his lips – a sure sign that something funny or devastating was about to be said.

The other side of the coin was his chaplaincy in the Bon Secours. Unlike teaching, which he carried out as conscientiously as he could but with no great enthusiasm or spontaneity, hospital chaplaincy work seemed to respond to some deep inner need in his nature, at least at this stage of his life. It was his true *métier* and *forte*. It was the sort of work he believed a priest should be doing. As far as he was concerned, a priest without humanity or compassion was only a hireling and not a true shepherd.

Hospital work seemed to change him, to raise his spirits and infuse new life and vigour. Normally he was not noted for his patience nor was he a good listener but when dealing with the sick it seemed as if he could call on unsuspected reserves of patience and humility and willingness to listen. Hospital work brought out hidden wells of kindness and thoughtfulness in him. Caring for wounded soldiers, one might say in three wars, had left its mark: it had given him a lasting insight into the needs and feelings of the sick. 'The sick are the same the world over,' he would say. By nature he was bright and cheerful and he was able to transfer these qualities to his patients. In his hospital work one saw a different Duggan, a more relaxed person, more patient, more at ease with himself, less inclined to live on his nerves.

He would be the first to admit that as well as giving to the patients he was receiving. Without meaning to be offensive, one might say that in attending the sick, strengthening their faith, raising their morale and soothing their anxieties he healed his own little ills and neuroses as well.

As time went on he began to involve himself more and more in the administration of the hospital and indeed in the Bon Secours Congregation in general, becoming their 'guide, philosopher and friend'. Dr. Jim Good recalls an occasion when, in the presence of a distinguished audience of Church and State he raised many eyebrows by prefacing his remarks with the words: 'We, the Bon Secours.'

He liked to operate a little outside of normal hospital procedure. Dr. Good gives a typical example:

> I was ordained in June 1948, and almost immediately became ill at home. An order came from TFD to enter the Bon Secours Hospital, Cork of which he was accepted guide and adviser. I got a full month's high-class medical care – and no bill. His word was law in the hospital.

Duggan loved this kind of doing good by stealth, his right hand not knowing what his left was doing.

At first sight one would not pick out Duggan for the role of hospital chaplain. It might be considered that he had too many sharp edges. But the fact remains that for a full fifteen years he devoted himself to this apostolate with exemplary dedication and a great deal of success. He always looked back nostalgically to his years in the Bon Secours and would willingly have stayed there indefinitely.

During all his years as a priest he concerned himself with the spiritual and material welfare of old I.R.A. men. Very often they were in sore need of help, especially in the immediate post-civil war period because few wanted to have anything to do with them. In official circles, they did not exist: they were outcasts and very little was done to restore them to normal civilian life. Duggan became their champion and stopped at nothing to uphold their rights: many a fiery letter came from his pen in defence of their rights as citizens. After de Valera became head of government he redoubled his efforts and if necessary approached de Valera personally. A draft of a letter he wrote to de Valera about one particular case of discrimination gives an insight into the type of causes he espoused:

> Dear Chief,
>
> Only that I have bad eyes, I should have gone straight up to see you. To amplify Sean Hegarty's memo re. X: [Sean O'Hegarty had been O.C. of Cork I Brigade of the I.R.A.]
>
> He became a whole time active service man from 1919 on. He was in the very thick of everything that happened in Cork No. I Brigade.
>
> He made a grievous mistake: he ought to have been killed and then the country-side would burgeon with monuments to the patriot hero.
>
> Instead he survived (the Lord knows through no fault of his own).
>
> In 1922 there was nothing in the bestowal of the Treaty Party that could not have been his.
>
> Instead he merely remained loyal to the decision of his Brigade.
>
> He emerged in 1924, a soldier broken by the tragedy of events.
>
> Some effort was made to set him up in business. The business wilted.
>
> A humble post was found for him in the barracks. Humble but satisfying. He never looked for much.
>
> Three years ago his position began to be attacked. Warriors, in a multitude of wars, became Accountants, and in spite of all the promises of the past (read the Hegarty note at this stage), in spite of most satisfactory service of the present, he was sacked.
>
> Revd. T.F. Duggan intervened. He took the facts to Defence Minister Sean McKeon and the man was reinstated. His reinstatement

> lasted till the recent change of Government; and a month later he was declared redundant.
>
> It is grievous that we should have to remind any Irish Government that commitments made at moments of History are being evaded.
>
> It is horrible when the Government which needs reminding is no heterogeneous collection of politicians but Fianna Fáil itself.

As far as his slender means allowed he tried to provide financial aid to old I.R.A. men who went into business. For instance, when some of his friends, including Liam Deasy and Dr. Tadhg O'Donovan, were instrumental in setting up Ideal Weatherproofs in Cork, he invoked the aid of a Cork priest in New York to advise on the possibilities of breaking into the U.S. clerical market with Cork-made waterproofs. In his letter he introduced Liam Deasy as the 'Liam Deasy of 1921 I.R.A. fame'.

Old Munster Fusiliers, down in their luck, were not turned away. It was not unusual to come across in the hallway at Farranferris an old I.R.A. man and an ex-Munster Fusilier in animated conversation as they waited for their mutual friend and benefactor.

The year 1935 brought a major and unwelcome change in Tom's routine. He had never made any secret of his fervent wish to be relieved of his teaching duties, so as to be able to concentrate on his hospital work. The continuing growth of the Bon Secours hospital brought extra pressure on the chaplain's time and gave him the opportunity he needed to make representations to the Bishop. In the summer of 1935, therefore, he approached the Bishop. Normally in such a situation the Bishop would try to accomodate himself if possible to the priest's wishes. The trouble in this case was that communication between the two had never been easy since the time of Duggan's ill-fated secretaryship. The Bishop had grown wary of what he regarded as Tom's deviousness and disingenuousness whilst Duggan, ill at ease in the Bishop's presence, tended to lose his natural fluency of expression and to make uncharacteristic *faux pas*.

It turned out to be a disastrous interview for Duggan. He started off on the wrong foot by saying baldly, 'The hospital needs a full-time chaplain'. The Bishop bristled, interpreting Duggan's remark as questioning his discharge of his pastoral responsibilities. 'Very well so,' he exclaimed dismissively. 'You can go into Farranferris. We can get somebody else for the hospital.'

Tom had only himself to blame. There was nothing else to do except to pack his bags and report to Canon Scannell in Farranferris. It was a grievous set-back for Tom. He had lost his chaplaincy and all contact with the sick. He had lost his home on the College Road where he had lived most happily with his mother and sister. The only redeeming feature of his appointment was that it brought him into closer contact with the students and so opened up a new kind of apostolate.

There was further disappointment ahead. Canon Scannell relinquished the presidency in 1937 and was succeeded by Fr. Denis Murphy, Duggan's old *bête noire*. But luck was on Duggan's side. As the war clouds gathered over Europe he saw his way clearly ahead: in the event of war he would offer his services once again as a chaplain. His opportunity came on 1 September 1939, when Hitler invaded Poland, and England and France declared war a few days later.

WORLD WAR II

CHAPLAIN TO THE DURHAM LIGHT INFANTRY (1939 - 1941)

Having decided to become a military chaplain with the British forces for the second time, Duggan did not allow the grass to grow under his feet. The age-limit for a chaplain was forty, and he was forty-nine.

He first invoked the aid of Fr. Christy Sheehan, a priest of the diocese of Cloyne, an old friend and fellow-chaplain of World War I who had remained on in the Reserve and was now senior chaplain, Southern Command in Britain. But when Christy wrote on 6 October 1939, the news was bad: 'I am sorry but the worst has happened and your application has been turned down on grounds of age.'

Some time later, however, he wrote again with better news, informing him that Bishop Dey, Chaplain-General (R.C.) to the British forces was prepared to accept him as chaplain to a hospital-ship. Tom wrote to Bishop Dey accepting his offer with certain reservations:

> I am in a difficulty. After twenty years service in a diocese, one gets entrusted with work of passing importance. I have indeed got permission from my own Bishop to serve as a chaplain but serving on a hospital-ship is only active service in a very tenuous sense. Besides (and more fundamental) I enjoy rude physical health and hospital-ship service seems destined more for invalids. Needless to say, I shall be delighted to start on a hospital-ship and establish my claim to something more strenuous.

Bishop Dey must have smiled to himself as he pictured the man behind the letter. Anyhow he relented and spared Tom the ignominy of serving on a hospital ship, and instead arranged that he be posted to the 13th General Hospital in southern England. The relevant information in Tom's official war-record is as follows:

> Appointed to an Emergency Commission as a Reverend into the Royal Army Chaplains Department, Southern Command 6.12.39
> Posted to No 13 General Hospital .... 9.12.39.*

Tom's tenure of office in the 13th General Hospital was very brief – having secured a foot-hold in the British Army his next step was to widen the breach he

* Imperial War Office, Records Department, Kew.

had broken through War Office regulations. It took him a mere twelve days to achieve his next objective, a posting outside of the hospital service. His War Office file has the following entry: 'Posted for temporary duty to Charlbury ... 21.12.39.'*

But why Charlbury, a remote town in Oxfordshire? At that time of year in a very bleak winter, the Cotswolds would have been an unlikely place to select as one's headquarters for Christmas. But Tom knew what he was doing. He had once been chaplain in the Durham Light Infantry for a six-month period (26 December 1918, to 9 June 1919) after his release from a German Prison-of-war-camp. He liked the Durhams: 'Though only 20% of them were Catholics he found it easy to establish a rapport with them. He must have heard of their present whereabouts through the grape-vine and immediately got to work to renew acquaintanceship.'†

The Durhams were a territorial unit as distinct from regular army. In other words, in peace-time they were only part-time soldiers. They consisted of three battalions, each with about nine hundred men. They had been called up to active service on 1st September as Britain prepared to declare war on Germany. After preliminary training, they arrived in Oxfordshire at the end of October 1939, with Charlbury as their headquarters. It is not known what strings Tom pulled but very quickly he succeeded in becoming attached to the 8th Battalion of the Durhams as their official chaplain. Even the War Office, so careful about details, is unusually coy about the precise date of his appointment: 'Attached to the 8th Battalion, Durham Light Infantry, 151st Infantry Brigade, 50th Division, 2nd Corps, exact date not recorded.'§

He duly arrived to take up duty just before Christmas 1939. The winter of that year was bitterly cold and when he arrived the Battalion was away on an artillery training course. It must have been a lonely Christmas: the silver lining was that very soon he would be on active service again.

Unlike World War I when Tom wrote many letters home there is a complete blank in that regard during World War II. Fortunately for his biographer, a very fine history of the 8th Battalion in World War II has been written by two if its distinguished officers, Major Ian R. English and Major P.J. Lewis. Major English, in particular, became a close friend of Duggan's and he very kindly supplemented the references to Duggan in the book with a personal memoir and copies of letters he received from him, all of which he presented to the author when he visited him in his hospitable home in the Yorkshire Dales.

* Ibid.

† Keegan, John, *The Second World War.*

§ Duggan's Official War Office File.

Cardinal Cushing sprinkles a handful of dust on the Archdeacon's coffin.

The final resting place.

Church in Lima which the Archdeacon christened 'The Dragon's Egg'.

House in which the Archdeacon lived during his time in Lima. It was the headquarters of the Society of St. James the Apostle.

Archdeacon and Fr. M. Fitzgerald with some young Peruvians.

The 'farewell dinner' party at Bishop Lucey's house.

Bishop's House,
Cork
17 10 61

DIOECESIS CORCAGIENSIS

My dear Dr. McCarthy

I am giving a farewell dinner for the Archdeacon on Monday next at 1.30 p.m. and hereby inviting you.

With all good wishes I remain — even if the Archdeacon doesnt.

+ Cornelius Lucey

Invitation from Bishop Lucey to farewell dinner for Archdeacon Duggan.

Boston – St. Patrick's Day, 1954. Archbishop Cushing on his way to celebrate High Mass in Holy Cross Cathedral.

Bishop Cornelius Lucey, Dr. Frank Creedon, Archdeacon Tom Duggan, Boston 1954.

Farranferris Hurling Team.

Farranferris College.

'Old soldiers together.' Archdeacon Tom Duggan, General Tom Barry and Chief Superintendant Philip Chambers at Collin's Barracks, Cork 1961.

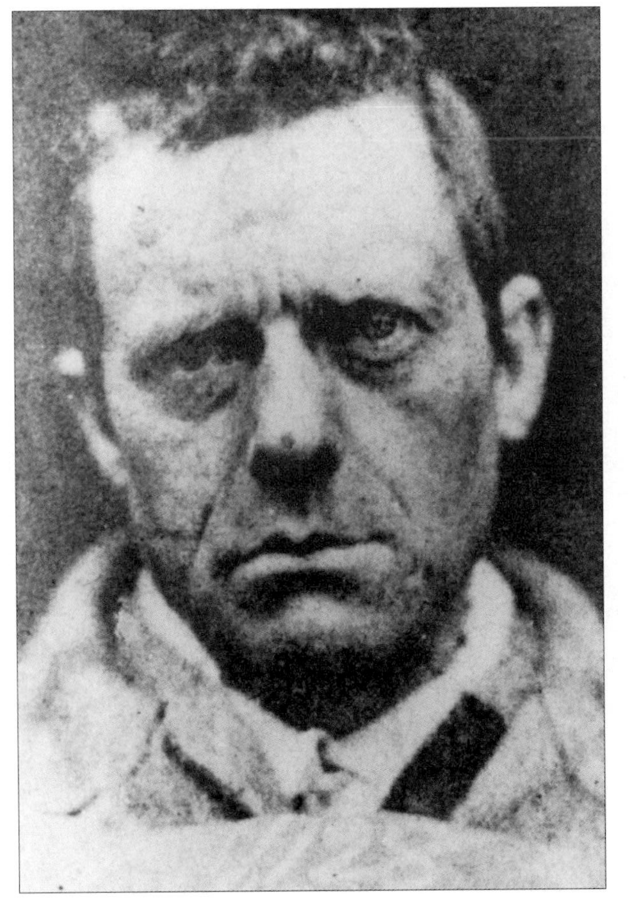

Archdeacon's grandfather in convict garb in Mountjoy, 1885.

Archdeacon's grandfather after release from his convict prison in Australia.

(L to R) Young Tom Duggan, his father, Thomas, and his brother, Jer.

Ordination photograph, Maynooth, June 1915.

Tom Duggan, Military Chaplain – World War I, 1914-1918.

Austauschstation Aachen.

J herewith give my word of honour not to make or to prepare an escape during the walks or other stays in open air, church-parade or any further outings granted, or to undertake anything, that could be of any disadvantage to the security of the German Empire or her allies.

J further give my word of honour not to hand this card over to any other prisoner of war, but to use it for myself only.

Signature: Thomas F. Duggan, C.F.

Rank: Chaplain,

Regiment: 1 Royal Muns. Fusiliers.

068

Prisoner of War, Mainz 1918.

General Tom Barry's wedding group.
(Notice de Valera seated between the bride and bridegroom.)

Before leaving for France, the Durhams received a visit from King George which turned out to be something of an ordeal for all concerned. The inspection took place on 12 January 1940, in the main street of Chipping Norton in Oxfordshire. The description in *Into Battle with the Durhams*, the Battalion history, is as follows:

> It is doubtful whether the King has ever inspected a healthier looking brigade of troops, for there was not a single man of the three D.L.I. battalions whose face had not been turned into the likeness of a rosy apple by the bitter cold....The dignity of the proceedings was somewhat marred by the band instruments freezing up and there was a pathetic series of the most extraordinary noises. Cpl. Fletcher and his bandsmen made a valiant but unsuccessful attempt to play 'Blaydon Races' as the 8th swung out of Chipping Norton and the Battalion left the village to surely the most ghastly wails which have ever been made by the instruments of a Regimental Band of the Durham Light Infantry.*

Tom Duggan must have been hard put to keep a straight face in the presence of his Majesty – musicians were never among his favourite people.

A few weeks later, on 28 January 1940, the Battalion left Charlbury for Southampton:

> It was one of the coldest days Oxfordshire had ever known, just the sort of day one would expect to leave England...By early afternoon the 8th had embarked; the trooper pulled out and anchored off the bar in the Solent until darkness blotted out the English coastline, then her engines throbbed as she got underway and moved out into the Channel. Next morning, after a somewhat stormy passage, dawn brought the coast of France and the port of Cherbourg into view.

Conditions were not much better in France when they arrived, the only difference being that instead of intense cold it was drenching rain. It was 11 p.m. before they boarded a ramshackle French train. After a seemingly interminable journey through Normandy they arrived at the billets prepared for them in a miserable little village called St. Remy du Plain. There must have been times during the journey when Duggan had second thoughts about the wisdom of leaving the 13th General Hospital.

* Major P.J. Lewis and Major I.R. English, *Into Battle with the Durhams.*

In January 1940, there was as yet no sign of the expected German offensive, if for no other reason than the appalling weather. The so-called 'Phoney War' continued. The 8th Battalion spent the next couple of months in hard training and it was not until the early days of April that finally and thankfully they moved northwards towards the forty-five-mile stretch along the Belgian border manned by the British Expeditionary Force. The 8th's headquarters was in a little town called Gondecourt, not far from the city of Lille.

When they arrived there was no sign of hostilities. A defence line consisting mainly of anti-tank ditches and pill-boxes was in course of construction by the British soldiers. The Battalion spent most of the next few weeks in denims and gum-boots doing just the sort of job the Durham coal-miners were accustomed to.

Ronald Atkin, the author of *Pillar of Fire: Dunkirk 1940* is critical of Lord Gort, the commander of the B.E.F. for his tactics during those weeks. He wrote:

> The BEF, allotted a 45-mile stretch of this frontier, built mile upon mile of trenches, anti-tank obstacles and concrete pill-boxes. It was named the Gort Line after the British commander, who could have been better advised, as it turned out, to press for more battle training and less labouring.

Perhaps the important phrase here is, 'as it turned out'. Atkin was writing fifty years later with the advantage of hindsight. Gort, without this advantage, was probably right in playing safe. The defences on which his troops worked were meant to be the Corps Reserve Line which should not have been left entirely defenceless.

The *Blitzkreig*

Hitler finally struck on 10 May 1940. The Germans were superbly prepared. The French and English in spite of the very forward thinking of Basil Liddell Harte and Charles de Gaulle were still living in the past, militarily speaking. Appalled by the frightful sacrifice of life in the dirty trench war of attrition fought out from 1914 to 1918, the Germans vowed that it would never happen again. For the next occasion, a completely new, more mobile and less wasteful form of warfare would have to be devised.

After a great deal of research they found the answer – next time it would be a *Blitzkreig*, a lightening war, which in one swift pre-emptive stroke would achieve total victory. They envisaged a massive two-pronged offensive. The less important prong would involve invading neutral Holland and Belgium in sufficient force to make the Allies believe that this was the main thrust. Simultaneously at the point least expected, at the weakest point in the French defence-line, in the far-away Ardennes, they would strike the deadly blow. It would be a massive attack, carried out by an élite, highly mechanised striking force, the core of which was the tank force, the armoured divisions called *Panzers*. These would form the cutting edge of the breakthrough.

The first requirement for the success of the plan was to lure the Allied armies deep into Belgium by making them believe that, as in 1914, this was the main attack. In other words, to use Liddell Harte's colourful metaphor, Belgium would be merely the matador's cloak to deceive the enemy while the lethal blow was being struck in the rough terrain of the Ardennes. Spearheading this mighty attack would be the Panzer divisions, led by brilliant generals such as Guderian and Rommel. They proposed to take full advantage of the foolhardy belief of the French that in terms of modern warfare the Ardennes was impassable.

Everything the Germans had planned worked like clock-work – up to a point. First of all the Allies swallowed the bait and advanced strongly into Belgium. When they did so, Hitler was ecstatic: at his headquarters, code named Felsennest in the Eifel mountains he was in lyrical mood on 10 May 1940:

> When news came through that the enemy was advancing along the whole front I could have wept for joy. They had fallen right into my trap. It was a crafty move on our part to strike towards Liege. How lovely Felsennest was! The birds in the morning, the view of the road up which our columns were advancing, the squadrons of planes overhead. I was sure everything would go right for me.*

The Ardennes offensive was even more spectacularly successful. The mechanised divisions swept through the Ardennes, stormed across the Meuse river and routed the weak French 9th Army pitted against them. The collapse of the 9th French Army had a snow-balling effect on the other French armies and on the British. Forced into a defensive position they soon found it impossible to hold their lines and a general withdrawal began which in the case of the British meant abandoning their front line in Belgium and trying to establish a new defence line nearer to the Belgian border.

The mechanised advance from the Ardennes rolled on inexorably. After crossing the Meuse the second phase of the operation began, the *Sichelschnitt*,

* Keegan, John, *The Second World War.*

the sickle cut, as they code-named it, the object of which was to cut an armoured corridor, like a giant snake, right across France from Sedan to the Channel, effectively cutting France in two. In a matter of days the Germans were at the Channel, the Channel ports were at their mercy. The British, withdrawing deeper into Belgium, now found themselves trapped. Wedged between the Germans advancing through Belgium and Holland and the Panzer divisions bumper to bumper across France they were firmly caught in an ever-decreasing salient. Under immediate threat from both north and south it seemed that only a miracle could save the beleaguered British Expeditionary Force consisting of about 250,000 men, the only army Britain possessed.

Hitler held all the aces. All he needed for complete victory was to tie up the loose ends, namely to mop up the British and French trapped firmly between his two forces, then march southwards, defeat the remaining French forces, occupy Paris and wait for the Allies to sue for an armistice. Was Tom Duggan's war experience on this occasion to be of even shorter duration than in World War I?

The Durhams Go Into Battle

On 10 May 1940, when Hitler struck, the bulk of the British Expeditionary Force moved deep into Belgium. Left behind were the 5th and 50th divisions, including the Durhams, to act as headquarters reserve. The British advance was initially so rapid that it was decided to bring G.H.Q. forward nearer to the French lines. Accordingly on the morning of 16 May, the Durhams advanced across the frontier. They were in high spirits. No word had reached them of the collapse towards the east. But suddenly they found themselves called on to cover the withdrawal of retreating British troops. Before nightfall the 8th Battalion of the Durhams itself received orders to withdraw. But priority of transport was given to the units returning from the Front; there was no transport for the Durhams, and so a very low-spirited Battalion began their weary march back the way they had so eagerly come a few days before. It turned out to be an agonizing experience. The weeks spent in gum-boots now took their toll: their feet had grown soft and began to blister.

Having finally reached headquarters, they received orders to prepare for combat: psychologically it was the worst possible time. But the German trap was closing in. Churchill had been insistently calling for a counter-attack on the German Panzers, to break through and link up with the French Forces to the south. Gort pointed out that the main body of his troops were already fully engaged in trying to hold the Germans to the east, leaving him only the reserve divisions, the 5th and the 50th for the proposed counter-attack.

A task-force was hastily assembled from these two divisions plus two battalions of tanks: some French help was also promised. All this was on paper and it seemed that such a force might just possibly succeed in cutting through the German formations. But next morning when the advance began it had been whittled down to the Durhams alone supported by seventy-four tanks. To allow such a tiny force to attack Rommel's élite Panzer divisions was almost suicidal.

Predictably, they failed in their main objective to cut the German lines. But the British tanks proved to be a far more effective weapon than Rommel expected and the Durhams fought valiantly in their first encounter with the Germans. Eventually the British withdrew in face of overwhelming counter-attacks. There had been little time for preparation; their counter-attack was little more than an improvisation, a shot in the dark, a sudden jab to catch the enemy unawares. It showed what might have been accomplished with proper preparation and adequate forces.

Years later at the Nuremburg trials, Field-Marshal von Rundstedt said of it:

> A critical moment in the drive came just as my forces had reached the Channel. It was caused by a British counter-stroke southwards from Arras on 21st of May. For a short time it was feared that our armoured divisions would be cut off before the infantry divisions could come up to support them. None of the French counter-attacks carried any serious threat as did this one.*

But the person most affected by the counter-attack at Arras was none other than Adolf Hitler. The Panzer divisions were his pride and joy. But ever since they had crossed the Meuse he had been saying that they were advancing too fast, leaving their flanks vulnerable to sudden enemy attacks. Now his worst fears were confirmed. He reacted violently. Whether the British attack south of Arras was the principal cause or not it certainly had a profound influence on a panic reaction he made a few days later. Out of the blue, with the Panzers practically in sight of Dunkirk which lay at their mercy, he issued a peremptory order to his Panzer divisions to halt.

Viewed with hindsight, this order was a disaster for Hitler's hopes. Dunkirk and the whole Channel coast to the north were within his grasp. By the time the order was revoked, three days later, the harm had been done, 'sickle-cut' had lost its momentum and the B.E.F. were in the process of extricating themselves from

* Horne, Alistair, *To Lose a Battle.*

the trap. It gave Lord Gort time to collect his thoughts and to concentrate on saving the British Expeditionary Force.

Along with the Royal Tank Regiments the Durhams could claim to have influenced the outcome of the war at a decisive moment.

The Miracle Of Dunkirk

On the night of 23-24 May, Gort began his move towards the sea. During the retreat to Dunkirk Tom Duggan gained the respect and admiration of every soldier in the 8th Durhams. At a town called Carvin, *Into Battle with the Durhams* describes Duggan's gallantry:

> During the morning Sgt. Carruthers noticed a British vehicle out in front and two khaki-clad figures walking away from it. The men turned out to be the Padre of the 8th, Father Duggan, and his batman, Pte. Deveney. They were obliged to abandon the Padre's car when it ran into a ditch and were not at all impressed when informed that they had been out in No Man's Land, nearer to the German positions than to our own. The Padre's infectious humour soon cheered everybody...
>
> Padre Duggan then established an unofficial regimental Aid Post in a house in the main street where he worked untiringly all day, tending the wounded and showing a complete disregard for the German shelling, which was most accurate and caused a lot of damage in the town.

By the night of 29-30 May the exhausted remnants of the 8th disengaged and withdrew into the small Dunkirk perimeter. There they set up headquarters in the chateau at Moeres, a little village inside Belgium. It was at Moeres that Duggan achieved his greatest claim to fame.

> The shelling in the area of the chateau, where 8th Battalion's H.Q. had been established, was intense; casualties came in fast and the familiar cry of 'stretcher bearers' became more frequent. Lieut, Wilkinson, the Battalion Medical Officer, with Captain Rutherford the Medical Officer of the 9th D.L.I. established a joint Regimental Aid Post in the cellars of the chateau which was soon blazing above their heads. Assisted by the redoubtable Padre Duggan they did some excellent work.

> Throughout the afternoon the figures of the Padre and Cpl. Fletcher, the stretcher-bearer Sergeant, could be seen wherever the shelling and casualties were the heaviest. Journey after journey was made by the two men to carry the wounded to the cellars of the chateau, where the Padre's cheerful humour was like a tonic to the long lines of men who lay on the floor waiting to be evacuated. He seemed quite oblivious to the heavy shelling, and his coolness, energy and courage undoubtedly calmed as well as kept up the morale of the wounded men in his care. Padre Duggan was awarded the Military Cross. The citation read as follows:
>
> For gallantry in R.A.P. during heavy bombardment. His coolness, energy, courage and example were outstanding and helped to maintain morale when the R.A.P. was heavily shelled and was full of wounded.
>
> This happened at Moeres.
>
> M.C. recommended by Comdr. 50 Div.

By this time, 31 May, the rescue operation by the British Navy was in full swing. At 2.30 a.m. on the morning of 1 June the Battalion withdrew in good order to the sand dunes some six miles east of Dunkirk: they were like men walking in a dream. The Battalion history describes their feelings:

> The feeling of tiredness, caused especially by lack of sleep, was unbelievable, voices near at hand sounding as if they came out of a mist. There was not a single man who was not tired to the point of exhaustion. The previous fourteen days had been a nightmare. The ceaseless bombing from the air and the continuous German shelling had shattered the nerves of some of the troops and the strain was beginning to tell on everyone. Those men who sat down for a moment's rest were almost instantly overpowered by an irresistible urge to sleep. The strain of fatigue and the lack of sleep will be remembered by those who took part in the campaign long after the fighting and dive-bombing had been forgotten.

All morning on 1 June the Germans bombed the beaches. Those men of the Battalion who were not too tired to watch saw the epic of the little ships at Dunkirk.

Just when the Durhams had begun to hope that all was well and that their turn for embarkation was near, a fresh order was received. A staff-officer arrived with the dreaded news that the Durhams had been chosen for another suicidal mission. With some units of the Grenadier Guards they were to try to create a diversion by smashing their way through the oncoming German forces massing for the kill. The object was to distract the Germans and buy time for the rest of the B.E.F. to escape.

Fortunately this order was never put into effect, largely because of increased pressure from the R.A.F. The result was that instead of having to fight a last-ditch rearguard action, at 2.30 p.m. the Durhams were ordered to move on to the mole at Dunkirk and get ready for evacuation. By 6 p.m. they had dug themselves in as they waited their turn. They were finally called forward to where a British destroyer was waiting. They scrambled aboard and set sail for Dover.

Into Battle with the Durhams whilst being pardonably sentimental is at the same time commendably honest:

> The embarkation was a complete anti-climax. Early that afternoon the men of the 8th expected to die fighting in a desperate break out from the Dunkirk perimeter, and now, less than twelve hours later, they were on a British ship on the way to England.
>
> The flames in Dunkirk reached up to the night skies and the dull boom of gunfire came from somewhere inland. The ship set course for Dover and suddenly everything seemed quiet and peaceful. It was, after all, the English Channel and to the tired troops on board the destroyer a bit of old England.
>
> Many battalion histories will tell a different story about Dunkirk but for the 8th D.L.I. there were none of these epics of supreme gallantry which were later pictured in the pages of *The Illustrated London News*. There was no swimming out to small boats, no murderous bombing and shelling of the beaches. In the quiet times of peace many a weekend tripper had a more exciting leave-taking.

Tom Duggan shared in this general feeling of anti-climax. He had no recollection of the sea journey, not, as he was careful to add, through any feeling of bravado but out of sheer exhaustion. He slept peacefully the whole way across and only came awake when a rough hand was placed on his shoulder and a voice said 'You'd better hurry up, mate, or you'll be back in France,' or words to that effect.

It was four o'clock in the morning as the Battalion arrived at the white cliffs of Dover. Light was just breaking as if to welcome them home.

Farewell to the Durhams (April 1941)

The spring campaign of 1940 was one of the greatest military defeats which Britain ever suffered but, paradoxically, the rescue operation from Dunkirk acted as a tonic for the British people. Two hundred and twenty-five thousand British troops had been rescued as if by a miracle. Their arrival in Britain lifted the gloom and enabled the British to brace themselves for the expected invasion by Hitler.

On 22 June the Battalion received orders to move to the south coast near Weymouth to take over duties of coastal defence. Tom Duggan joined them there, his official war-record stating: 'Posted to 8th Battalion, Durham Light Infantry Southern Command, Dorchester Road, Weymouth...... 22.6.40.'

The 8th had fourteen miles of coast-line to defend – fourteen miles of vital coast defended only by riflemen – it was typical of the general situation. As *Into Battle With The Durhams* comments: 'It was only one step removed from bows and arrows and there is no doubt that only the Channel and the courage of the British people stood between England and Nazi Germany.'

It was back to the early days of April for the Durhams. Once again they were digging, constructing beach defences, a boring and monotonous task. But the men did not complain; there was a great sense of urgency all over England at the time. There were many false alarms and many visits from eminent celebrities like General Bernard Montgomery, now corps commander, to break the monotony.

The aerial Battle of Britain was now in full swing. On 1 September news came that the long-awaited invasion was now imminent. The troops girded themselves for action; the code-word 'Cromwell' was received at Brigade headquarters of the Durhams on 1 September, which meant 'stand-to' in battle positions. For seemingly interminable days the 8th 'stood-to' until finally, after nearly two weeks, storms broke in the Channel on 15 September heralding the end of the threat of invasion. On the 18th 'Cromwell' was cancelled. Hitler had lost his chance, celebrations were in order!

Soon afterwards the 8th Battalion was moved inland to different locations where the troops were being trained for foreign service. Months passed without any word of the 8th's destination which was an official secret. But early in 1941 the troops received a lecture on 'The Wonders of Egypt', a pretty strong hint that North Africa would be their destination. Once again Tom Duggan tried to get into the action but this time it was beyond even his powers of persuasion. He was transferred from the 8th in April 1941, a month before they left for overseas.

The Battalion history describes the feelings of the Durhams at his departure:

> Another grievous loss was Padre Duggan; his gallantry and continual cheerfulness during the hopeless situations which were all too characteristic of the French campaign earned the respect of every member of the Battalion.

The final entry in the unit's history concerning Duggan is worthy of note. In September, 1944, some survivors of the 1940 campaign found themselves treading familiar ground in the north of France. *Into Battle with the Durhams* relates:

> That evening (1 September 1944) Majors Chambers, Beattie and English, all of whom had been with the 8th in 1940, visited the villages where the Battalion had been billeted. At Oissy they were recognised by the people, who remembered even the numbers of the unit vehicles. They had a good memory for names and asked after Commandant Raine, the Padre Duggan and Captain Walton.

On 14 February 1950, Tom Duggan wrote to Major English to thank him for sending him a copy of *Into Battle with the Durhams*. He said:

> You have done a wonderful job....You have made history and made history live.
>
> You have been entirely too kind to an old chaplain. I am old, I am worn, in lots of things I have been futile. But I have one boast; I received kinship and friendship from brave men.

Some years later, Major Ian English wrote the following personal memoir of Tom Duggan:

> Father Duggan was one of the most remarkable men I met in the Second World War. We first met in December 1939 when he joined 8 D.L.I. as the Padre. It was soon obvious that he was something special, very different from the average officer and indeed from the other Army Padres. First he was over-age, though he was cagey about his age, and also it was probable that he was not fully fit for active service. But somehow he had persuaded the authorities in the War Office they should employ him as a Regimental Padre.
>
> He must have been very much at home with fighting men. He had been an Army Padre in the First World War. In 1919 he had been

deeply involved in the I.R.A. campaign against the British in the Cork area. He is reputed to have produced an outrageous plan to 'spring' a number of I.R.A. prisoners from Cork jail, which fortunately or unfortunately was not adopted by the Sinn Féin command. He had no obligation to join the British Army in 1939, particularly in view of his age and health. So it must have been his strong desire to take an active part in the war against Nazi Germany.

There were three padres in the 151 (Durham) Infantry Brigade, one from each denomination – Roman Catholic, Church of England and Methodist. So although Father Duggan was attached to the 8th Battalion, he had responsibility for all Catholics in the 6th and 9th Battalions, in fact throughout the brigade. But inevitably he had more contact with the soldiers of 8 D.L.I. who came to know him well, not only Catholics but also other religions, and men who had no belief at all.

In 1940 the Battalion was mainly made up of Durham men, many of whom were miners. We also had a draft of militiamen from the King's Own Scottish Borderers most of whom proved to be first class soldiers. Both the Durham lads and the Scotsmen could quickly see if an officer was genuine or not, and no one could pull the wool over their eyes. They knew who they could follow when things got difficult. So it was that Father Duggan soon earned the respect and later the love of men of all ranks. He had an air of being a rather peculiar old Irishman, but one quickly saw that this was merely a façade. He had an ability to spot a problem or an injustice and he went straight to the person who he thought could best deal with it. In many cases it was the Brigade or even the Divisional commander who received a piece of his very persuasive lobbying. He would not have hesitated to tackle the Commander in Chief if he thought that was the only way.

We joined the B.E.F. in France in January 1940. Whenever we were in one place for more than a short time Father Duggan established a rest room where men could come to discuss their problems or perhaps just to sit and chat. But he was strict about his flock attending to their religious devotions. Church services were held every Sunday unless operational requirement made it impossible. Later in the months after Dunkirk when we were busy

> digging defences on the Dorset coast, and every weekend training with the Home Guard, several weeks passed without proper church services being held. The Padre said this had to stop, and went straight to the Divisional Commander and gained an assurance that unless and until an invasion occurred time must be set aside from training for proper religious observance.
>
> The Germans attacked on 10 May 1940 and from the 16th until we left Dunkirk on 2 June the Battalion was either in action or moving from one place to another. The strain of this was tremendous even for young men. How much worse for Father Duggan? But his morale never faltered, and he always radiated cheerfulness and resourcefulness. His place was in the Regimental Aid Post with the medical officer and orderlies. But he was frequently in the forward area collecting casualties.
>
> When we returned to England the Padre remained with us until about April 1941. The Battalion was then under orders to move overseas. The authorities now insisted that Father Duggan should not go abroad again. Therefore he could not remain with the Battalion. So it was a sad farewell to a most lovable and staunch friend.

Tom kept up his contacts with his friends in the Durhams right up to his death in Peru. His letters to them are poignantly touching. For instance, his Christmas letter of 1960 to Major Ian English:

> Our friendship has come of age. Twenty-one years ago we joined forces at Charlbury. At this time of year the world is full of memories. As for myself, I feel like an old galleon, battered but sound, on the verge of dropping in to port....Yours with loving memories.

His last letter to Ian was written soon before he left for Peru; it is dated 15 September 1961 and says:

> I had a stab to achieve your 'semi-retirement' but it worked in contrarium. I have a big parish here and (between real work and bad filing) I have to work 16 hours a day.
>
> I am just back from South America, in Peru and in Bolivia. If I haven't to go back (and that is still in the lap of the Gods) I might make the 15 Brigade Re-union in London.... It would be nice to meet everyone again.

There is a postscript to this letter: 'I have sudden news that I am posted back to South America so I shall indeed be at the Re-union but only in spirit and in prayer. At the rate I am going, my retirement won't take effect till I am ninety.'

Possibly the most touching letter of all was sent a few days later to another friend in the Durhams, Major George Chambers:

> Thanks for yours of the 10th. I should have been delighted to have been with you but I am off to South America this week for a four year assignment.
>
> Somewhere (all going well) about May 1965, a sprightly and sunburned septuagenarian will report back to you.
>
> Give my regards and my affections to everyone. If the Lord of Heaven takes me to His heart in the way the Durhams did, in the next world I shall be high among the angels.
>
> The Lord love you all.
>
> Yours ever gratefully
>
> T.F. Duggan

Northern Ireland

In May 1941, Tom Duggan received his new posting: he was to be head Chaplain (R.C.) to the British Forces in Northern Ireland.

In British Army circles generally Tom Duggan's transfer to Northern Ireland was regarded simply as a well deserved promotion (he now enjoyed the rank of major) but in the chaplaincy department it was looked on as a singularly difficult assignment in which religion and politics were inextricably mixed.

In a divided community, tensions between Catholic and Protestant, Nationalist and Unionist, Orange and Green, were never far from the surface, and a war situation naturally increased the risks of confrontation. Northern Ireland, *de facto* if not *de iure*, an integral part of the United Kingdom, was expected to play its full part in the war effort. Though conscription had not been introduced in deference to Nationalist sensitivities, the province was on a war footing when Duggan arrived in May 1941. There was a very considerable British Army presence. Later, as D-Day drew near, there was also a strong United States consignment of troops, particularly in the Derry area.

In these circumstances, part of the head-chaplain's role was to keep relations between Catholic Army chaplains and the local Catholic clergy and people as amicable as possible. Some of the chaplains in his charge were British but many also were Irish bred, in itself a dangerous mixture in time of war and a potential cause of internal tension. An English-bred chaplain was at a severe disadvantage *vis à vis* the population of Northern Ireland: he could not but be aware of the tensions around him but he knew very little about the historical background. His insensitivity in regard to the feelings of local Catholics could, therefore, be a source of conflict. On the other hand, Irish-bred chaplains might err in the opposite direction by becoming over-identified with the local Catholic community, and, in extreme cases, with the local I.R.A.

Whether those responsible for sending Tom Duggan to Northern Ireland knew it or not the fact was that he was an inspired choice. In spite of a certain abrasiveness he possessed exceptional diplomatic skills. From his varied experience of life and especially of soldiers he knew he was a good communicator with people and that it made no great difference whether they were Irish or English or French or German: he took them as he found them, and there was no trace of racial prejudice in his dealings with men. He had charisma: one could not ignore his presence. He had the gift of words, a turn of phrase, a sense of humour and a drollness which the English in particular could not resist. He could be fiery and irascible but only for a moment. All in all, he was the sort of chaplain that the troops, both officers and men, could respect. It might be said of him that he was a good advertisement for the religion he proclaimed.

He had no illusions about the magnitude of his task. Afterwards he summed up the risks attached to his position in his own droll way:

> For the Senior Chaplain to-be it meant higher status and home horizons. Yet Northern winds were said to be harsh, Northern speech incisive, and Northern life full of pit-falls to one of this Chaplain's antecedents. He could but comfort himself with the advice given by a German queen to her princeling son, dubious of accepting a Balkan throne: 'Take it, son, it will be such an interesting memory when they have kicked you out.'

Normally Tom would have hated any sort of desk job with little contact with the troops and few opportunities of exercising any sort of pastoral ministry amongst them. But this particular appointment had compensations. The intermingling of religious and political dimensions called for exceptional diplomatic skill and he felt that in this regard he could cope better than most. He was his own master to a considerable extent with a great deal of freedom of movement and considerable power and influence. The Army raised no objections to his absences in the South which allowed him to keep up his contacts with Maynooth and Dublin.

Somewhat to his surprise, Tom found the Unionists (or Loyalists) a fine people. He mourned at the historical causes which had made them a people apart:

> They are a grand people. Their tragedy is to have been born into a heritage of hatred; to the confusion of themselves and their neighbours, they wriggle uneasily in their unblessed Kingdom. They cling to England and their English connection but their 'loyalty' does not translate itself into any spontaneous affection for individual Englishmen. Broadly speaking, it is true that Northern Ireland likes England and dislikes Englishmen, whereas the rest of Ireland curses England and welcomes Englishmen.

These generalisations hardly stand up to close examination but the fact remains that in the exercise of his duties Tom never encountered any unpleasantness from local Unionists.

Of course he had a greater affinity with the Catholics:

> The Nationalists (or Catholics) comprise the remaining 40%. For centuries much perverted ingenuity has been devoted to the task of keeping this 40% the hewers of wood and the drawers of water in the land of their fathers.
>
> A race so virile and so vigorous will have to get justice. Go to a Nationalist hall in Derry or in Belfast or in any place in between. Look at the audience, the prideful men, the glorious women. Look at them and pity any bemused tyrants who would deprive them of their lawful rights.

This was Tom's brand of nationalism which would be regarded by some people today as old-fashioned or even as the cause of much of the present trouble.

Tom spent two and a half very happy years in Northern Ireland. At the time Northern Ireland, militarily speaking, was a hive of activity and to his desk at headquarters in Lisburn came a stream of problems but he was in his element, pouring oil on troubled waters, getting people out of scrapes, keeping the peace generally as between Army and Church, and in the process endearing himself to everybody.

One of his main problems was to keep the relationship between the British Army and the local Catholic Church on an even keel. There were bound to be incidents which called for common sense on both sides and this was not always forthcoming.

The most dangerous situation was when a local Catholic priest with strong feelings about the British Army presence in Northern Ireland clashed with a British officer who looked down on the Irish. In such cases of conflict, Tom usually found himself in the middle but generally managed to restore calm without hurting either side's feelings too much.

Typical of the sort of problems he encountered was the following: due to the illness of the local British Army chaplain, a local priest was called in to officiate at Mass. He was not a great admirer of the British Army. The first Tom heard about any unpleasantness was in a report which arrived at his desk from a very high Army source, namely, the Assistant Adjutant-General at H.Q., British Troops in Northern Ireland: it spoke about certain expressions used by the local priest in the course of the Mass.

The report was as follows:

SUBVERSIVE COMMENTS

> The following extract from the Weekly Security Report for the week ending 27th June is forwarded for your information:
>
> On Sunday 14 June the above-mentioned priest, before beginning his sermon, requested a group of civilians and soldiers standing at the back of the church 'either to remove themselves or to take a seat'. Two or three of the soldiers did not accept the invitation, whereupon the clergyman said: 'The British Army will not remove itself. For once in its life it stays put.'
>
> The congregation, largely composed of British and American soldiers, appeared to resent this.

In the aftermath of Dunkirk, it was a provocative remark. Though a veteran of the famous retreat, Tom would probably have smiled to himself at the priest's neat turn of phrase but publicly he had no option but to take a serious view of the incident. Umbrage had been taken at high level and though word had been passed on to Duggan by way of information only, clearly he was expected to take action. A less sensible man might have gone straight to the unfortunate priest's bishop but this was not Tom's style: for one thing he knew the bishop would probably be better pleased if the matter could be settled without recourse to him. Tom moved quietly, spoke to the priest in question and then wrote to headquarters:

> The fact is the man's bark is worse than his bite. Our R.C. chaplain is loud in his praise of the help and co-operation he has got and is getting from him. In church he allows himself a certain liberty of utterance. His own people readily understand this. So would any Irish congregation but the impact on strangers may well be disquieting.
>
> I myself have interviewed him about this particular incident. He readily admits that on that particular morning events had conspired to aggravate him. The final straw was the obstinate refusal on the part of some soldiers to leave the door and move up the church. Any remarks he made, he made them in a mood of grim facetiousness. It was furthest from his mind to offend anyone. He expresses his regret and undertakes that an explanation will be made in church at the first possible opportunity.
>
> The matter may well be allowed to rest here. It is conceded that there was a little effusion of petulancy. It is making a mountain out of a mole-hill to label it subversive comment.

Duggan's letters were quite famous at headquarters. Their Victorian phraseology was a source of wonder to less literary-minded colleagues.

Only once did he fail to find acceptance of his views:

> One day I was urgently summoned by a fussy little Brigadier. He produced not one but both organs of local opinion [Catholic and Protestant]. In one the caption: Courageous Words of a Patriot Priest.. In the other Outrageous Outburst of a Cleric.
>
> In both there was the same letterpress:
>
> In the event of conscription being enforced, the Revd. X. is prepared to take on the whole British Army with the R.A.F. thrown in.
>
> We might have expounded the doctrine of duality of priest and citizen; we might have quoted famous statesmen to the effect that hypothetical treason was no treason. We did not. We felt that the Brigadier was too upset to be receptive of fine distinctions. Instead we said Mass ourselves in the camp till the ordinary Chaplain returned. This was the nearest approach to an incident in the whole four years.

Occasionally he found it necessary to intervene when one of his chaplains was being discriminated against or unjustly set up. In one instance a chaplain under his jurisdiction drove an army vehicle outside his area without a permit. It was hardly a heinous crime but his C.O. was a stickler for rules and all hell broke loose. The chaplain's explanation was not accepted. A file was opened headed 'Improper Use of War Department Transport'. A witch-hunt began and by the time the incident came to Duggan's ears the chaplain was accused of:

1) Having a brother in the I.R.A.
2) Running messages for the I.R.A.
3) Having curious associates.

The final conclusion was that 'Enniskillen should have an English-bred chaplain'. Tom saw in the whole incident pretty solid traces of old-fashioned anti-Catholic and anti-Irish bigotry. It was lucky for the priest concerned that he had such a formidable personage as Duggan to defend him. Tom wrote to the A.A.G:

> On the occasion of the recent Enniskillen unpleasantness there are a few observations I would like to make. I am not (at the moment) concerned with the rights or wrongs of the quarrel. What does concern me is the dossier produced or rather the mentality behind it. Crude unconcern about inherent probability, childish credulity in rumour! And they call it evidence.

He cast aside with contempt the I.R.A. allegations, saying that the person who made them seemed unaware of the fact that at different times there were four separate I.R.A. organisations: he failed to specify which one he had in mind. If he meant the I.R.A. that fought the Black and Tans, Tom had no apology to make for the man – in fact the reverse:

> All that means is that the chaplain's family was no exception to 90% of Southern Ireland.
>
> One could go on quoting from this dossier but enough has been given to press home my point, namely, that at least 50% of the R.C. Chaplains could be implicated on 'evidence' of this kind.

As regards the charge of having 'curious associates' Tom permitted himself a little sarcasm:

> He has curious associates. In fact, to put it plainly, he mixes with the local Catholic clergy. Like every other Catholic Chaplain he has a

> strict duty to maintain liaison with the local officials of his Church.
> Far be it from me to minimise the difficulties, still less the importance of an Intelligence Service. The point we make is that, under the stress of anxieties, Intelligence has ceased to be intelligent. It is degenerating into a low form of witch-hunting.

However he reserved his greatest wrath for the final recommendation: 'Enniskillen should have an English-bred Chaplain.'

He commented emotionally:

> The directing executive of the 17th Brigade have concentrated so much on their own wretched little potato patch that they obviously regard the place as the centre of the cosmos. It is not. If the request did have validity for Enniskillen, it would have equal application for every other part of Northern Ireland. It means just this – Irish-bred Chaplains are not to be trusted.
>
> The man who wrote this is, I hope, too muddle-headed to be conscious of the logical implication of his words. Otherwise, all that I can say, veteran as I am of two wars, is God forgive him for a foul aspersion on the living and the dead.

He concluded by giving the Army a little advice about their relations with the local Catholic population:

> We have got to live here it may be for years. We cannot needlessly offend the Catholic population. They may not be enthusiastic about us. They many regard ours as the bayonets which uphold what they call the oppression of Stormont.

His final warning is to be careful not to turn the Catholics of the North into pro-Germans: 'Do not force such a decision on them.'

It was one thing to try to browbeat an ordinary chaplain: it was quite another matter altogether to offend one of Tom Duggan's stature. Various people ran for cover. A soothing reply came from the very top:

> I have received a letter from the General Officer Commanding 5 Div. and there is no charge whatever against Father X. I agree with you that 1920 is a long time ago and even if he had a leaning towards the I.R.A. in those days, there is not reason why he should still retain these views. I think, now, that he is under your eye, all will be well,

> and we can put aside the file and never again refer to it unless there is just cause.

In view of the very strained relations which existed between the Nationalist population and the R.U.C., Tom was extremely cautious about any dealings he might have with the police. Any suggestion of any form of co-operation with them in their activities would be fiercely resented by the local Catholic community. In Tom's papers there is a very interesting draft of a letter he sent to Monsignor Coghlan, the Chaplain-General, about this matter:

> A few days ago I ran into the R.A.F. Chaplain. He told me the Inspector-General of the Police was anxious to meet me. He led me into the presence. The I.G. had departed but we had converse with the head of the Intelligence, one Captain Moore. Moore professed himself very anxious about some I.R.A. activities directed towards sapping loyalty of (1) U.S.A. troops, (2) British Air personnel. Having no time to think I said nothing and kept saying it. Interview fizzled out into a vague request for co-operation from Chaplains.
> Having thought things out it seemed to me:
> (a) That the very slender evidence proffered did not even purport to prove that the British Army was aimed at.
> (b) Even if the Army were aimed at, Army Intelligence and Administration might well prefer that the Chaplains did not butt in to anything so delicate.
> (c) That whatever the Army thought or wished, our chief consideration was the reaction of the *Ecclesia Catholica* in Northern Ireland. To the priests of the North, active co-operation with Captain Moore would only be construed in one way – felon-setting.
>
> If it ever got out (and it would) that the Chaplains were helping the police, the local clergy to a man would boycott us. All this I put before the R.A.F. Chaplain. Its effect on him I am not so certain. He seems a reasonable, prudent person himself but he is swimming in (for him) uncharted waters.

There was not, it seems, any further effort to involve Catholic Chaplains as auxiliary policemen.

One of Tom's priorities was to defend to the last the right of Catholic servicemen to fraternise with the local clergy and people. He held strongly that even if it were workable it was contrary to the universal mandate of the Catholic

Church to set up local self-contained ghettos for Catholic Army personnel only. As a corollary, he would not countenance any form of discrimination by the local Catholic Church against Army personnel who wished to avail of the facilities of the local Catholic Church.

A minor instance of discrimination was brought to his notice – a few members of the ATS (a women's auxiliary group) were refused admission to a dance in a local Catholic hall. If tolerated by Tom, it might well become a precedent. Tom wrote a letter of protest to the secretary of the Hall Committee:

> The net result of excluding these children will be to force them into dance-halls of more than doubtful reputation...
>
> It would help if I was in a position to assure them that the exclusion was the individual act of two half-baked morons, and had no support from the Catholic population of Lisburn.

He received a full explanation and apology from the secretary of the committee and wrote a grateful letter of acknowledgement:

> *Ex imo corde*, I thank you and your Committee for your gracious letter. I know full well the trials of the Catholic body in Northern Ireland.
>
> That makes me all the more proud and more appreciative to have it exemplified once again that when it comes to a question of safeguarding the spiritual interests of strangers in your midst every tragic memory is forgotten.

But the happy days in Northern Ireland were coming to a close towards the end of 1943. The first sign of discontent on Tom's part is found in a letter he wrote to Lady Franklyn, wife of General Sir Harold Franklyn, a former high-ranking general in the B.E.F. evacuated at Dunkirk, later G.O.C. Northern Ireland and now returned to active service:

> I hope life is using you both very, very gently. After a sojourn in Northern Ireland it must be nice to be back in the centre of things.
>
> Not much doing here. America is now, of course, in these regions, the predominant partner. All that is left here is a nice carefully-culled collection of cripples. The blessed place looks like an annex to a Chelsea Home.
>
> I am making the remote preparations to going home. In 1939 I broke away from the neutrality of my neighbours to do something

> active. Instead of activity, I find myself sitting in comfort in a back area. My present participation in the war would not arouse conscientious scruples in a pacifist.

The cause of Tom's discontent was the changed role of the British Forces in Northern Ireland. It was now a quiet back-water with a comparatively small number of troops engaged in routine garrison duty. According to Tom Duggan, the sole reason for their presence was 'to control the more potentially turbulent of my own kith and kin'.

Tom wanted no part in it. He was not an army chaplain in the usual sense of the word: he belonged to that more specialised breed, a war chaplain. As an Irish Republican and Catholic priest he dreaded the thought that sooner or later the garrison status of the British Army would lead to confrontation with the Catholic minority. He did not want to be in Northern Ireland when that happened.

To get back on active service once the invasion began became an obsession with him. But it was quite unreasonable for him to expect to be put back on active combat service. He was forty-nine when the war broke out; an exception had been made in this regard though he was at least five years above regulation age limits. Now in 1944 he was ten years above the limit and his category was high on the priority list for demobilisation.

Unfortunately he channelled all his efforts into a continuous effort to force Monsignor John Coghlan, the chaplain-general, to use his influence on his behalf. Although a contemporary of Tom's in Maynooth, Coghlan was not prepared to be a party to bending the rules. The result was an increasingly acrimonious correspondence between the two. Duggan blamed Coghlan for lack of co-operation. One can sympathise with him to a certain extent when he complained that between Coholan (his bishop) and Coghlan (his chaplain-superior) he was 'between the devil and the deep blue sea'.

Tom fired the first shot in his campaign for a transfer to active service in a letter to Monsignor Coghlan on 20 May 1944:

> When I saw you in Dublin...in a passing way I did mention myself and my future. I thought I saw a gleam in your eye that I did not like.
>
> You were good enough to speak of indispensability, continuing successful liaison with Northern Bishops, etc. All very flattering but now devoid of significance. The fact is, N.I. no longer exists as a military force. We are now merely an insignificant enclave in the midst of an American Transit Camp....

> Only four short years ago I, literally and metaphorically, did as good a gallop as most. [At Dunkirk.] My façade of external achievement is not entirely unimpressive.
>
> This much I permit myself to say. An application on parallel lines to mine would be acceded to in any other Branch of the Service. I also should be listened to but I happen to have as Principal Chaplain a College contemporary and a good friend. And that Principal Chaplain is unduly sensitive lest men think he favours his own.
>
> This much at least you can do. Get me out of Northern Ireland. As a volunteer from a neutral country, if I am to be in this war at all, I have to be in it up to my neck. The extent of my participation for the last three years would not suffice to arouse scruples in a Conchie. Needless to say, I am quite prepared, if it facilitates you, to serve again as a 4th Class Chaplain.

In August he wrote to an American chaplain-friend: 'Things here are in the usual doldrums. I'd like one final gallop and then I'd come home in peace.' In September 1944, Bishop Neil Farren of Derry, interceded for him with Monsignor Coghlan:

> I am writing about our mutual friend, Fr. Tom. Please do not consider me interfering. Fr. Duggan has done excellent work since he came here. I doubt if any other could have kept relations all round so excellent. Apart from local difficulties he has steered the Americans through a difficult course.
>
> Now he is straining at the leash for other work and pastures new. For more than a year I have used my influence to make him realize the good work he is doing. Now the truth is there is little to be done that any sensible man cannot handle. He has become quite discontent and restless.
>
> I understand the difficulties. Still I make bold to suggest that if it is not possible to give him permanent duty abroad it would solve many difficulties if he could be given some mission that would take him further afield and so remove his discontent.
>
> The motive urging him, I think, is not ambition, but self-justification.

In view of Bishop Farren's representations Monsignor Coghlan applied for a transfer for Duggan to active service but his application was turned down by higher authority. He wrote to Duggan:

> In my reply to the Bishop of Derry I told his Lordship that I would do my best and yesterday I gave instructions for you to be posted to an overseas Command, only to have them returned to me with the comment that 'personnel placed (as you are) in Group 1 for demobilisation may not be sent out of U.K.'

But Duggan continued to pester Coghlan who finally lost patience and wrote brutally but frankly to Duggan terminating their correspondence:

> I shall not demote you; to do so would certainly militate against your interests in your own diocese and elsewhere; no explanation from you or from anyone else would effectively prevent your demotion being interpreted as an indication of a lack of confidence in you.
>
> If, however, your conscience, your background and antecedents are, as you seem to imply, really proving obstacles to your continuing to minister to the spiritual needs of the Catholic personnel in H.M. Forces in N.I., I will, at your request, though very unwillingly, do what I can to facilitate your return to your own diocese.

Having failed to get a transfer through chaplaincy channels, Tom tried another avenue: working on his friendship with Sir Shane Leslie he tried to organise a lecture tour in the U.S.A. Before anything concrete emerged, word came to headquarters in Lisburn on 8 June 1945 that: 'In accordance with paragraph 330 of Release Regulations sanction is hereby given for release of Roman Catholic Chaplain T.F. Duggan Group 1 - 3 (incl.) on the appropriate date.'

Effectively this meant the end of Tom's career as a military chaplain. Tributes poured in from Church and State. Cardinal MacRory voiced the feelings of the Northern bishops when he wrote: 'You have won golden opinions, and you can always count upon a welcome if you return in any capacity to the North.'

Bishop Magean of Down and Connor wrote: 'God bless and reward you for all you did while in Down and Connor.'

A few months later when Duggan had been appointed president of Farranferris Bishop Neil Farren wrote:

> I am very glad of your appointment as President of the College. I do not know what your reactions are but I think you could not be better placed at the moment.
>
> Put your whole heart into it and make a good job of it. Show a proper deference to the Powers that be and do not engage too much

> in work *ad extra*. Your position entitles you to take a keen interest in the University. That and the College should keep your hands full.
>
> I wish you every success. You will be free around Christmas. You know there is a bed here: so come along when you can. There is always a welcome.

This was sound advice but very difficult to follow for one of Tom's disposition.

The most tangible token of appreciation from the British establishment came in the form of a high decoration from Buckingham Palace, the Order of the British Empire, (O.B.E. for short). The citation appeared in the New Year's Honours List, dated 4 January 1946:

> The King has been graciously pleased to give orders for the following appointments to the Most Excellent Order of the British Empire:
> To be Additional Officers of the Military Division of the said Most Excellent Order:
> THE REVERENED THOMAS FRANCIS DUGGAN, M.C., M.A. (144948),
> CHAPLAIN TO THE FORCE, THIRD CLASS (TEMPORARY),
> ROYAL CHAPLAINS' DEPARTMENT

Tom wrote to thank Major General Bucknall, G.O.C. Northern Ireland District to whom he gave credit for the award:

> News has just reached me that I figure on the current O.B.E. list. As the responsibility is ultimately yours, you will permit me to write to you.
>
> I beg to thank you *ex imo corde* for thinking of me. It is not the reward itself (God forgive me, I am unregenerate enough to prefer one mention in the field-of-battle dispatches to all the back area decorations in the world) – it is not the reward itself but the kindliness of spirit which actuated it. I know how scantily these decorations are doled out, how selective you must be in awarding them, the richness of merit which had to be passed over before my name could be even thought of.
>
> I came into this war a stranger and from afar. I have had already a rich reward in six full years of warm-hearted co-operation in my pastoral work. And now you pile honours on me. To you, to all the magnanimity that you embody and represent, I tender my heartfelt thanks.

He did not actually go to Buckingham Palace to receive the award in person.

Perhaps he was afraid of the local reaction in Cork or maybe he pictured his Fenian grandfather's spirit coming back to haunt him. He sent his apologies and asked that the decoration be sent to Farranferris. With his tongue in his cheek and knowing how his staff in Farranferris would enjoy the joke he wrote by way of explanation: 'From a College such as this, the unfortunate President can be absent only to attend his own funeral; no other exception made.'

Subsequently in the place of honour over his fireplace in the President's room in Farranferris he hung a photo-copy of the minute of the Commissioners of Education dismissing his grandfather for the crime of being a Fenian, a framed copy of General Tom Barry's wedding group and his O.B.E. medal. This collection of memorabilia says much for the breadth of his horizons.

The *Belfast Telegraph* gave the news of his demobilisation.

> When the demobilisation scheme commenced in Victoria Barracks, Belfast, yesterday, one of the first to pass through was Rev. T. F. Duggan; in common with the other soldiers leaving the Army, he was presented with an ordinary civilian suit.

It went on to give the prosaic details of each man's entitlements in the way of dress:

> Each demobilised man is entitled to one suit, one raincoat, one shirt, two collars, one tie, one hat, one pair of shoes and two pairs of socks. He can have a sports coat and a pair of flannels in preference to a suit.

It is unlikely that Tom emerged from the barrack resplendent in a trendy sports coat and flannels. More than likely his first call was to a priest-friend's house to ask for some more becoming clerical clothes.

His career as a military chaplain was well and truly over but not so his wanderings. The remainder of his life is largely the story of his peregrinations.

PRESIDENT OF FARRANFERRIS AND AMBASSADOR-AT-LARGE IN THE U.S.

PRESIDENT OF FARRANFERRIS

After six years' absence, Tom Duggan arrived back in his home diocese on 20 June 1945. The War in Europe had ended officially at midnight on 8 May 1945. Like hundreds of thousands of others he was now technically unemployed.

He did not expect any sort of sentimental reunion with Bishop Coholan or any word of recognition for his services as a military chaplain. The old scars in their relationship had not healed with the passage of time; if anything they had grown farther apart. When they met, after the opening, 'So you are back,' there was little in the way of small talk. There was no indication of when he might expect an appointment or what it might be. He would be sent for 'in due course' he was told.

'Due course' turned out to be nearly six months. The house on the College Road was lonely: his mother had died in 1943 and Lucy, his sister, was taken up with her teaching. Tom was not a good waiter: time lay heavily on his hands. He became increasingly frustrated, as a note written by him in late September shows:

> I got demobbed in June, 1945. It is now September, 22nd and there is not even the distant vision of work. I have read every 'shocker' I could find in the house.
>
> On September 22 I find myself: (a) half blind
> (b) nauseated
> (c) bankrupt of occupation.

But there was still a long purgatory ahead: Bishop Daniel was not going to hurry diocesan changes just to suit Duggan. At last on 1 December the call came from the Bishop's House where he received news of his appointment to the Presidency of Farranferris. He was not exactly overjoyed but anything was better than the vacuum in which he had been living.

The Seminary had seen better days. War-time shortages had made life difficult in all boarding-colleges. Shortages in such vital areas as food and fuel made life very difficult, especially for the kitchen staff. But Farranferris had suffered more than most. Despite obsolete cooking facilities and wet turf as the principal form of fuel, the Sisters had struggled hard to maintain standards, but notwithstanding their best efforts the food situation had seriously deteriorated. The health of the students was giving serious concern, and for the first time ever tuberculosis began to make inroads. Inevitably the reputation of the College began to suffer: students were under-nourished and some in bad health, parents were complaining, and the staff was powerless and embarrassed.

This was the situation which faced Tom Duggan on his appointment as President at the end of 1945. He wasted no time in recriminations.

In fairness to Denis Murphy, he left one important legacy to his successor, one valuable monument – a considerable credit balance in the bank.

Even without this financial cushion it is unlikely that Tom Duggan would have hesitated to take the urgent remedial action which was needed. He identified two areas for immediate attention, the provision of better and more wholesome food and the introduction of some sort of comprehensive health service.

First he concentrated on the kitchen. Modern cooking equipment was sorely needed and he made it his first priority. But due to the shortages of the time it was not possible to obtain luxury items such as Aga cookers locally. He found it necessary to have recourse to his military and political contacts in Northern Ireland and Britain.

It took a little time, but soon the hard-pressed Sisters had reason to admire his determination. Gleaming new or nearly new items of cooking equipment arrived to transform the appearance of the kitchen.

Decent cooking equipment was now in place but an even more difficult problem remained – how to improve the students' diet both in quantity and quality. Basic commodities such as potatoes, vegetables and fruit were still hard to come by. He called for an all-out effort from staff and parents, and he himself travelled far and wide in quest of food. It was a long and a hard struggle but eventually he was satisfied that reasonable progress had been made and that the famine was over!

He next set about providing an adequate health service for the students. For the first time in history, a College physician was appointed. The Sisters co-operated in securing a trained nursing sister from their headquarters. The services of a dietitian from the North Infirmary were called upon to work out a balanced diet. A little room was set apart as a clinic, and regular X-rays were introduced.

Soon T.B. became a thing of the past but he still continued to keep a sharp watch for students who appeared to be under-nourished. Despite modern refinements in the way of tonics, he always trusted in the efficacy of raw eggs as nature's pick-me-up.

In many such ways he gradually brought the College into line with other educational establishments of its kind. Staff, parents, and especially students appreciated his efforts and admired him for the broad humanity which lay behind. He hated meanness of any kind but especially in regard to food. If students felt they had a grievance, he was prepared to listen. On one occasion a boy was late for dinner owing to a dentist's appointment. Some unthinking person refused him his food and he complained to Duggan who stormed into the kitchen and told the first person he met there that 'this sort of treatment would arouse comment in a concentration camp'.

It was only to be expected that in spite of all his good points there were some human failings. He was short-tempered, he could be rude, and sometimes his jokes were inclined to be hurtful as, for instance, when a parent complained about her child being in 4C (the lowest class in that particular year), he replied that the reason he was in 4C was that 'we have no 4D'.

While sometimes he offended people's sensibilities, he managed at the same time to change the spirit of the Seminary, and students were no longer treated as an anonymous herd. It was extraordinary how many of the parents he knew personally, and this form of contact with the students' home situation helped him in his personal relationships with them. Many of his former students, now no longer young, recall the personal interest he took in them and how he tried to build up their self-confidence and self-esteem.

The boys in Farranferris quickly discovered that under the new regime it was wiser to look neat and tidy at all times. The new President insisted that hair be kept short and shoes polished.

Naturally he was very interested in the spiritual formation of the Seminary students. Each morning he celebrated Mass personally for the students and always gave a little talk beforehand, usually a few practical applications of the gospel of the day. It was always very clear that he had special devotion to Our Lady.

He taught Christian doctrine to the senior classes, using these class periods as occasions for providing a spiritual basis for the students' lives. Mindful of the fact that the majority were unlikely to become priests, he looked on the religion class as being their last chance of getting to understand the faith and of gaining an insight into the person of Christ. He tried to impart the principles of right living and the importance of being manly and honourable. He believed that Christian doctrine at senior level should be more a spiritual experience than an academic exercise.

Naturally he was keen on fostering vocations – it was part of his job – but he did not push students unduly in that direction: 'I don't want to be responsible for bad priests,' he would say. Occasionally he suffered disappointments when a boy who showed every sign of a vocation to the priesthood decided otherwise. On one such occasion he went to his friend, Fr. Michael Roche, for consolation. The only consolation he got from Roche was, 'But Tom, he is far too good to be a priest'. Roche, possibly from his study of the classics, was something of a cynic.

He tried as best he could to introduce as much variety as possible into the students' lives. He brought in external celebrities to lecture, and they heard the story of Kilmichael from General Tom Barry himself and the epic of Crossbarry from Jim Hurley, a prominent participant.

If life was becoming even more monotonous than usual, he would find some excuse for giving a half-day. A military-style time-table appeared on the notice board with each class period cut down to half:

For 9.00 a.m. read 9.00 a.m.
For 9.45 a.m. read 9.20 a.m.
For 10.30 a.m. read 9.40 a.m.
and so on.

He inherited a splendid staff and under his leadership and motivation they found great fulfilment. In Mathematics there were Fr. Mitchell Kelly, Dr. Jerry O'Sullivan and Dr. Edward Hegarty; in Classics, Dr. Dan Connolly and An Doctúr Sean Mac Cárthaigh; in History and Geography, Fr. Michael Roche and Mr. John A. Murphy; in English, Fr. Jerome Kiely and Dr. C. Mac Cárthaigh; in Irish, Risteard uasal O Luineacháin and an tAthair Tadhg O Murchú; in French, Dr. Laurence Kelleher. Relations were very good between the President and staff. Duggan usually presided at every meal except breakfast which he did not regard as a social occasion. Very often the meals were most entertaining. There was food for the mind as well as for the body. Conversation was brisk and uninhibited. Professor John A. Murphy is on record as saying that the open nature of the discussion was remarkable for its time in a predominantly clerical gathering.

Each Wednesday Fr. Christy O'Flynn arrived to take elocution classes with the students. He and Duggan were great friends and when class ended Christy usually went upstairs to have lunch with the staff. It often turned into a long session during which, sooner or later, Christy introduced his favourite topic: how hard it is to tolerate the wailing that one sometimes hears masquerading as sean-nós, Irish traditional singing. After one such session, Duggan summed up Christy's contribution: 'Sometimes he prophesies, and sometimes he brays.'

An indication of Tom's high standing in neighbouring dioceses was the fact that the diocese of Killaloe sent priests who were studying for the Higher Diploma in Education to live in and to take classes in Farranferris. When one of them, Kevin McNamara, led the class in the examination, followed by two nuns, Duggan commented: 'Our little horse cantered home, followed by two fillies.' When his opposite number in St. Flannan's, Canon Tom Maxwell, offered some form of monetary compensation in return, Duggan was horrified at this slur on his hospitality, 'Maxwell,' he said, 'I always knew you had the breed of a huckster in you'.

He always had a special grádh for an tAthair Tadgh. Normally they were the best of friends but there were occasional hiccups in the relationship as on the famous occasion when following a Fianna Fáil defeat in a general election Duggan noticed an exceptionally large group of students parading in the hated detention area. On inquiring about the nature of the crime he was told, 'Fr. Tadhg sent us out, Canon'. 'Dismiss,' he said, 'We can't have political prisoners here.'

He did not always agree with the team-selection picked by the College trainers. On one occasion he inquired of Steve Kennifick, the College maintenance man of the time, 'Steve, who picked that young man?' Steve said, 'Fr. Kelly, Canon'. And Duggan replied: 'Mind you, he's not bad but he's easily the worst I've seen.

The lack of playing fields was still acute when Duggan became President so he decided that something had to be done. He first thought of approaching his great friend, Fr. Christy O'Flynn, who owned a large farm in Churchfield. Duggan called at what he considered the most propitious time to broach the subject of buying or leasing one of the fields. The moment Duggan introduced the subject, Christy sprang up and turned on the radio, 'I think it's news time, Tom,' he said. So obviously there were limits to the great friendship.

He next turned to the Corporation who owned a hilly field of $8^1/_2$ acres adjoining the College land. He applied to his friend, Philip Monahan, the City Manager, to buy the field, and the matter was referred by Monahan to the Department of Local Government. The Department had no objection provided that, before selling, the Corporation had the land valued. In due course, Monahan communicated with Duggan: 'The value of the property in fee simple is £1200. May I take it that this is acceptable to you.'

Duggan replied indignantly:

> In spite of the figure, we are firm in our desire to proceed with the purchase. The fact is, we have no alternative...But let it be said most emphatically, we are dismayed at the suggested purchase price.

> We had good reason for believing that the land would be transferred at the price originally paid for it. Instead this is what is to happen: land acquired at £75 per acre, the 'buildable' that is to say, the valuable portion used up, and the unusable remnant offered to us at £150 per acre.
>
> The valuation is arrived at by the application of standards of only too widely held acceptance in the market place. The chief of these is, a thing may be appraised not at its native worth, but at what can be squeezed out of the man who needs it and must have it.
>
> Nothing could be more unethical. Needless to say, we do not blame you. It is sad that strangers on an issue trivial in the perspective of a whole programme have threatened to disrupt the cordial relations between the Municipality and the Church which you yourself have so steadfastly maintained.

The Manager was won over and he appealed on Tom's behalf to the Minister and in due course was able to report back to Tom: 'I attach, for your information, copy of a letter from the Department surrendering to our blandishments.'

At one stroke, therefore, Tom had succeeded in doubling the College land at an extremely favourable price. But the saga was not yet over. In due course he posed the next question to the Manager, who is going to pay for the boundary wall which it will be necessary to erect between Corporation and College land? The Manager replied: 'We estimate the cost of building a boundary wall to your land at £1130. We think your contribution should be £565.'

Tom was outraged:

> When we negotiated the new field we were certain that you would segregate the holding not merely on the map but with a stoutly-built Corporation wall. That, we were given to understand, was the usage. If we had envisaged anything else, we would never have thought of acquiring the property.
>
> The simple fact is: we can pay for the field or we can pay for the wall. We cannot pay for both. In the perspective of your commitments an extra piece of wall is a matter of small moment, to me it is bankruptcy.
>
> Bearing this in mind, won't your please reconsider?

Monahan duly relented and wrote to Duggan: 'In all the circumstances I agree that the Corporation should build the wall at its own expense.'

Entirely due to Duggan's dogged persistence, therefore, generations of students have benefited. In due course, two splendid playing pitches were laid out in the land acquired by Duggan. Duggan was dead and gone when Farranferris won its first Dr. Harty Cup and Croke Cup in 1963. But those with long memories recalled how vital a part Tom Duggan had played in making these and future victories possible.

First Visit To America

After four years of Duggan's presidency, Farranferris was back on an even keel. The food situation had improved dramatically and there were no further major health problems. Spiritually also the students seemed more at peace with themselves; disciplinary worries were few. Morale was high and a far happier atmosphere prevailed. Pride in the College had been restored.

During these years Duggan had sedulously avoided outside involvements. But after four years he felt that he could spread his wings a little. The outside world began to obtrude itself. The first distraction came in the from of an invitation from his old friend, General Richard Mulcahy, Minister for Education, to serve on the Council of Education, a review body of the educational system at national level. Though this entailed many journeys to Dublin it was nevertheless quite compatible with his fulfilling properly his role as President.

A more serious distraction came his way when he was elected President of the Maynooth Union, the association of Maynooth priests. He appreciated the honour but he soon found that it was going to be a very onerous responsibility. A major and overdue restoration and modernisation of the old buildings had taken place. A national collection had been held and though it had brought in a great deal of money, much remained to be done. Now, as President of the Union, Duggan felt it incumbent on him to give a lead. After some consultation he decided to spear-head a major fund-raising drive among the Irish Catholic laity in the United States, working through the Irish societies in the various cities.

But first of all it would be necessary to obtain Bishop Coholan's permission. But this in itself would not be sufficient. Foreseeing long absences from Farranferris he concluded that it would be necessary to appoint a Vice-President who would take over when he was absent. But at this stage, and not for the first time, he over-stepped the mark as far as Bishop Coholan was concerned. Duggan had always hoped that Fr. Michael Roche would succeed him as President and this, he felt, was his chance. When Tom saw the Bishop he asked, in the most innocent way possible, for a vice-president to be appointed and suggested the name of Fr. Michael Roche. It was a fatal mistake. Though now aged 92, Bishop Daniel still held the reins of control resolutely in his own hands: if there was one thing he disliked it was when someone attempted to manipulate him. He told Duggan he needed time to consider. A few days later, two letters from the Bishop arrived at Farranferris, one for Duggan and the other for Dr. Dan Connolly, a junior member of the staff compared to Fr. Roche. Connolly's letter was as follows:

> Dear Dr. Connolly,
>
> There is need in the College of an Administrative Council. I hereby appoint you Vice-President of the College and a member of the Administrative Council, with your present duties as Professor. The accompanying statement to the President will indicate what the Administrative Council will have to look after.

It was brutal treatment for Duggan but it was his own fault. He was very upset but after a period of extreme despondency he began to look on the bright side. He decided that he would give the new Vice-President every opportunity of gaining experience in running the College. At this stage, when he needed it most, his morale received a great boost. On 8 December 1950, an announcement was made that his friend Dr. Cornelius Lucey had been appointed coadjutor to the Bishop of Cork with the right of succession. Tom was elated, expecting and hoping for a happier relationship with authority in due course. A happy augury came in a matter of days in the form of an invitation to accompany the Bishop-elect to Rome for the closing ceremonies of the Holy Year on Christmas Eve.

During the early part of 1951 he continued to seek out ways and means of getting his campaign in the United States under way. The American bishops had grown tired of seeing so many clergymen arriving in their midst in pursuit of money for various good causes and had tightened up regulations considerably as regards outsiders collecting money in their dioceses. Tom contacted a friend in the American hierarchy, Archbishop Robert Emmet Lucey of San Antonio, Texas, and asked for his advice: 'There is an ever-flowing stream of ecclesiastical bandits from Ireland in your midst collecting for the activities of their various hen-runs, but this is different.'

Nothing came of this contact. Tom now realised that he himself had to find some pretext for entering the United States for reasons not connected with raising money for Maynooth. Just about this time, February 1951, Fr. Patrick Peyton, the famous 'Rosary Priest' arrived in Cork. Duggan had met him previously and entertained him in his usual hospitable way in Farranferris. It transpired in the course of conversation that Peyton belonged to the same religious Congregation that administered the famous University of Notre Dame in South Bend, Indiana. Tom pricked up his ears. One thing followed another, culminating in a warm invitation to Tom to deliver the St. Patrick's Day address to the Irish Cultural Society of the University. Dr. Cornelius Hagerty, director of the Society wrote: 'It will be an inexpressible favour to us to have an address from one so deeply versed in Irish culture as yourself.'

Tom may have cringed a little at the description but he accepted the invitation with alacrity, writing to Dr. Hagerty:

> Unless my hand has lost its cunning I shall be with you before March 16....I thought of speaking of 'Ireland's Contribution to the Second World War'. There has been much misunderstanding and misrepresentation. During the period, I was rather in the middle of things. I knew the British point of view and I knew de Valera's point of view even more intimately.

Unfortunately for Duggan, Hagerty was the type of Irish-American who did not even want to hear that there was such a thing as an Irish dimension to World War II. He found it difficult, consequently, to restrain himself when writing back to Tom:

> So far as I am concerned personally, I admire Ireland for staying out of both world wars...Why should Catholics in the U.S. be occupied with hearing that the Irish were friendly to England in the past world war? What good came out of it for the Christian Faith? Had Germany won could we be worse off? The Faith of Poland, Czechoslovakia and Lithuania is being suppressed.
>
> The only reason that the U.S. went into both world wars was to save England, and England's foreign policy is not something to make any Catholic in the U.S. proud. Ireland has nothing to apologise for because she did not jump on the English band-wagon.

It was a salutary lesson for Tom, teaching him to tread more carefully where Irish-American sensibilities were concerned. He hastily back-pedalled as regards his choice of theme, substituting the comparatively innocuous topic 'Ireland's Spiritual Heritage', in place of the one which had given offence.

Tom now had achieved his primary purpose, gaining entry into the United States with the ostensible purpose of delivering a lecture in Notre Dame but with the real purpose of spying out the lie of the land as far as the proposed collection for Maynooth was concerned. He delivered his lecture and availed of the opportunity of visiting some of the key centres of Irish-American influence.

After a month he wrote to Bishop Patrick O'Neill of Limerick with some progress to report:

> Availing of my presence in Chicago I presented myself to His Eminence, Cardinal Stritch. I had first been to see the Auxiliary Bishop, Most Rev. W. O'Brien. Dr. O'Brien finished up by being very interested in the project. He spoke to the Cardinal on my behalf, and the Cardinal very graciously received me on Monday, March 24th. Dr. O'Brien assured me if I could get a gathering of significance together, either himself or the Cardinal would address it. I suggested both, nor was I contradicted.
>
> I went next to Washington. His Grace the Archbishop was kindness itself. He gave me full permission but told me to inform him in advance when our project was maturing.
>
> For Baltimore, I had a letter of introduction from the Irish ambassador to His Grace of Baltimore. His Grace was out of town but I was assured at high level that there would be no lack of welcome there.
>
> Philadelphia came next. Thanks, I should say, to grateful memories of Bishop Farren's services to American troops during the War I was received with the utmost cordiality. Full co-operation was promised.

A careful reading of the foregoing shows that it is long in promises but very short in terms of real commitments. The fact was that at the time Cardinal Francis Spellman of New York wielded exceptional influence over the rest of the United States hierarchy, due in particular to his very close friendship with Pope Pius XII. Unless some signal of support from New York emerged for Duggan's cause, he was only wasting his time elsewhere.

When he went to interview Cardinal Spellman he met more than his match: Spellman was a practised politician:

> New York next. I arrived in New York when His Eminence, the Cardinal was more than usually busy. In spite of that he graciously

> accorded me a short interview. I explained our project. He pointed out that New York had already been very generous in the matter of the Maynooth collection. That I assented to with the uttermost emphasis, and, switching ground, I asked his blessing and permission, not for a collection in New York, but for the whole general scheme. He assured me that there would be no objection on his part to any action taken in other dioceses.

It was a very half-hearted endorsement of Tom's plan. Effectively it cut the ground from under his feet and marked the end of his campaign. But he would not yet concede defeat. Writing to Archbishop Lucey of San Antonio, he told him the bad news:

> I am afraid the blow has fallen – with the induration of heart prevailing in New York I appear to be ham-strung. I don't like being beaten (like the Luceys, the Duggans come from Macroom). Not even Eminential induration casts me down. It merely challenges me to seek solvents.

But in spite of his brave front, the writing was on the wall. He returned home soon after without a penny to show for his trouble. But at least he was a much wiser man in the ways of the Catholic Church in America. He would not make the same mistakes again – especially the grievous error he had made in not making it his business to approach Archbishop Richard Cushing of Boston personally. In fact Cushing was worth all the other Graces put together when it came to supporting Irish causes.

In his letter to Bishop O'Neill, Duggan made a feeble attempt to justify the glaring omission of Cushing: 'I did not visit Boston. If I made the visit it would have to be in Holy week, and Dr. E. Maguire of the Chinese Mission has promised to make arrangements with His Grace of Boston.'

To most observers at home, Duggan's failure was absolute. There was one exception, Bishop Cornelius Lucey, coadjutor Bishop of Cork and, at the time, parish priest of Bantry. Duggan visited him in Bantry soon after his arrival and left him a voluminous file on his American trip.

Bishop Lucey went through the correspondence minutely – and one particular letter caught his attention, a letter from Dr. Maguire of the Columban Fathers to Bishop O'Neill:

> What should be done – in Ireland or out of it – to meet the needs of Maynooth is, of course, the business of the Irish Bishops, and I have

> no intention whatever of advising men who are quite capable of handling and solving their own problems.
>
> But I will say this: if our organisation (i.e. the Columbans) in this country had a man of the Canon's ability, versatility and persuasive powers, he would almost certainly find himself with a roving commission from the Holy Ghost. He would function as our ambassador-at-large, a man whose task it would be to explain the financial needs of our Society by word of mouth to members of the hierarchy and to prominent lay folk.

This unsolicited testimonial and the manner in which it pinpointed Tom's talents greatly impressed the Bishop. Already a great design was maturing in his mind which would come to fruition when he became Bishop of Cork – *The Rosary of Churches* which would gird the city. He could see a place for Tom Duggan in his future plans.

The Rosary Of Churches

The old patriarch, Bishop Daniel Coholan, died on 24 August 1952, and, in accordance with the terms of his appointment as coadjutor with the right of succession, Bishop Cornelius Lucey automatically became Bishop of Cork. Foremost in his list of priorities was a massive church building programme in the city of Cork. In loyalty to his predecessor's memory he was careful to point out that:

> The need for a big church building programme just now does not arise through any neglect in the past. The need has arisen simply because houses are going up so rapidly so recently. And let me say that we welcome that – the quicker the slums are cleared and the more houses that are put up by the Corporation and private builders the better.

During the winter and spring of 1952-53 he finalised his plans. Among his priorities was the launching of an appeal to the Irish Catholic population of Greater Boston to support his church-building programme. He called on Tom Duggan to advise him, and, on Tom's recommendation, he sought advice also from Dr. Frank Creedon who had practised as a doctor in the city of Brockton near Boston for many years. It was decided that Dr. Creedon, like the dove from Noah's Ark, would first be sent to Boston to test the waters and, if his report were favourable, then Tom Duggan would follow to organise the actual collection.

Frank Creedon was the ideal choice. Outgoing and gregarious, he was a highly respected figure in Brockton and the surrounding areas.

By May 29 1953, only months after becoming Bishop of Cork, Bishop Lucey was ready to launch his great church building project. To a packed audience in the City Hall he unveiled his plans; they were breath-taking in their extensiveness:

> To meet the needs of these new suburbs three new churches are needed at once; if the city develops as it is scheduled to develop, at least two further churches will be required very soon.
>
> The churches presently needed are for Gurranebraher on the North side, Ballyphehane on the South side, and the Model Farm Road on the West; two further churches envisaged are for Spangle Hill and the Mayfield area respectively.
>
> I may add that sites for the first four churches mentioned have already been acquired and plans for the first two finally approved – we should see a beginning made in the actual building in the course of the next few months.
>
> As I looked round the city and thought of these new developments, I had the inspiration to put the new city that is so rapidly rising under the protection of Our Lady of the Rosary. With a Rosary of churches – the Church of the Resurrection, the Church of the Ascension, etc. – encircling it, Cork can hopefully face outwards and upwards!

As Bishop Lucey spoke that night in the City Hall, Dr. Frank Creedon was already in Boston, carrying with him a letter of recommendation from Bishop Lucey:

> We in Cork are desperately in need of new churches and we are desperately in need of the money with which to build them.
>
> The city has grown by leaps and bounds in the last few years. All these newly built-up, suburban areas – many of them housing the families hitherto condemned to the slums – are without churches. To bring God's Mass and Eucharistic Presence to those areas at least five new churches are called for. Five churches will cost more than £500,000. That is a sum far beyond the reach of the people settled in the new houses, people with big families, big hearts, big faith but little wages.

> Consequently I am appealing to Cork people everywhere but particularly in Boston to come to our aid. I am appealing to them for the sake of the old country, for the sake of their own kith and kin at home, for the sake of God for whom the churches are going up, and I am empowering the bearer, Dr. Francis Creedon, Pope's Road, Cork – a good Corkman and a good worker for the Church here – to seek and accept donations for the *Cork Churches Fund*.
>
> To all who hear our appeal and answer it, be their answer great or little, I say, 'God bless you, many times over, for remembering His houses and your own people'.

Bishop Lucey, being a patient man, was prepared to wait for Dr. Creedon's return for news of the Boston project. Tom Duggan, however, did not share his Bishop's gift of patience. He found himself unable to resist the temptation of journeying to Boston to find out how Dr. Creedon was progressing. Having arrived there early in May he wrote post-haste to Bishop Lucey in wildly over-optimistic terms:

> My Dear Lord,
> I arrived in Boston only an hour ago but I'd like you to know the marvels which Frankie has accomplished.
>
> Frankie had only landed when he realised that, unless he was prepared to content himself with chicken-feed, the Archbishop had to come into the picture.
>
> Accordingly he took a courageous military decision. He got hold of an old friend of his own who is also a very intimate friend of the Archbishop and they went straight to the A.B's House.
>
> The A.B. was not at home so, then and there, they sent the following letter:
>
> Your Excellency,
> Dr. Creedon is a dear friend of mine.
> We took a chance and called at your home to-day.
> I know personally of the wonderful work Dr. Creedon is doing for the Church and Ireland. Anything done for him will be a big favour to Devotedly yours,
> Fr. Matt.

Fr. Matthew Miller, O.F.M. was the friend in question. Following this note of introduction, Dr. Creedon addressed an appeal to the Archbishop, which concluded as follows:

> Knowing your great love for Ireland, and cognizant of the part played by the Irish in bringing the faith to America, we feel confident that you, as the son of a Cork father and mother, will assist us with your blessing and invaluable advice.

Cushing replied to Father Miller:

> I have your letter and the appeal. It comes too late. I just promised the Pastor of Glanworth, Ireland, some five thousand odd dollars to equip his Church with pews. It will be a memorial to my beloved mother and father.
>
> The only way Bishop Lucey can get money is to come here and appeal in the churches. Unless he does that tell him he wouldn't get anything. If he does that I am sure he will be successful.

Duggan's letter to Bishop Lucey concluded as follows:

> Frank has taken this [the Archbishop's letter to Fr. Millar] as an indication of the benevolent attitude of the Archbishop, sufficient for him (ie. F.) to communicate our needs to the papers and to the people of Boston.
>
> I can't claim to have contributed one iota to the triumph. I do take pride in thinking of Frankie.
>
> Plan a half dozen more churches.
>
> Expect further bulletins.

That Duggan could interpret as a 'triumph' a polite letter from the Archbishop to an old friend turning down his request is an example of his extraordinary power of self-deception or self-persuasion. The Cork Churches, in fact, were in the rear of a formidible queue, waiting to gain the Archbishop's ear, a queue which included the pastor of his father's native parish in the diocese of Cloyne and Mother Mary Martin of the Medical Missionaries of Mary.

Duggan was so carried away that he wanted to start the collection there and then. Frank Creedon, however, persuaded him that the seed sown needed time to germinate and it was agreed between them that they would report back to

Bishop Lucey and suggest that Tom Duggan be sent back to Boston in October to organise the actual collection.

Meanwhile planning went ahead apace for the building of the new churches. The first site was blessed in Gurranebraher on 25 August. In the course of his address Bishop Lucey prayed for all those who had helped in the work:

> Today has seen the start made on the Rosary of Churches wherewith we hope to girdle this fair city and bind it fast to Our Lady. It is the church of the second decade, the Ascension. God grant that we may see the completion in this our day of all the five decades of that Glorious Rosary.
>
> God bless the work. God bless the workers, both that will do the building and those whose efforts and sacrifices the money to pay for the building will come. And God bless all this generation and the many generations to come who will come to His Mass and His Presence in this Holy Place.

The Bishop's joy on this happy occasion was somewhat marred by an incident which occurred in the same week. *En route* for Dublin after landing from an American liner at Cobh with a group of pilgrims, Archbishop Cushing was to change trains at Cork. Bishop Lucey was on the platform to welcome him but scarcely got an opportunity of doing so. When the Archbishop set foot on the platform he was immediately engulfed by his pilgrims lustily chanting, 'Happy Birthday, dear Richard, happy birthday to you' and other such anthems. The Archbishop, accustomed to this kind of familiarity, gave every indication of enjoying the proceedings to the full, but Bishop Lucey, standing forlornly apart, was not impressed.

Just before boarding his train, the Archbishop had time only for a brief word with the Bishop of Cork: there was no mention of the Cork Churches' appeal. It put in perspective the so called 'triumph' of Tom Duggan and Frank Creedon in Boston! Bishop Lucey took it as a calculated slight and was in two minds about calling off the whole Boston project. But wiser counsels prevailed after Frank Creedon had made him aware of a more casual relationship generally prevailing between American bishops and the laity.

About the middle of October Tom Duggan returned to Boston accompanied once again by Frank Creedon who came to train him in, so to speak, into the ways of the Irish in Boston. The city of Brockton where Frank had practised medicine from 1926 to 1932 became Tom's headquarters and John Collins (a friend of Frank's and, like him an old I.R.A. man and a native of Ballyvourney) volunteered to act as his host and mentor. After a couple of weeks Frank returned to his medical duties in Cork and from that point on Tom Duggan ploughed a lonely furrow. And for a while it was very lonely. For the first time he began to realise fully how much was at stake – for the Cork Churches and for his own credibility. It seems that to some extent he lost heart. There was no glamour attached to being a fund-raiser in Boston at the time – the pool was over-fished. The target which had been set was 25,000 dollars: it was hoped to raise it by public appearances, lectures and private donations.

As the weeks slipped by, Tom became increasingly despondent: the 25,000 dollars looked like a mirage in the far distance. Much – indeed almost everything – depended on the Archbishop. He was a much loved prelate, possessing enormous personal influence. He was the soul of generosity but he was getting tired of being generous. Latterly he had begun to feel imposed upon by numerous suppliants, with the Irish well to the fore. Understandably, in view of the advice he was receiving from many quarters, he felt the time had come to call a halt. For the time being at least he was wary about becoming involved in any fresh projects such as the Cork Churches' appeal.

Tom Duggan, in consequence, found himself confronted by a stone wall. Normally when he wanted to meet a person he was not an easy man to keep out, but on this occasion when he tried to reach the Archbishop he found his way firmly barred by a resolute and watchful Praetorian Guard.

Sadly he reported his lack of progress to Frank Creedon. A weekly correspondence began which on Tom's part consisted mostly of brief notes in telegraphic form, more or less in the nature of military communiqués. These letters are most interesting and some of them are quite hilarious. To Frank he could reveal his inner self and his many disappointments and frustrations:

4 November:

> There is to be a Men's Ball on the 20th, promoted by the Cork Ladies Association. I am going to be the belle of it. God save all Christians!

7 November:

> Sunday evening to Lawrence where I had the effrontery to lecture to 500 students of Merrimac. I got away without being lynched.

21 November:

> Are they all dead in Farranferris – or merely paralysed?

22 November:
Still chasing 'big' money but many disappointments.

24 November:
(He was worried about some Bon Secours problem):
Over thirty years of meddling with their affairs and it has become, I suppose, a habit.

8 December:
In Natick Sat. night. I fixed on my smile at 6.30 p.m. and I scraped it off at 1.30 a.m. 351 dollars.

18 December:
Meeting began at 5.30, I got speaking at 9.45 and I got 30 dollars.

Some idea of the kind of function he had to attend week after week can be gleaned from the following report in *The Boston Traveller*.

> Brockton residents were thanked for their generosity by the Very Rev. Thomas Canon Duggan, M.A., M.C., personal representative of Bishop Cornelius Lucey of Cork, Ireland, Saturday night in the Hibernian Hall where he was tendered a reception. Special guests were Mayor Lucey and Police Chief O'Donnell. Mayor Lucey presented Canon Duggan with a pair of Brockton-made shoes.
>
> Canon Duggan has been touring in the United States raising money for the construction of new churches in Cork and while he has been in this country he has made Brockton his headquarters.
>
> After the Canon made his appeal, there was a musical night. Featuring at the reception were Pride of Erin dancers...the girls clad in green costumes with gold sashes did a horn-pipe, four-hand reel and jigs. Mrs. M. Holland gave several solos which were well received by an appreciative audience.

Coming up to Christmas, the situation had become critical. The bargain with Bishop Lucey was that Tom was to try to raise twenty-five thousand dollars (15,000 in the hub, Boston, and 10,000 in the surrounding towns) and that Bishop Lucey would travel to Boston on St. Patrick's Day for the presentation.

But now Bishop Lucey seemed to be having second thoughts about going to Boston because, in Duggan's words, 'He does not want to submit himself to the boisterous embrace of Big Brother'. Apparently the debacle at Glanmire Station still rankled. Duggan wrote him a strong letter of protest, openly ascribing his reluctance to appear in Boston to the fact that 'the Boston Circus visited Ireland in August and, quite evidently, dismayed you'. Bishop Lucey was a shy and undemonstrative man and he was probably afraid that he might look out of place in Cushing's entourage. But eventually he relented and agreed to fulfil his promise.

By Christmas, all Tom had to show for his months of toil was a paltry 6,700 dollars. Obviously the clouds were gathering over his venture: A blood transfusion was needed to save it. Tired and dispirited, at the end of his tether physically and psychologically, he decided to take a complete break and travelled down to Baltimore to spend Christmas with the Bon Secours Sisters. It was a wise decision: the few days away did him the world of good. He came back a new man, ready to do battle once again, prepared to endure any number of reels and jigs.

The long awaited break-through came just at this point. Archbishop Cushing was in hospital, recuperating after a serious operation. Tom managed to gain admission to his bed-side. The Archbishop was in despondent mood and scarcely wanted even to talk. Soon he had no need to talk because Tom embarked on a flood of reminiscences and funny stories. Calling on all his experience of dealing with sick people, he set about raising the Archbishop's spirits. He must have given a virtuoso performance because soon the Archbishop was sitting up in bed, laughing at Duggan's stories.

From the very start they seemed to empathise. They had a great deal in common. They were two eccentric geniuses, very much alike in temperament and outlook with the same strong sense of mission from God and fierce loyalty to the Church. They were both unusual characters, extroverts, individualists, radical and unconventional in many ways but warm-hearted, emotional and impulsive; compulsively generous, absolutely detached from money or possessions, Spartan in their way of life, wanderers for Christ. At heart deeply compassionate men yet there was also a lighter side, a mischievous streak in their natures. They could not resist commenting on people and things with a dry and sardonic sense of humour. They both had a gift of words and a turn of phrase, a *penchant* for irony and epigram.

In Cushing's case this impish touch shone through on even the most solemn occasions. For instance, during President John F. Kennedy's inauguration ceremony in Washington smoke began to issue from the lectern as Cushing was reciting the dedicational prayer and he loudly ascribed it to 'the devil being up to his tricks again'.* Some of his more memorable remarks were quoted nationwide in the American press, even in such prestigious magazines as *Time* and *Life*. For instance, when asked for his views on women-priests he said: 'I've supported many lost causes in my life-time but this one is not for me. I could never confess my sins to a woman: it would be like doing it on television.' On another occasion he stood on a stage flanked by the usual group of clergy and begged the laity to become more involved: 'You see the dead-wood I have around me.' Or perhaps the funniest story of all, one which he told against himself, was about the time he was called to anoint the victim of a road accident and he solemnly asked the poor man, 'Do you believe in God the Father, God the son, and God the Holy Ghost?' and the man said, 'Ah, Father, here I am dying and you bother me with riddles'.

One cannot help thinking that Tom was lucky to have made a friend of Cushing at the time he did because otherwise his last years might have lacked purpose and direction. They certainly would have been less entertaining.

Tom Duggan's visit to the Archbishop in hospital (to be followed by many more) was the turning point as far as the Cork Churches' Appeal was concerned. Within days the Archbishop made a series of most generous offers – he would contribute 25,000 dollars if Tom could collect 25,000 before St. Patrick's Day; he would also hand over the collection to be taken up in the Cathedral on St. Patrick's Day, and finally he would assign a staff reporter from the *Boston Pilot*, Ellen Sullivan, to publicise the Cork project. Ellen was of Bantry stock and turned out to be of tremendous help. Years later when Tom was boarding the aircraft at Idlewild airport in New York on his way to Peru she broke through all barriers, shouting 'Press' and she was the last to shake his hand before he climbed the steps of the aircraft.

All this was great news for the Cork Churches fund but for Tom personally it meant added pressure. His credibility was heavily at stake once again: he knew that Cushing was not the sort of man to stick to the letter of his contract but that was all the more reason why he was determined to reach his target of 25,000 dollars. He confided his fears to Dr. Frank Creedon, writing on January 21:

> I undertook to collect 25,000 dollars and I would hate to get a fool's pardon (from Cushing if I fail).
>
> I am dating these letters like battle dispatches and a bloody battle it is.

* *Time* magazine, August 21, 1964.

But soon his letters to Frank were becoming markedly more optimistic:

> 23 January:
> In two months I'll take off my cursed smile and burn the damn thing!
>
> 28 January:
> Money is rolling in satisfactorily. Think I made 2,500 dollars at St. Andrew's (five sermons). Then made the Eire Society and made 00.00.
>
> 1 February:
> I am nearing the end of my tether – preaching at all Masses in five big churches for the next five weeks. Eyes troubling me.
>
> 28 February:
> I'll probably go mad (tension increasing every day). Even if I do, THE WORK IS DONE. In fact if a final spectacular departure from sanity can be arranged it would be worth some thousands of bucks.

He knew that his main troubles were over and that the over-all target had already been attained but he was of such a nervous disposition that he did not relax until Bishop Lucey duly arrived in Boston on 15 March, was royally received by the Archbishop, preached at Pontifical High Mass in the Cathedral on St. Patrick's Day and received the promised cheques from the Archbishop and Duggan.

As far as the Archbishop was concerned, his contribution was only a first instalment. Several further donations were made by him to the Cork Churches Fund, including 25,000 dollars when he preached at the opening of the new church at Farranree, and a further 25,000 dollars when visited by Bishop Lucey some years later. In terms of money contributed, no other benefactor of the Cork Churches Fund could compare with him.

If it were not for Tom Duggan it is almost certain that the Archbishop would never have seen his way to making these huge contributions. But for some strange reason, Duggan never received full credit.

In the pages of the *Boston Pilot*, he bade an emotional farewell to Boston:

> I went to Boston forlorn and friendless. I gave nothing, I had nothing to give. For six months I dedicated myself to the most unpopular of all avocations: I attached myself like a leech to the pockets of the people.

> I came away with my target munificently reached. And in spite of all these handicaps the people of Boston not only tolerated me but gave me their affection.
>
> In the light of all that, how can I be objective?

Before leaving Boston Tom made a personal request to Bishop Lucey which in the circumstances could hardly be refused: he would like, he said, after all his years of involvement in academic affairs, to be given a pastoral appointment in the diocese. Bishop Lucey readily complied with his request and promised him the first suitable parish to become vacant.

RESCUE MISSION TO KINSALE

Providence decreed that the first parish to become vacant was Kinsale. A calculating clergy would not have looked on it as exactly a 'plum' parish. This was by no means a reflection on the people of Kinsale but on the place itself at the time. It came, therefore, as a pleasant surprise to Bishop Lucey to discover that someone of Tom Duggan's stature was interested. He had hesitated about offering it to Tom in case he might not think it suitable and it was a great relief when Tom made the first move.

Why did Tom find Kinsale attractive at the time? He was afraid that an ordinary run-of-the-mill parish might not be to his liking. Even at the age of 64 he was young at heart, he still yearned for challenge. He would certainly find a challenge in Kinsale: if ever a place needed the kiss of life it was Kinsale in 1954. The opportunity of breathing new life into an ailing body was more than he could resist.

There were also sentimental reasons. His memories of Kinsale went back to his early childhood. As a young Ballyheeda boy at the turn of the century, it was the first town he had ever known – in some respects it was 'town' for the people of Ballyheeda. It was there at Cionn tSáile, the head of the sea, the quiet sea, that he had seen the sea for the first time, where he had first breathed the pure sea air, smelled the tang of the sea. In those days there was magic and romance in the atmosphere of Kinsale to stir the heart of a child. There was a buzz and bustle about the busy streets; the sight of the fishing boats returning to harbour, the animated scene at the new pier as they landed their colourful catch, the schooners with their varied cargoes, the seeming myriads of boatmen with their navy jerseys and colourful caps, these were his first contacts with that great big world he was told about at school and saw pictured in the encyclopaedias at home. He had marvelled at the quiet sea in the inner harbour, it was so calm:

> It is a slow sea,
> Mare tranquillum.*

And though the schooners might be only 'dirty British coasters with cargo of Tyne coal'† they could still fire a boy's imagination and perhaps give him the first stirrings of a wanderlust which he would carry with him through life.

* Turner, Walter James, 'The Seven Days of the Sun', *Oxford Book of Modern Verse*, 1952.
† Masefield, John, *Cargoes*.

Although the child was unaware of the fact, Kinsale was already sinking slowly into obscurity. The primacy it had long enjoyed among the fishing centres of the Cork coast had been lost to Baltimore and Berehaven, and foreign fishing boats with the advent of steam no longer needed a haven like Kinsale when storms raged.

By the time Tom Duggan arrived as parish priest in May 1954, the process of decline was almost complete. Kinsale was a ghost town, a mere shadow of its former self. Several factors had contributed to its economic collapse. The sea had been its life-line and now the fishing industry had almost disappeared; the trade in the harbour had dwindled to a trickle; there had never been a tradition of manufacturing industry in Kinsale except for the celebrated and very beautiful Kinsale lace. The departure of the British Army garrison, several hundred strong, however desirable politically, was a sore blow to the town's economy. The once thriving grain mills such as Jagoes Mills and Browns Mills no longer ground the local corn to supply the busy bakers of Kinsale. Once a feature of the countryside around Kinsale, they were now a symbol of its decay. As a centre of life and vitality Kinsale had been brought to its knees. All it had left was its own matchless unspoiled beauty, breathtaking then as now.

As well as for its beauty, Kinsale had always been noted for its unusual lay-out, its peculiar architectural features, its projecting bay windows and ornate wrought-iron balcony-railings, its slate-covered houses, its tiers of houses rising sharply from sea level, its maze of narrow streets and laneways. It was more Mediterranean than Irish in its appearance, an Irish Positano or Sorrento. No wonder it was looked on as unique among the seaport towns of the south of Ireland.

Kinsale had still another distinguishing feature, its majestic ruins. The noble piles of Charles Fort and James Fort dominated its inner harbours. The town was alive with history, a treasury for scholars and antiquarians. Picturesque ruins abounded giving an old-world charm to the place.

But all this had changed utterly by 1954. The rank smell of decay was in the air. Kinsale had become shabby and down at heel, like an ageing woman careless of her appearance. Derelict sites abounded in the silent streets; ruined and abandoned buildings reflected the apathy of the people. There was nothing particularly romantic about the new ruins; they were just gaunt skeletons, empty shells which disfigured the landscape, pathetic reminders of a glorious past. One could have acquired a house for a song and nobody minded very much what became of the derelict sites.

Kinsale, which once boasted a teeming population with several thousand engaged in the fishing industry and ancillary services was reduced to less than two thousand people. The emigrant ships were now her only contact with the sea. Kinsale had indeed become a quiet place, quiet with the tranquillity of death. Like Venice, she was no longer the Bride of the Sea but a decrepit widow. Even the Boatman of Kinsale was only a memory:

The wind that round the Fastnet sweeps
Is not a whit more pure –
The goat that down Cnoc Sheehy leaps
Has not a foot more sure.
No firmer hand nor freer eye
E'er faced an Autumn gale –
De Courcey's heart is not so high,
The Boatman of Kinsale.*

Bishop Lucey had made it abundantly clear to Duggan that he expected him to revitalise the town. It was easier said than done. Writing to Dr. Beddy of the I.D.A. soon after his arrival, Tom was brutally frank:

> I was appointed parish priest of Kinsale not to restore the spiritualities (these were in an eminently satisfactory condition) but the economic life of the town which was in a dreadful state. It was hoped that I could be the instrument to attract an industry.

To a friend who inquired about Kinsale he wrote: 'The tide comes in and the tide goes out – it is the only sign of life.'

At first he concentrated on getting the feel of the place, every detail of it. He wanted to find where its pulse beat however faintly. He made it his business to master the very complicated local topography from Scilly to World's End and the heights of Compass Hill, colourful names, redolent of its seafaring past. Soon he came to know all the local landmarks, so vividly evoked by Phil O'Neill in his ballad The Holy Stone:

The strangers ne'er fail when they visit Kinsale
to admire every beautiful scene,
Compass Hill and Kippagh, World's End and the Dock,
Joaney's Garden and famed Scilly Green.†

* Davis, Thomas, 'The Boatman of Kinsale'.
† O'Neill, Phil, 'The Holy Stone'.

Tom's predecessor, Canon James O'Brien, was a most saintly man, a classical scholar and a bibliophile but not cut out for parish work. He rarely set foot on the streets or involved himself in public life. The new parish priest could not have provided a greater contrast. He was scarcely ever at home, always in motion. In his second-hand Morris he was a constant menace to unwary pedestrians on the narrow streets or around sharp corners.

As an old soldier and amateur student of history it was natural that he had always been fascinated by the riddles surrounding the battle of Kinsale. How had the Irish leaders failed so completely to alert their Spanish allies in the town of their imminent attack? How did it come about that a mere skirmish with comparatively few casualties came to be regarded as a decisive battle in Irish history? He read how a contemporary, Lughaidh O'Clery had expressed his wonderment about this very subject: 'Though there fell but so small a number of the Irish at the battle of Kinsale that they would not even perceive their absence ... yet there was not lost in one battle ... so much as was lost here.'

Tom now found himself in the happy position of being able to study the battle terrain at his leisure. He haunted the little stretch of land from Whitecastle to Ballinvard cross-roads; he followed the course of the stream which was alleged to have run red with blood. Soon he was in a position to identify and mark the locations of the different stages of the battle. Later he published his findings:

> In the modern sense of the word, the Battle of Kinsale was not a battle. It was more like a company raid of the First War – a company raid in which everything went wrong. There was a half-hearted attack, a vigorous counterattack with artillery backing. Some limited use of cavalry to exploit the confusion which resulted when O'Neill's forces fell back to mingle confusedly with O'Donnell's men.*

To a certain extent he blamed the rivalry between O'Neill and O'Donnell for the disaster, refusing the easy option of blaming the Spaniards. In fact, he paid high tribute to the fighting qualities of the Spaniards: 'Aquila was a competent soldier. His men were the pick of the Spanish army, and the Spaniards then (as probably now) the toughest infantry in Europe.'

He found a modern counterpart in the O'Neill-O'Donnell incompatibility: 'A sixteenth-century Montegomery-Paton situation but with no one to knock their heads together.'

* Archdeacon Tom Duggan (under the name of Didymus) *Blarney* Magazine, Volume 12, Summer 1957.

Possibly the fact that he was reared only a few miles across country from the site of the Irish camp at Coolcarron may have given him almost a personal stake in the disaster. This may account for perhaps a slightly exaggerated summing up of what might have happened if the battle of Kinsale had gone the other way:

> Kinsale, as a defeat in arms, was insignificant; Kinsale, in its consequences, was one of the decisive battles of the world.
>
> If Kinsale had gone right:
>
> 1. The hitherto hesitating Irish clans would have come down decisively against their natural enemy.
> 2. Success would beget success: the English would be driven back to the Pale – and not be able to hold it.
> 3. James I would be the founder of the Stuart Catholic Dynasty of England.
> 4. The Counter-Reformation, instead of 50%, would have been 100% successful.
> 5. A Spanish hegemony would have been established over North-Europe.
> 6. North America would have been divided between the Spanish and the French.
> 7. New Amsterdam changed not to New York but to Nuova Barcelona.
> 8. Boston today with less evidence of English culture than present day San Francisco has of Spanish.
> 9. And dictating peace to a twentieth century world, not Dwight Eisenhower in English, but Don Duarte Ferrofabrico in Spanish.
>
> If Kinsale had gone right, these are the might-have-beens of the Brave New World.

Perhaps he might have added that if Kinsale had gone right there would not have been any Plantation of Ulster or any need for Partition!

After a few months in Kinsale he considered that he had seen and heard enough of the past and present to form a reasonably balanced view of what should be done for the future.

His first conclusion was that there was little point in inviting industrialists to the town in its present dilapidated condition. Somehow the town would have to be made presentable. A cosmetic exercise to cover over the ugliness and decay was useless: the axe would have to be applied to the roots. But where to start in the uniform picture of desolation? The answer came readily to his mind – he would start in his own back-garden

St. John's, the parish church, shared only too fully in the general air of faded gentility. A once lovely building which among its treasures contained a masterpiece of the sculptor, Hogan, in the course of time had become surrounded and cluttered up by ruined buildings, overgrown shrubs and brambles. The first task was to remove the ruins. He looked for voluntary labour but his first efforts were not a conspicuous success. The youths from the town who volunteered lacked experience in the use of pick and shovel: it was a case of: 'The hand of little employment hath the daintier sense.'*

He saw that what was needed was a few strong country lads. In due course a suitable team was assembled with the help of Donal Desmond of Tisaxon. Soon the wilderness disappeared and the area leading up to where the curates' houses now stand was transformed into landscaped terracing. Similar work was carried out on the other side of the church and, as a centre-piece, a beautiful drooping elm from Farranferris was set in place.

He next organised the construction of a ramp leading up to the main entrance of the church. The purpose was two-fold, to make the climb easier for the elderly and to ease the passage of funerals. As a final embellishment, some lovely stone, arrived from no one knew where to face the sides of the ramps. Soon the parish church began to look as it had looked originally, an imposing building in suitable surroundings.

The interior of the church was not forgotten and a general clean up began. Again he had recourse to voluntary labour and many young ladies of the town rallied round. Some of them still recall the boxes of 'Black Magic' they received in token of appreciation.

He grew to love the church. He thought that the galleries and the 'grand and poor returns' gave it character and atmosphere. The beautiful Hogan monument to the builder of the church, Fr. Justin Foley McNamara, a nephew of the then Bishop of Cork, Dr. John Murphy, aroused his admiration and, to some extent, his curiosity. Why does the monument include an angel holding an upturned mitre? He used to say that it was a great help when he was doing his meditation on the vanity of human wishes!

It is said that 'example is the best sermon' and Dr. Johnson speaks about 'the salutary influence of example'.† Others gradually began to follow Tom's lead and

* William Shakespeare, *Hamlet* V,i,69.

† Dr. Samuel Johnson, *Lives of the English poets*, Milton.

people began to take pride once more in their surroundings. One by one the first hesitant tentative efforts were being made to turn Kinsale into a tidy town. Local pride was the spur once the example had been given.

Before long Kinsale was ready to face, without flinching, the critical gaze of unsentimental industrialists. Phase two of Tom's campaign was about to begin, the wooing of industrialists to set up business in Kinsale. He did not stand alone: the local Development Authority were more than willing to help. Some public-spirited business people were prepared to put their money where their mouths were.

It may be that Tom at first underestimated the difficulties. He first thought in terms of a textile industry. Somewhat prematurely he acquired some looms and the services of a Swedish instructress to begin a hand-weaving class for the women of Kinsale. To his great disappointment he found that local textile chiefs considered they had stretched themselves enough and were unwilling to extend their operations to Kinsale. He then approached a prestigious up-country firm, Gentex of Athlone, and invited its managing-director to Kinsale. Mr. Linehan came and appeared to be very impressed but subsequently wrote: 'From our point of view, Kinsale is rather too far away. It would not be possible for me to have any part in your project, much as I would like to and much as I liked Kinsale on my recent visit there.'

This brought the cold winds of reality home to him. It was the type of letter which would be repeated again and again in the years ahead, soft words in plenty but the bottom line was always the same: 'We'd love to come but...'

But Duggan was a trier. Soon a constant stream of industrialists and politicians wended their way to the parochial house where they were dined and wined by his long-suffering housekeeper, Nora Aherne.

The first Inter-Party Government was in office and it might have been expected that this would prove a handicap for a person with such well-known Fianna Fáil associations. It did not turn out so. Among Tom's early visitors was General Richard Mulcahy, while the local TDs, Dan Desmond and Tadhg Manley, were most helpful.

Having failed to attract a textile industry, he next turned his attention to deep-sea fishing. He went as far as procuring a suitable boat. James Dillon was Minister for Agriculture and his junior Minister with special responsibility for Fisheries was Oliver Flanagan. Writing to Dillon, Tom made a heart-rending appeal for Kinsale:

> Mr. Flanagan and the officials of the Department made Kinsale the object of a particularly detailed study. By the time they left us, Kinsale had the first message of hope which came its way for a generation.
>
> We are all conscious and weighed down with the responsibility that Kinsale, old historic Kinsale, is having its final fling with fate. If any industry starts and that industry fails, Kinsale is finished for all time. In twenty years time it will not be even a cross-road reference on the map of Ireland.

Even this *cri de coeur* fell on deaf ears. In spite of his high-sounding principles Dillon was a politician at heart. He was a Westerner and it transpired that at this very time he had arranged a government grant of £350,000 for developing inshore fishing off the west coast. What chance had Kinsale of competing? Dillon wrote in his usual florid style:

> The proposal turns out to be essentially similar to a number of others which have come before my Department over the past few years. I cannot see my way to support such projects as I am satisfied that to have deep-sea trawling enterprises operating here in a complementary way with the inshore fleet would be to the serious detriment of the latter.
>
> Plans for the development of the inshore communities around our coasts have been made and I believe that our fishermen, when these plans come into execution, can be relied upon to supply in great measure the national needs in the matter of fish and fishery products.

The letter failed to include even the ritual expression of regret for being unable to help a dying town.

At this depressing juncture, Duggan was prepared to grasp even at straws. An inquiry arrived from a Captain Carson, based in Kent, which seemed to offer possibilities. Duggan replied: 'You are the first person from outer space who has shown an interest in us.' Unfortunately there was no further communication from outer space.

On 24 September 1955, the Canon wrote to William Norton, Minister for Industry and Commerce, with news that he had secured a guarantee of local financial aid to help towards the establishment of a rubber-processing plant in Kinsale. He subsequently wrote to Norton: 'Your message of encouragement, as brought by Deputy Desmond, has helped to tide us over days which were dark.' Again there was no follow up.

Success nearly came his way in 1956 when a Danish firm called Dansk Stoker, specialists in the manufacture of heating appliances became very interested. Negotiations with the I.D.A. were at an advanced stage only to falter at the last hurdle. Tom wrote sorrowfully to Dan Desmond:

> It comes to this: Dansk Stoker and the I.D.A. are full of designs benevolent to Kinsale. They are severally dead honest but owing to sad experience on their respective parts they live in climates of distrust.

But better days were drawing near and his travail was nearly over. A French firm, Messrs. Saupriquet of Nantes, well known internationally in fish-processing circles, was anxious to come to Kinsale. Foras Tionscail agreed to provide a grant and local businessmen, Sean Barrett of Kinsale and Tim O'Mahony of Cork, were prepared to invest money. Negotiations were slow and painful, entailing many journeys to Dublin, and when the day came for the formal opening ceremony of the factory on the sea-front on 11 September 1959, the Canon had moved to Ballyphehane. However he was invited back for the occasion to assist Bishop Lucey in the blessing ceremony. The Bishop spoke in glowing terms on the significance of the occasion for Kinsale:

> This is a great day for Kinsale which was once a big and busy place but in recent years had shrunk almost to the proportion of a village. But now the tide has begun to turn and we have here today what I hope is only the beginning of a great future, a future of industry and seafaring welded together.
>
> Not all enterprises are equally worthwhile; those that are worthwhile are those which work on our own materials and for the most partly employ men who will be the heads and supports of families; these are much more worthwhile than industries mostly occupied in packaging and assembling what comes from outside and which give employment in the main to girls and women.
>
> Today we have a well-balanced industry which, while largely giving employment to girls and women, draws its harvest from the sea, and the harvesters are the seafaring men, men of stout hearts who give hope of raising good families and building a seaport town

> that will be a credit to themselves, to their country and to their religion.
>
> I am happy to see established here a well-balanced industry that gives employment to both men and women and which tills the largest field, the boundless ocean which supplies the fruits for the harvesters and which for so long has been harnessed by others than ourselves. So it is good to see the field of the sea being tilled and the harvest being reaped and processed in our town.
>
> I am particularly pleased at the help they have got from the Government, and the help they have got from our local men of industry, Messrs. Tim O'Mahony and Sean Barrett, but I have not been surprised and I have not been taken unaware by the fact that Archdeacon Duggan also had a hand in this kettle of fish. I am grateful to him and to all who have made this day possible for Kinsale.

Success begets success, as Tom Duggan might say. A few days before the fish-canning factory opened, *The Cork Examiner* carried a feature-article entitled, 'Kinsale is Hive of Industry' with the following text:

> The factory of Kinsale Canners, which has been building up stocks of canned mackerel, herring, pilchard, etc for the home and export markets will be blessed and opened on Friday next.
>
> To date the factory employs 300 women and girls, in addition to the technical personnel and executive staff. The employees work under very congenial conditions in the spacious factory which is equipped with the most modern machinery and has its location along the picturesque harbour frontage at Kinsale.
>
> The West German firm of Friedrich Graepel and Son, Loeningen, who selected a site at the Barrack Green several months ago ... have got a considerable number of men employed preparing the ground for the laying down of foundations...
>
> It is expected that the old walls which surround the derelict military barracks site will soon be demolished to make way for the erection of a completely new building for the manufacture of ladies' frocks for export. This industry, sponsored by the Kenrose Manufacturing Co. Incorp., of New York will open up further employment for approximately 300 people. In this connection a new

> company, 'Kire Manufacturing Company' has been registered here to run the industry.
>
> Inquiries from Decorative Products Corporation, Chicago, have also come in and information has been supplied.
>
> There is no shortage of employment in Kinsale at the present time and apart from industrial developments a number of business and private residences are reconstructing or extending their premises.

In lighter vein, the local newsletter commented on the changed industrial picture in Kinsale:

> Now that the canning factory is almost ready, a German light steel factory ready to commence building near Barrack St. and an American company measuring Tom Good's field we can soon start exporting factories.

The accompanying cartoon bore the words:

> Man Spricht Deutsch
> Nous Parlons Français
> Má Tá Gaeluinn Agat, Labhair í

In spite of his continuous involvement in the campaign to promote industry for Kinsale, the Canon did not neglect his pastoral duties. Kinsale is a comparatively small parish and he soon got to know everybody. He particularly liked the old tradition of Station Masses in the houses of the people. As a raw newcomer to the pastoral scene at parish level, he was not so foolish as to think that he was not in need of help or guidance. This was readily forthcoming from his curates, Dr. Stephen Harte and Fr. Charlie O'Connor, and, later, Fr. Michael O'Riordan, men of wide pastoral experience, and congenial companions.

He was not an innovator in regard to the pastoral field – it was all too new to him. In such things as liturgical practice he was a traditionalist rather than a seeker after novelties.

Person to person contact was his chosen form of communication. He distrusted committees and felt that too often they were ineffective. Laity involvement, so much a lauded feature of post-Vatican II thinking, had not yet come to the fore. It is hard to imagine him coming to terms with the proliferation of committees and meetings which has become a feature of the contemporary pastoral scene, the holding of meetings becoming almost an end in itself when carried to its logical conclusion. Tom had not the sort of patience necessary to listen to long and repetitious speeches or to wait indefinitely for a consensus to emerge.

At heart he was an individualist who liked to deal with people as individuals and not as members of committees. Consequently he regarded regular visitation of the homes of the people as far more important than setting up committees and attracting the same sort of people no matter what the purpose was.

He lived very frugally, always ate at home in preference to restaurants or hotels. His house was very simply furnished, his bedroom in particular was easily recognisable as an old soldier's. As regards cars, he described himself as a person with Rolls Royce tastes but a Ford pocket which meant that in buying cars he had to compromise, usually ending up with large second-hand models.

The people of Kinsale soon learned that he was a kind and compassionate man with two categories of people specially important to him, old soldiers and the poor. As regards the ex-soldiers, he did not distinguish: the flag under which they had fought made no difference. This sometimes gave offence to the great 'patriots' but he took no notice. One of his frequent calls was to see an old Connaught Ranger named Johnny Dillon whom he had known well in Flanders and who lived close to his house. He couldn't do enough for Johnny and his family. There were many children and times were bad.

The older Sisters in the convent remember his kindness to the poor, and how the poorer children waited around outside to meet him, knowing that he would empty his pockets of small change for them. He could not resist a crying child. He often said there were enough tears in adult life without bringing sorrow into the lives of little children.

The sort of unstructured charity in which the Canon indulged might not meet with the approval of sociologists but it was his way of doing things and nothing was going to change him. As in the matter of committees, he felt that charity can become over-organised and lose its humanity and freshness. In a small town, he claimed, it was easy to know the genuine poor.

He was not a good preacher in the generally accepted sense of the word. His sermons were not really such but rather a series of little vignettes, usually spiced with local references and anecdotes. It was as if he were holding a personal conversation with his listeners in the church. They always listened if only to hear his funny remarks as when he referred to a group of boys who had disturbed his sleep on the previous night as 'our local nightingales who never sing during the day'.

He took a particular interest in the future of boys (and to a lesser extent, girls) of school-leaving age and did his best to secure employment for them. On Saturday morning he sometimes invited Leaving Certificate boys to his house for private coaching for the examination. This sort of informal teaching appealed to him more than standing before a class.

A habit of his that did not endear him to local officials was his tendency to go over their heads if they refused him their co-operation. An instance of this occurred at Summer Cove when a few boys harassed a wandering goat. Some local ladies were appalled and reported the matter to the Gardai, who took a serious view of the crime. Having seen and scolded the culprits the Canon took up the cudgel on their behalf and intervened with the Gardai but to no avail. He then took the matter directly to the Garda Commissioner in Dublin, his former pupil, Dan Costigan. It happened that about the same time a young girl of the poorer classes disappeared and in her case there was no fuss at all. To satisfy his feelings Duggan wrote a little verse to contrast the different reactions to the two events but it had better remain unquoted.

His desk was anything but tidy. A Scot named James S. Adam wrote a book entitled *My Private War with the Army.* He had been a war-time comrade of Duggan's in Northern Ireland. A very methodical man he was horrified by Duggan's lack of system:

> A senior padre, he ranked as a major, called me in one day. He was a marvellous man, a Father Duggan from Cork, the first padre to win the M.C. If I have time I'll tell you about it.
>
> 'You're the efficiency expert', he said, 'Tell me how to organise my files.
>
> His desk was a shambles of loose papers. I suggested that the first step was for him to prepare a list of numbered titles for his secretary and then to instruct her to put all incoming letters in the appropriate files .....
>
> When he realised that I wasn't going to do the job for him he lost interest and said: 'See that tray over there', pointing to a petrol can cut on the bias and filled to overflowing with letters. 'That's my pending tray. All the letters that come in go there. And I generally find that after about six weeks I can tear the damn things up'.
>
> It conjured up an awesome picture of frustration and fury reaching from the unit in Northern Ireland right up to the boss padre in the War house.

The picture may be slightly overdrawn but it certainly had a basis in fact.

On a personal level Tom's days in Kinsale were not without their share of hurts and disappointments. They came in various shapes and forms.

A letter he received out of the blue from Bishop Lucey towards the end of 1955 was the first shock: he could scarcely believe that the Bishop who had entrusted the Kinsale project into his hands and given him, as it were, exclusive competence in that area could have written such a letter:

> I want you as a matter of urgent business to let me know (a) what sites for factory building are available in Kinsale; (b) what numbers leave school and are available for employment each year.
>
> As regards (a) there is question only of sites of two or three acres in or adjacent to the town, more or less square in shape and obtainable here and now at a reasonable price. Once there is talk of purchasing for a new industry there is always thought of raising hitherto reasonable prices to astronomical levels. I want firm information.
>
> As regards potential labour supply I want just an approximate figure of the number seeking an opening each year plus the number presently available. I believe, however, that a new housing scheme would ensure an adequate supply of migrants from elsewhere even if locals ran short. Would the Council undertake to build forty new houses for instance, if an industry were to be located in the town?

The tone of the letter suggested that some dramatic development was in the pipe line. But when Tom provided the required information once again there was no follow up. It showed that there was no magic formula for solving Kinsale's problems. The net result was a temporary hiccup in the relationship between the two men.

Tom had less foundation for his second grievance. The death of Archdeacon Jeremiah Coholan left two vacancies, the parish of the Lough in the city which in terms of importance and desirability ranked second only to St. Patrick's, and the title of 'Venerable Archdeacon' which was largely an honorary title among the canons who made up the Chapter. In the eyes of the priests of the diocese Tom Duggan was a strong candidate for both. But it was not to be. Canon Denis Murphy, parish priest of Bantry, was given the vacant parish and Tom Duggan became Archdeacon which meant staying on in Kinsale.

The Bishop was not without strong reasons for appointing Murphy. First of all, he was the senior man by a number of years. Secondly, Tom had unfinished work to perform in Kinsale.

Nevertheless Tom was disappointed though he joked publicly about his new title, describing 'Venerable Archdeacon ... as an also ran prize whose main advantage was that its sheer length frightened off potential enemies'. Unfortunately in private and among his friends he was less guarded. The old habit of looking for the colourful phrase, the *bon mot* asserted itself: 'Dinny got the pint and I got the froth.' It certainly was a striking phrase and might be said to have hit the nail on the head. But whether is was appropriate in the circumstances is another matter. Inevitably Bishop Lucey got to hear of it and was not amused. It would turn up again in the future to haunt Tom.

As a distraction from these disappointments he began to interest himself more and more in Boston and its charismatic Archbishop with whom he had so much in common. To his great joy Cushing broached the subject of another visit by Tom to Boston. It was the tonic he needed: it would be good for soul and body.

When Tom wrote in June, 1957, to say he had offered up his Lough Derg pilgrimage for him, Cushing was very appreciative: 'Any chance of the good Lord sending you this way? If there is, we'll roll out the red carpet for our favourite Irish Canon.'

Writing again on 13 July 1957, he was more specific:

> When will you come and walk once more amongst us? If your good Bishop will let you come towards the end of the year I will give you the duplicate of that cheque to bring back to him. Any time in the early part of December would be the idea. You could fly both ways and send me the bill. Returning you would be another Santa Claus. I get a little fun out of giving gifts; somebody ought to get a little fun in carrying them around. You are my man!

Not surprisingly, in view of the fairly obvious carrot attached to the Archbishop's invitation, permission for the trip was duly granted and the Archbishop was delighted: 'I am delighted that there is a hope of seeing you before the snow flies. Write anytime before the fall and let me know your plans. You won't go back empty-handed.'

In the meantime Tom wrote discreetly to Monsignor Reily, Cushing's secretary:

> Will you quietly find out how long I should be expected to stay around. I could see myself becoming a nuisance after a few days. I haven't St. Paul's experience in sail-making but I could earn something.

The Archbishop wrote again towards the end of September:

> You will be welcome around the latter part of November. Let me know just when you will be here. One hundred thousand welcomes to you. As St. John the Baptist prepared the way for the Master, I will do the same for you.

Tom duly arrived about mid-November and stayed with the Archbishop for a few weeks before embarking on a whirlwind tour of the States, taking in Maryland, Pennsylvania, Washington D.C., South Bend and Chicago. His visit rekindled the old restlessness in him. After returning home he began to review his options for the future. The situation in Kinsale was now well in hand. An easier parish might be a temporary solution and give him time to think.

Luck was on his side when the time came. The parish of Ballyphehane became vacant; from what he knew of it, it would suit his plans admirably. On making his wishes known to Bishop Lucey, there was no difficulty about securing the appointment, though the Bishop was very surprised at his request.

Before leaving Kinsale he drew up a will and sent it to the Bishop:

> My dear Lord,
> In making you heir to my estate, you are not getting much. I hope there will be enough to pay off my debts.....
>
> If there is anything left for general charitable purposes, give a priority to the poor of Kinsale.
>
> Please have me buried in the crypt in St. John's, Kinsale: it is near the Foley-McNamara monument. Directions where to look and *non obstat* from Dept. of Health appended.
>
> If impracticable: the Friars have promised me sleeping room in their vault in the Abbey, NOT in the new St. Eltin's cemetery; too far away; the old women who, I hope, will pray for me, have cruising ranges of not more than two hundred yards.
>
> Pray for me.

The people of Kinsale remembered him affectionately for what he had tried to do for them. According to one cynical view of life:

> The evil that men do lives after them;
> The good is oft interred with their bones.*

* Shakespeare, William, *Julius Caesar*, III, ii, 80.

It was not so with Duggan in Kinsale. Many years after he had left, a magnificent new bridge was erected to span the river Bandon near its estuary at Kinsale. They called it 'Archdeacon Duggan Bridge'.

When all is said and done, all Duggan did was to start the ball rolling, to get the people of Kinsale to believe in themselves, to cast aside their lethargy and to look to the future. But in his wildest dreams he never could have imagined the sea change which came over Kinsale in just a few decades transforming a shabby and decaying town into a busy cosmopolitan centre, an architectural show case, a tourist Mecca, a gourmet capital, and all this without sacrificing any of its natural charm and attractiveness.

Kinsale proves not so much that miracles can still happen but that they can be made to happen.

THE SHADOW OF THE THIRD WORLD

THE QUIET YEARS IN BALLYPHEHANE

Ballyphehane in the south side of Cork city was a complete contrast to old and historic Kinsale. A new suburb, it was largely made up of a very extensive Corporation housing scheme. It had a teeming population and children abounded. As in many such areas, the shadow of unemployment hung heavily on Ballyphehane and as a result life was a daily struggle for many couples trying to make ends meet and to provide for their children.

The parish of Ballyphehane had been established as recently as 1956 and Archdeacon Tom Duggan was only its second pastor. Its church, the second of the 'Rosary of Churches' to be built, was dedicated to Our Lady of the Assumption. It was large and commodious, accommodating some 1400 people. Speaking at the blessing ceremony on Easter Monday, 1956, Bishop Lucey had summed up its importance for the people of Ballyphehane:

> Today God has come to dwell among the people of Ballyphehane. You have given him this house as his own. You have promised him that young and old alike will make it their place of worship and prayer.
>
> Bless, great Master of the House, all who have helped by their sacrifices to build it.

From the beginning the Church of the Assumption at Ballyphehane held a special place in Bishop Lucey's heart. On becoming coadjutor bishop in 1950, the Marian Year, he had chosen as the motto on his coat of arms *Assumpta est Maria*, and now he took particular pleasure in dedicating a church to honour Our Lady under that title. It was fitting also that Tom Duggan who had worked so hard to provide money for the 'Rosary of Churches' should now be pastor of one of the five.

The first team of priests to labour in the new parish had done their work well. In an amazingly short period of time it had become a parish with a soul, a warm vibrant parish unit. Its church, convent and school formed an imposing array of buildings; they stood out among the rows and rows of corporation houses all almost identical in outline. They were the heart of the new parish where, from the start, everybody was welcome. From them there radiated a dynamic parochial spirit which made Ballyphehane the envy of less organised parishes.

Though Tom had been more familiar with the north side of Cork city up to that time, he quickly felt at home among the people of Ballyphehane. He found them warm-hearted and friendly. The children fascinated him: they were far more numerous, more precocious and outgoing than the shyer children of Kinsale. They were not in the least overawed by the new parish priest. Whenever he went for a walk or to call on a parishioner they materialised out of nowhere and accompanied him on his walk, drawing on their intimate knowledge of the neighbourhood to impart such little gems of information as 'She's in all right, Archdeacon, but sometimes she does not answer the bell if she is in a bad mood'. Even when he tried to make his way around the Stations of the Cross in the church they followed him around, their little knees bobbing up and down in time with his genuflections.

The majority of the householders were young married couples, living in rented accommodation. Tom marvelled at the dedication shown by the mothers. Writing to Cardinal John d'Alton he could not restrain himself from praising the mothers in extravagant terms:

> As far as I can make out, the small boys of Ballyphehane have three deities: in order of importance, my mam, Holy God, the nun.
>
> Some fine day, please God, I'll put up a statue to the representative mam, the unchanted heroine of Ballyphehane. She will be:
>
> 1. Aged about thirty.
> 2. Many children looking up to her with complete dependence.
> 3. Herself healthy but lean as a greyhound.
> 4. No wonder lean: she never has four hours unbroken sleep at the time and I doubt if she ever sits down to a meal....
>
> I could write and keep on writing for ever on the glory which is the mothers of Ballyphehane. I could write but you would not go on reading.

Whether he was aware of it or not when he penned these lines, Tom Duggan was here chronicling a way of life which was already disappearing before the advance of a more materialistic way of life.

It was a poor community, materially speaking, in Ballyphehane in 1958. But in spite of economic deprivation it was a happy community. There was however, one lowering cloud which threatened its well-being: there was an ever-growing dependence on illegal money-lenders. It was like a blight which poisoned the whole social fabric of Ballyphehane. Family after family were being swept into this vortex. Harassed housewives paid over and over again the price of the household furnishings and equipment they had bought on hire purchase without a care in the world. The subsequent nightmare of trying to keep up repayments was an ever-present and gnawing worry. If this situation were allowed to continue it would present a frightening threat to the stability of family life.

The underlying cause of this dependence on money-lenders was that many of the mothers had received no training in home economics or forward planning: this was foreign territory to them. Saving for the rainy day was unknown. Usually they got by from day to day – just about – but from time to time a crisis manifested itself. Sometimes it was foreseeable, like a child's First Holy Communion outfit for which they should have made provision, but often it came without warning, or, for instance, when an essential kitchen appliance suddenly needed replacement. Sooner or later for many families panic set in: there did not seem to be any avenue of escape except through recourse to the money-lender.

Tom Duggan was horrified by the extent of the exploitation. If unchecked he knew it would destroy the whole fabric of family life in his parish. What could one man do? In desperation he approached Bishop Lucey. To his great relief he found that the Bishop was well aware of the problem. Better still he had a solution in mind. In the course of his visits to the States he had come across a financial institution called 'credit unions'. It was being put forward as a great boon – if not a necessity – for working-class families. Archbishop Cushing of Boston, the champion of the small man and enemy of exploitation in any shape or form, persuaded him of the inherent advantages of the scheme and urged him to introduce it into his own diocese. As a result Bishop Lucey was only waiting for a chance to introduce a pilot scheme in his diocese.

He now suggested to Tom Duggan that he should get the priests of the parish and a chosen band of lay helpers to help him to launch the scheme. Duggan went home, read all the literature the Bishop had given him and decided that he would be doing an injustice to his people if he did not try out the scheme.

He considered that at the age of sixty-eight he was too old to become involved personally in implementing the practical details of the scheme. He decided that he would become its public relations officer. In his Sunday sermons, in his talks, in his ordinary encounters with the people he would carry the flag of the credit union. He was fascinated by the vision underlying the scheme, namely, that the people's money, whatever little of it they could spare on a regular basis, would be invested to benefit not only themselves but the whole community. He saw that the key to success lay in numbers, hundreds of people investing small amounts – many a mickle makes a muckle as the old saying went, many small amounts accumulating to make a large sum. It seemed too good to be true but with all his mathematical expertise, try as he would, he could find no flaw in the scheme.

For the practical management of the scheme he called on the services of one of his curates, Fr. Edward Fitzgerald, a man of immense patience and tenacity with the sort of methodical mind necessary for the task.

Initial progress was painfully slow. It was very easy to count the first lodgement. But Tom Duggan kept urging on Ned Fitzgerald: 'For God's sake, Ned, keep the doors open. The parish will back you.' In view of the critical state of the parish finances, it was cold comfort. Duggan also had recourse to scripture, reminding the worried founding members about the mustard-seed of the Gospel, so tiny at first but which 'grew and became a great tree and the birds of the air lodged in its branches'.

Soon the scheme proved itself and went from success to success. Speaking at the first A.G.M. Bishop Lucey could not contain his delight at the progress which had been made:

> The Ballyphehane Credit Union is the first in these parts. In forming it, the parish has lighted a torch which I hope and pray will be carried from parish to parish in these dioceses. For credit schemes are almost a necessity in this age of so-called 'easy payments' and hire purchase.
>
> Credit schemes have proved a boon wherever they have been introduced. But it was hard to establish them here where the whole idea of them was so new. All credit, then, to Archdeacon Duggan, the parish priest, and the founder members who started the pilot scheme.

Many parishes subsequently had reason to be grateful to Ballyphehane Credit Union for the headline it had set. Credit Unions became a feature for many parishes especially in the city. It saved very many families from financial ruin. It gave people the habit of saving, of having the little 'nest egg' in the credit union which could be called on in time of need. Having established their financial credibility to the credit union, people could borrow within reason and depending on the amount they had invested. The borrowing rate was low. But the greatest achievement of the credit union was to inculcate the habit of regular saving among people who never before thought of saving. This was its key to success: this was how it prevented human misery from becoming the norm in Ballyphehane.

Like all new parishes Ballyphehane had its financial problems. The parishioners were still trying to pay off the debt on their new church. A parishioner recalls: 'The Archdeacon never scolded us. He had a grand soft way of asking for money. When the weekly collection dropped he joked about it in his Sunday sermons. "Too many tired soldiers here, I'm afraid." He was a big man and you couldn't refuse him.'

With the moneylending problem solved, the Archdeacon could now relax somewhat. The parish was running like a well-oiled machine. He concluded that he could afford to give the curates a free hand, interfering as little as possible. The result was that he found himself in the unusual position of having time on his hands. He was delighted, therefore, to hear from the Bishop that he had invited Archbishop Cushing to bless and preach at the opening of the third of the 'Rosary of Churches' scheduled to take place in August, 1958. The church was in Farranree, hitherto known as Spangle Hill. Bishop Lucey deputed Tom to make all the necessary arrangements.

It was the kind of assignment Tom loved. When he began his rounds he found a great deal of good-will on all sides. The Corporation proposed to confer the Freedom of the City on the Archbishop (the first member of the American hierarchy to be so honoured) and to name a street in his honour in Farranree. Not to be outdone, the University authorities would confer on him an honorary doctorate and host a garden party at the College. Tom also arranged that the Lord Mayor would formally welcome the Archbishop at Patrick's Bridge and drive with him to the City Hall.

The Archbishop was delighted though in a letter to Tom he put on a show of reluctance:

> I will be there to receive the Doctorate. I am not enthusiastic, however, because I have always believed that if you want to live to be an old soldier one must keep away from the big guns.
>
> We will be in Cork, please God, on August 26th and 27th. I don't have much time but that is long enough for a nervous character like me.

For a nervous character he set himself a daunting schedule. The first step would be to Rome for his formal *ad limina* visit to the Pope to present his regular five-yearly report. After Rome there would be a two-week pilgrimage to the Holy

Land, followed by a pilgrimage to Lourdes before arriving to spend a few days in Ireland before embarking by liner from Cobh.

Tom Duggan was invited to join the party for the whole trip but declined on medical grounds. Old friends had noticed a decline: the first tell-tale signs of age had appeared. His shoulders were more stooped and the bounce was gone from his step. They wondered if the reasons were psychological rather than physical:

> The foot less prompt to meet the morning dew,
> The heart less bounding at emotion new,
> And hope, once crush'd, less quick to spring again.*

Monsignor Reily, Archbishop Cushing's secretary, wrote to say that the Archbishop was very disappointed: 'Your decision re. the pilgrimage to the Holy Land very much disappointed us. However, I realise that it is wise and prudent to follow the doctor's advice.'

Before arriving in Cork the Archbishop wanted to be sure that he had met all his financial commitments to Bishop Lucey. He asked Tom to find out quietly:

> Check up sometime, and find out if I owe Bishop Lucey any money. I don't know whether we have received all the bills we were supposed to pay. I would like to have all this business clarified before we leave for the 'promised land'.

Apparently the Archbishop was worried in case he would find himself blessing a church for which he owed money. He had asked to be involved in the provision of furnishings for the new church. In response to his wishes Bishop Lucey had gone personally to Ortisei in the South Tyrol, a world famous wood-carving centre, to commission a hand-carved high altar and side altars with several life-sized figures including the Sacred Heart and Our Lady, all to be carved in polished oak. The finished product which greeted the Archbishop on his arrival in the church is possibly the single most distinctive artistic ensemble in the whole 'Rosary of Churches'.

Before setting out on his journey the Archbishop wrote to Tom on 3 July 1958, to tell him about a great new venture he had in mind, a venture which was to have profound repercussions on the remaining years of Duggan's life:

> Did I tell you about my new project? I am inaugurating a new Pious society of St. James the Apostle for recruiting of priests and the training of future priests for South America. To the present, fifteen

* Arnold, Matthew, *Thyrsis*.

> have volunteered. They will leave for their mission in the later part of February. We have been assigned a territory, Yauyos, with about one hundred thousand priestless, baptised Catholics. It is about seventy five miles outside the Archdiocese of Lima, Peru. I will visit it in the late fall before our priests start on their apostolate.
>
> Please keep the project in your prayers...

He wrote again on 25 July: 'I will be seeing you unless they put me in a Vatican prison. The Pious Society of St. James is keeping me busy, hence the brevity of this note.'

He wrote again a few days later: 'We will be leaving by liner on Saturday for our memorable tour. I hope I will make out better than did Jonah of the Old Testament. When we get to Rome I hope they won't detain me too long.'

There was a postscript: 'Please don't kill me with gifts and receptions. *I don't want anything.*'

The Archbishop's visit was something of a triumph. He arrived in Dublin on Monday, 25 August 1958. He was welcomed by Frank Aiken, Minister for Foreign Affairs, and, according to *The Cork Examiner* 'was especially welcomed by the Venerable Archdeacon Thomas F. Duggan, P.P., Ballyphehane, representing the Bishop of Cork, Most Rev. Dr. Lucey'. The following evening he arrived in Cork by car in the midst of a torrential downpour. Nevertheless he received what *The Cork Examiner* called a tumultuous welcome:

> Oblivious to the torrential rain which swept the streets of the city, he stood for long in the centre of St. Patrick's Bridge in Cork last night, and responded to the cheers as the crowd heaved and swayed all around him.

Introducing him to the crowd which thronged the City Hall, Bishop Lucey said:

> All Cork is honouring the Archbishop. To-night, the civic authorities: to-morrow evening, the University authorities, and all the time, all the people of Cork, young and old, who have been so long looking forward to seeing and hearing and cheering so good a friend.

Later in the Bishop's House, the Archbishop presented Bishop Lucey with a cheque for 25,000 dollars for the new church. On the following day, having solemnly blessed the new church, he spoke with some emotion:

> Above all this new church so appropriately commemorating the mystery of the Risen Christ by which the Saviour reveals his power to make all things new – is a symbol of the old in the midst of the new, the modern growing out of the ancient.
>
> This is the lesson we shall carry away from this holy, historic occasion, we who have come back from one of the newest of the nations to visit in one of the oldest of the nations, here to find the old Faith preached in new temples, the old saints remembered at new shrines, the old truths taught with the aid of new techniques. *Non nova sed nove*, not new things but in a new way.

On his return to Boston the Archbishop wrote to Tom Duggan: 'Kiss the soil of Ireland for me. We will certainly never forget the recent visit to Cork when even the skies wept for joy.'

A few months later, on 9 October 1958 the long twilight of the pontificate of Pope Pius XII came to a close. For some time the government of the Church had been effectively in the hands of a small group of Curia cardinals whom the Italian press referred to as 'The Pentagon'. There was much unfinished work facing the new Pope, John XXIII. One of his immediate priorities was to call a Consistory to nominate new cardinals. There had not been such an event for years with the result that many of the great Catholic cities of the world were without a cardinal. Among the newly created cardinals was Richard Cushing of Boston.

Initially he was not over-enthusiastic about the new Pope. He wrote to Duggan: 'The new Pope looks rather promising. I never met him, in fact I never even heard of him.'

Writing to Tom he insisted that he should travel to Rome for the great occasion:

> Thanks for your note of congratulations. For one of my character it is going to be a cross but I am willing to carry it for the sake of the priests and the little people. I cannot imagine anyone going to Rome for the purpose who would be less inarticulate than I.
>
> Nothing pleases me more than to know you are going to Rome.

On meeting the new Pope the new cardinal from Boston was most impressed. It was not the usual formal meeting he expected but a spontaneous meeting of minds. He discovered that like himself Pope John XXIII came from a humble background, and was proud of it. Cushing found to his delight that the new Pope shared fully his own passionate concern for Latin America.

It was the beginning of what was to be a most happy relationship between the two men.

Tom had never before seen a glittering Papal ceremony at close quarters. Seated among the Boston party he could not but be deeply moved. The inclusion of a black African cardinal and of the very first Indian to join the Sacred College made the occasion a dramatic manifestation of the universality of the Church.

Back in Boston the new cardinal complained to Tom that his new honour brought new troubles in its wake: 'This "Red Hat" rests heavily upon my head. Since I got it, everybody thinks that with it I received the United States treasury, hence from all over the world people are writing for very substantial help.'

He was immensely heartened by a letter he received from Cardinal Mimmi who wrote on behalf of the Holy Father:

> It was with particular gratification that the Holy Father learned of the zealous initiative of your Eminence in establishing recently in the Archdiocese of Boston a Pious Society under the name and protection of the great Apostle who evangelized Spain....
>
> His Holiness could not but be specially pleased that Latin America should be your choice for this wider action, for his loving care, his hopes and his anxieties as the head of Christiandom for Latin America are well known.
>
> The Holy Father sends his most particular blessing, imparting it to those priests about to leave for South America, to the entire Pious Society, its directors and moderators, and especially to Your Eminence, its founder and continual inspiration.

Writing to Tom Duggan at this time the Cardinal invoked his aid in recruiting priests and seminarians. When Tom organized a novena of prayer and a spiritual bouquet for the departing missionaries from the children of Ballyphehane, he was delighted:

> Thank all the boys of the parish for their magnificent spiritual bouquet for the Apostolate in South America.....Please God, many of the small boys who made it possible will one day become priests and missionaries.

During that summer of 1959 Tom entertained many friends of the Cardinal during their visits to Ireland, including three Jewish ladies about whom the Cardinal had written: 'Since they represent the highest in Jewish culture I wanted them to meet an Irish priest who personifies Irish scholarship, wit and optimism I selected you to fill the bill.'

Later the Cardinal's own immediate relatives arrived, his sisters, a brother and a nephew. From Ireland they wrote back to the Cardinal describing Tom's great hospitality and many kindnesses. The Cardinal was overwhelmed and wrote warmly to Tom:

> I had a letter from my folk. They said you were wonderful to them. You did everything for them.
>
> Buy a pipeful of tobacco with the enclosure. It is a little material token of my personal gratitude and appreciation.
>
> Come over and walk among us once more in the late fall or the spring of '60. Let me know and I will send along the money.

During the summer the Cardinal suffered a long and agonizing bout of shingles. Writing to Tom he revealed his plans for 1960:

> We will arrange for your trip to the States after Christmas. If I lead the pilgrimage to the Eucharistic Congress in Munich and Oberammergau I will take you with us. That is about a year from now.

Recurring bouts of illness forced him to change his plans: his health was beginning to cause serious concern. He wrote to Tom in September:

> I send you my heart's full measure of love and gratitude for all your kindness to the visitors whom I inflicted on you during the summer.
>
> Your note arrived on the day that Bishop Lucey and Father Barrett left for Ireland. I gave the former 25,000 dollars and told him to contact you with regard to your coming visit.
>
> Since 'Galway' is coming here in the spring I think you should postpone your visit until later in the year. We will be in touch with one another and I will take good care of you.
>
> I think I will bow out of the Pilgrimage to the Eucharistic Congress and Oberammergau. Travelling doesn't agree with me. I am better when I stay close to home base.
>
> I hope Bishop Browne leaves something for us.*

* Bishop Michael J. Browne, Bishop of Galway, who was collecting in the States for his new cathedral.

For one who up to then had led a very active life, the years '59 and '60 were uncharacteristically quiet for Tom. It seemed to his friends that he had grown more introspective and less desirous of becoming involved in outside activities. His interests seemed to be more supernatural: he was definitely spending more time at prayer.

Perhaps his Retreat-like silence of those years was connected with Latin America. Cardinal Cushing's letters were a constant reminder of the crisis in vocations there. His final decision to become a missionary in Peru was no sudden impulse – it was not the result of a blinding revelation from God such as Paul experienced on the road to Damascus. It came from long and laborious meditation and from much prayer. Putting together various little hints and indications one might conclude that its roots went back to those quiet years in Ballyphehane.

In sharp contrast the year 1961 was a year of great activity and many disappointments, leading finally to peace and fulfilment.

It began with a letter from the Cardinal in January to say that he would be coming to Ireland in March:

> I am happy to tell you that I have accepted the invitation of Cardinal d'Alton to preach at the opening of the Patrician Year in the Cathedral at Armagh in honour of the fifteen hundredth anniversary of the death of St. Patrick. My programme is to stay about a day in Armagh, then to go to Bishop Lucey's house for a few days, visit St. Colman's Seminary in Fermoy, and Glanworth, and then return home.

Soon there was further news of Latin America:

> I am overwhelmed with commitments and the Holy See wants me to go to Bolivia in the summer time.
>
> I will go wherever they send me because after my experience in Peru I am convinced that the Lord chooses the foolish to confound the wise.
>
> I hope to see you in March. Keep the faith.

As a result of the Cardinal's next letter Latin America began to take on a personal dimension for Tom:

> We will be seeing you for a couple of days during our stay in Cork after our mission is accomplished on March 17.

> With regard to Bolivia. I have yet to receive the official assignment. All I have is the word of the Nuncio of that country that I will be invited at a later date.
>
> If the assignment takes place at the same time as the one in Peru it would be in August. In any event, as soon as I receive the commission I shall contact you and bring you along as a member of the Pontifical Commission.

Meanwhile there was big clerical news at diocesan level. Dean Joseph Scannell passed away on 25 February 1961. He had held three important positions, vicar General of the diocese, Dean of the Chapter, and parish priest of St. Patrick's – a parish which though it might have lost some of its attractiveness, still ranked as number one in the diocese. These vacancies created awkward problems for Bishop Lucey: was he to dismember Dean Scannell's 'empire' or give it again to one man?

Cardinal Cushing duly arrived for St. Patrick's Day, and during his few days in Cork he visited Ballyphehane, the first cardinal to set foot in this new parish. The Ballyphehane Parish Annals tell the story:

> To honour the Patrician Year, Cardinal Cushing of Boston came to Ireland and in the course of his journeying, paid a visit to Cork. He called on his close friend, Archdeacon Duggan, at whose suggestion he appeared in all his glory during the Lenten Retreat to address the men.
>
> Later the Cardinal was entertained in the Parochial House where he kept his audience of prelates and local clergy regaled until the small hours with his wide repertoire of stories and events.

Soon after Bishop Lucey contacted Tom and offered him the vacant parish of St. Patrick's and the title of Dean which would make him the premier dignitary in the Chapter. There was no mention of the most important appointment, that of Vicar General of the diocese. Duggan, reading between the lines, surmised that history was about to repeat itself: Denis Murphy would be the new Vicar General.

Tom replied in writing to the Bishop's offer:

> Since I saw you last evening I have gone up (and down) various alleys of thought but what I tried to say is abiding.
>
> My spontaneous preferences are Archdeacon of Cork and P.P., Ballyphehane, rather than Dean of Cork and P.P., St. Patrick's.

> As to St. Patrick's a parish is important and in that matter I regard the Bishop's wishes as mandatory. I abandon Ballyphehane.
>
> On the other hand, as between Dean and Archdeacon, in the petty matters of rivalling dignities I should like, subject to Your Lordship's approval, to exercise my personal preference.
>
> However, *prius, pendente et post,** I am at your disposal.

Only Bishop Lucey would have been able to interpret fully all that was said and left unsaid in that cryptic communication.

At Dean Scannell's Month's Mind on 12 April 1961, Tom Duggan was installed as parish priest of St. Patrick's, retaining at his own wish the title of Archdeacon. Denis Murphy was appointed Vicar General. In spite of Tom's protestations that he was entirely at the Bishop's disposal he firmly refused the title of Dean, and eventually Canon Timothy Cullinane was appointed in his stead.

A few months later when Archdeacon Duggan gave up his parish of St. Patrick's so as to work in Latin America there were people who said he acted out of pique: there were murmurings of 'sour grapes'. In some circles Duggan was pictured as a sort of modern Scholar Gypsy:

> A man of pregnant parts and quick inventive brain
> Who, tired of knocking at Preferment's door,
> One summer morning forsook his friends...
> And roam'd the world.
> And came, as most men deem'd, to little good
> But came to Oxford and his friends no more.†

It is a view which does not do justice to Tom Duggan. He was too deeply spiritual a man to be so deeply upset about lack of promotion as to leave his diocese, using the Missions as an excuse to get away. Frustration and disappointment did not cause his departure to the Missions though they may have played some little part in its timing. Before ever the question of appointing a vicar general arose the missions were at the back of his mind. It was his visit to Latin America a few months later with Cardinal Cushing which brought matters to a head and finally triggered off his decision to become a missionary. The actual experience of the parlous state of the Church in Latin America devastated him and forced his hand.

* 'before, during and after'

† Arnold, Matthew, *The Scholar Gypsy*.

His missionary vocation had deeper roots than his critics were prepared to admit. He had thought about it in Maynooth forty years before. His military chaplaincy was a form of missionary activity. He had held back, waiting until he was sure, 'waiting for the one clear call,'* waiting 'for the spark from Heaven to fall'.† The Lord had kept him in suspense until his race was nearly run.

There was a side to his character which inclined him towards the dramatic. Like all good soldiers, he aspired to the *beau geste*, the gallant deed. He liked to *fare la bella figura* as the Italians say, to cut a dash. Up to a point he looked on life as a great adventure. He had done many tremendously brave deeds in his life, his courage was legendary. Was it not entirely in keeping with his quixotic nature to make his last hurrah the most striking deed of all, a kind of one man Charge of the Light Brigade? Tom's decision to opt for missionary life at the age of seventy-one did not make any kind of sense by any worldly standards but he, and we, would hope and believe that it was magnificent in God's eyes.

As he bade farewell to Ballyphehane and crossed over to St. Patrick's the Ballyphehane Parish Annals paid him this simple tribute:

> Scarcely before he had time to get to know us all, we learn that our very kind Archdeacon has been taken from us. Though only a short time here, he effected a tremendous amount of good in the district and has endeared himself to everybody, old and young alike, whose affection and gratitude he now takes with him to his new parish of St. Patrick's.

As epitaphs for parish priests go, it was high praise indeed.

The Big Decision

Not surprisingly in the circumstances, Tom never settled down in St. Patrick's for the few months he was there. His mind was on other things. He knew that there would be no shortage of priests willing and anxious to serve in St. Patrick's if he were to vacate it but that there were very few who were fully *au fait* with the plight of the Church in Latin America and prepared to offer their services for that distant apostolate.

As in his final years in Ballyphehane he seemed to have withdrawn into himself. Canon John Forde, an old friend who was working at the time in Mayfield in St. Patrick's parish, saw a change in him: he had become more serious, more contemplative:

* Tennyson, Alfred Lord, *Crossing the Bar.*

† Arnold, Matthew *The Scholar Gypsy.*

> There was a deeply religious man inside him which he secretly cherished and fostered and which the world did not know about. Actually he was a man of deep faith in God who liked to spend time thinking after the evening meal, praying maybe or thinking. Maybe this was why he gave up a desirable parish to go to Peru.
>
> In St. Patrick's, in a sort of way, I recall he shut down in the evening, kept to himself, to his own thoughts and prayers. He discouraged visitors, he wouldn't answer the phone – this was very uncharacteristic. He did much thinking. I have no idea how long this went on. All I remember is that he pushed things aside so that he would have time to think.
>
> This was reasonable enough when you think of what he was going to do. It was done with thought. It was not done on the spur of the moment.
>
> I think he did a great deal for God... He seemed to have a thing about forgiving and forgetting. If somebody injured him he seemed to strive to forget about it. Those who injured him had a special claim on his kindness.
>
> He was a great Christian, a very lovable man, one of the best.

Cardinal Cushing was surprised at Tom's decision to leave Ballyphehane:

> I was surprised to learn that you have a new parish. I thought Ballyphehane was the best in all Ireland.....
>
> When you come to Bolivia bring with you all the robes of your office. You wear them with dignity and you will 'steal the show'. I am sending the names of all the members of the Pontifical Commission to Rome for approval....
>
> I hope you have settled down in your new parish. I can't understand any parish greater than the one you had but I suppose things are not always what they seem.

There was exciting news about the missions when he wrote on 19 May:

> I am happy to tell you that Bishop Lucey is giving me two priests for the Missionary Society of St. James the Apostle.... I expect them in July. If by any chance we go to Bolivia stopping first at Peru and then getting a plane for Bolivia I would probably bring these two men with us and place them in the hands of the Peruvian group.

A few weeks later he wrote to say that the number of Cork priests had gone up to three:

> I am happy to tell you that Bishop Lucey wrote me and offered me three of his priests for Latin America. They are coming here in July. If we leave here early in August I will keep them around here and can get reservations for them on the jet plane on which we shall travel.

The three Cork priests in question were Fr. Michael Murphy, now Bishop of Cork and Ross, Fr. Michael Crowley, now P.P., Curraheen Road and Fr. Paddy Leader, since deceased.

Approval of the Commission came from the Holy See at the end of May. The Cardinal wrote:

> The members of the Commission to Latin America have been approved by the Holy See. You are one of them. The dates of the Congress are August 10-13, but we will be in Bolivia, Peru and probably Venezuela over a period of ten days.

Tom replied in high spirits:

> Ready and raring to go whenever you want me. My Hispaniolization is taking longest. I have a most elaborate record-playing machine. Pure Castilian ought to emerge but it sounds more like a dog-fight.

On 27 June he was told:

> Come any time after the fifteenth of July. That will give you two or three weeks before we go. Stay at my house and take over the entire Commonwealth of Massachusetts. Let me know when to expect you. Come soon.

By 19 July all was ready for Tom's arrival:

> I note the time you are leaving Shannon and will arrive in Boston on Wednesday, 26 July .... The three Cork priests have been in New York in recent days but they will be returning this week and staying at my house until we depart.

For the two weeks Tom was in Boston the Cardinal arranged a busy schedule for him and the other Cork priests. He took them with him on his official engagements and introduced them to such notabilities as the Kennedy brothers.

The jet flight to Lima took off on 8 August. The following morning before boarding the plane Tom bade farewell to the three Cork priests. Fr. Michael Murphy and Fr. Paddy Leader were due to leave in a few days for the language school in Cochabamba, Bolivia whilst Fr. Crowley was to begin missionary work straightaway as he was already a fluent Spanish speaker. Tom never saw them again.

At the Eucharistic Congress in Bolivia, Tom encountered Latin American conditions in the raw for the first time. The Congress took place in Santa Cruz, a comparatively small city. The liturgical ceremonies took place at a safe distance from the poorer quarters but Tom made it his business to see the other side of the coin, and he was horrified at what he saw: the people there seemed to be living in a different city in a different age. It was hard to make an informed judgement after only a few days but he saw enough to convince him that the neglected poor in Bolivia were in dire need of spiritual and material succour.

It was the same story when he returned to Lima. He asked Fr. Michael Fitzgerald, a Columban priest originally from Turner's Cross in Cork, to show him around Lima: he wanted to see the Lima the tourists never saw, 'warts and all'. It was not a pretty sight: the misery and degradation, the hordes of half-naked hungry children, the prevailing attitude of hopelessness, the fatalistic and mute acceptance by the poor of their miserable lot. He remembered reading a book by Carlo Levi about an impoverished town in Italy entitled *Christ stopped at Eboli*. Surely, he thought to himself, this is Eboli on a massive scale: the unfortunate people seemed abandoned by God and their fellow human beings.

Fr. Fitzgerald described graphically the uphill battle the Columbans were waging: they had accomplished a great deal but it was only a drop in the ocean. Before leaving Lima, Tom asked him, 'Fitzy, do you think I'd be of any use here at my age?'

Back in Boston Duggan informed the Cardinal of his firm wish to join the Society of St. James the Apostle. Cushing was dumbfounded; he tried to dissuade him but to no avail. Duggan pointed out that even as a gesture his going to Peru would do a great deal for the missions and would encourage younger men to follow his example. Cushing argued that even if he agreed a formidable obstacle still remained in the person of Bishop Cornelius Lucey. The Bishop might interpret Tom's request as a reflection on his diocese, as a defection brought about by disillusionment and frustration. Considering Duggan's advanced age and frail health he might feel in conscience bound to refuse him. Eventually they decided that the Cardinal would write to Bishop Lucey, making the case for Tom's secondment to the Missions.

The Cardinal (as Bishop Lucey revealed to Fr. Kevin O'Callaghan years later in Peru) telephoned Bishop Lucey immediately after Duggan's departure and begged him to refuse Tom's request. Bishop and Cardinal then played a waiting game, hoping that Duggan would change his mind. Instead he wrote to Cushing a few days after coming home more determined than ever:

> Waited till to-day to attack the Lord of Cork. I miscalculated the time. I had counted on your letter having arrived and that I would find the earth-works pulverized.
>
> Your letter had not reached him. There was I – an old soldier at that – attacking without a bit of artillery preparation.
>
> To put it mildly, he resisted grace but not altogether. My resulting impression is:
>
> (a) he hates the idea.
>
> (b) he would not summon up defiance enough to refuse you.

Tom's dogged determination eventually won the day. The Cardinal and the Bishop accepted defeat: the former wrote:

> The Holy Ghost was with you or with my letter. In any event, it is a good thing I wrote to the Bishop for unless I did I doubt if you would receive permission to go to Latin America. I thought I made it clear to you before you left Boston that he would have the letter in two or three days after you arrived in Cork. However, all is well that ends well.
>
> Now let me know as soon as possible when you will have all your affairs straightened out and you can come here for a few days and probably leave for Lima in the early part of the New Year. At that time it will be summer there.
>
> Meanwhile, I will write to Father Masciarelli [the local Superior of the Society] and tell him you don't need to go to any language school, unless they need you there for special work. Whatever Spanish you need you can pick up in the meantime or learn enough of it from contact with the people. If you spend a month here and gave one hour a day to Spanish at Boston College, you could learn more of the language in that time than you would in six months at the language school.
>
> You and the Bishop of Cork are going to make history.

To Tom, ever in a hurry, the New Year seemed an eternity away. He wrote to the Cardinal appealing to him to bring forward the date of his departure and the Cardinal did so:

> I suggest, therefore, that you come along around the third week of October, spend a week or ten days here preparing for your trip, or longer if you wish, and then you will be on your way.
>
> By the time you come to Boston I will have a letter from Father Masciarelli, the Latin American Superior of our men, who will take good care of you. By the time you arrive in Lima the new Language School and Retreat House for Men will be finished.
>
> You can skip the language school, if you wish, because you can be understood in any language.
>
> God love you and be with you always. I feel like going back with you myself. If the third week of October is a little late, come any time. I'll pay all the expenses from Ireland to Peru and support you while you are there.

He also wrote to the American Embassy in Dublin:

> This is to advise you that Archdeacon T.F. Duggan of St. Patrick's, Cork, Ireland, has volunteered to serve with our Missionary Society of St. James the Apostle in Lima, Peru, for three years. During that time he will be under my immediate jurisdiction and I guarantee that all his needs will be adequately, and, indeed more than adequately, supplied by me. He will not be dependent on anyone save myself.
>
> Anything you can do to expedite his visa to come to the States will be appreciated.

Tom wasted no time in settling up his affairs: it was not a difficult job. An auction of his belongings was out of the question for such a man. He simply divided his belongings among his friends, and took with him only a few favourite books and his clothes.

Following the official announcement of his departure he was overwhelmed with invitations from old friends and associates. One such occasion which he greatly appreciated was a farewell function put on by the Old I.R.A. in the course of which he was presented with a solid silver missionary cross by General Tom Barry on behalf of all present.

On 23 October Bishop Lucey gave a farewell dinner in his house to which he invited diocesan dignitaries and Tom's closest clerical friends. There were no representatives of the laity. The invitation card sent by the Bishop was typical, his wry humour shining through:

> I am giving a farewell dinner for the Archdeacon on Monday next at 1.30 p.m. and hereby inviting you.
> With all good wishes, I remain
> *(even if the Archdeacon doesn't)*
> Cornelius Lucey.

Before the dinner the Archdeacon handed to the Bishop his written resignation from the parish of St. Patrick's as required by canon law:

> I, the undesigned, acting in full liberty and after mature deliberation, resign the office of Parish Priest of the Parish of St. Patrick's, Cork, and I beg the Lord Bishop to accept my resignation.
>
> Reason I am resigning St. Patrick's parish is because I am being temporarily attached to the Missionary Society of St. James the Apostle.

At the foot of the document Bishop Lucey wrote: 'I hereby, with regret, accept this resignation. 23:10:'61.' The legal formalities were now complete.

An old friend, Fr. Tim Connolly, Superior General of the Columban Fathers in the course of a tribute to the Archdeacon after his death under the title of *Adios, a Shagairt, Hasta Luego*: goodbye, priest, till we meet again: said:

> Tom came to me a week before he left Ireland for Peru. As was not uncommon in discussion with Father Tom we found ourselves in active disagreement on several points. He asked me what I thought of his decision at the age of seventy-one to go to Peru.
>
> My answer had to be carefully considered, but also knowing my man, it had to be frank. I told him three things:
>
> 1. I told him that he could never hope to run a parish in Latin America. The work was incredibly hard and he was too old.
> 2. In spite of this I told him that he would be of immense importance for the morale of the young priests.
> 3. I disagreed with his conception of where the work in South America was to begin.
>
> He was all for the rural districts, I was all for the slum areas in the cities. His idea was that in rural areas families stay together, propagate themselves and form a truly Christian nucleus. I agreed but pointed out that time was of the essence. Rural people are

> moving in – thousands of them – to the big cities in the hope of employment they cannot get at home. They move into incredibly bad slums and horrible living conditions.
>
> In rural areas the Catholic Faith, such as it is in rural areas at present, will persist in this way for forty years, not so in the cities.
>
> Rural people are scattered, few and inarticulate. In the cities they begin to have an impact on the political life of the country. They have votes and the Communists seek their votes.
>
> In rural areas the priest spends 80 per cent of his day travelling on mule back. In the slums all this time is spent in meeting those who need him so badly.
>
> I don't believe that either of us converted the other. Or perhaps it would be more true to say that both of us were half converted to the other's point of view. Indeed, the rural areas will have to be tackled; actually they are easier than the cities. But time is of the essence, and now there is none to spare.

Though Tom did not know it, he also had little time to spare: his spell of life was closing in:

> The Bird of Time has but a little way
> To fly – and Lo! The Bird is on the Wing.*

He planned to leave Shannon for Boston on the evening of October 27. He wanted his departure to be as low-key as possible but when the time came it was in keeping with the rest of his life – it was full of drama.

It was a miserable day. He set off from Cork with Canon Jim Kelly driving. Canon Kelly was a fast driver. On a previous occasion on a similar mission he said to Jim Kelly when they reached Shannon, 'Thanks, Jim. The worst of the journey is over me now'.

This time there were no jokes. Flooding had taken place on the road near Bunratty and Tom, impulsive as ever, insisted on trying to get through. As a result they were held up for a considerable time before a bus arrived to take him the rest of the way. When he finally arrived at Shannon there was barely time for the formalities to be concluded before it was time to board the aircraft. There was time only for the briefest of farewells to his friends. This suited Tom: he was never one for emotional farewells.

His last glimpse of Ireland was through the mist and rain of a miserable October evening.

* Rubaiyat of Omar Khayyam, translated by Edward Fitzgerald.

THE LAST HURRAH

When Tom Duggan arrived in Boston he found himself already a celebrity. It seemed that everybody he met wanted to shake his hand and wish him well. He found it all slightly embarrassing and half jokingly complained that he felt like a prize animal on show.

All he wanted was to be on his way now that the die had been cast. But there were various formalities to be attended to before he could leave. By 6 November, all was ready. He felt a great sense of elation. It was the feast-day of All the Saints of Ireland, so many of whom had made themselves voluntary exiles to spread the Kingdom of God. He felt that this was a good omen.

Before leaving Boston he wrote a hurried note to Bishop Lucey:

> My dear Lord,
>
> A final word.
>
> On my way and feeling on top of the world. I'd have looted Boston if I stayed here longer. Tell Frank Creedon that I appeared before the Eire Society and they contributed 300 dollars. That will shake him.
>
> Do you know? I feel so elevated that I could see out 1965 and be still alive.
>
> The Lord ever bless you.
>
> Your venerable son,
>
> TFD

The stamp on his passport shows that his flight landed early next day at the International Airport of Callao, situated beside the Pacific Ocean, a few miles downstream from Lima. It was 7 November 1961. His odyssey was over. The wanderer had come to his final home: he'd go no more a roving.

He had exactly forty days to live, a mystical number in biblical terms. For a man who loved scriptural symbolisms it was strangely fitting.

Next day in a letter to Bishop Lucey he gave his first impressions of his new home:

> Here I am safe and sound.
>
> This seems to be the best climate in the world, like a July day at home with a cool breeze blowing from somewhere and no such thing as rain.

> The Cardinal came all the way down to New York. Fortified by his holy presence, I got away with over a hundred-weight in baggage.
>
> Don't let your sense of humour overcome you but I am slated to give a Retreat. Don't forget, for Heaven's sake, to keep me in your prayers.
>
> P.S. I am within screeching – but not reaching – distance of a Doctorate in Church and/or State. It would be of value here. I spoke to H. Atkins about one and I wrote to Kevin McNamara about the other. If either could be pushed.

He must have been regretting the chance of a doctorate in Theology he had let slip in Maynooth.

A few days later he heard from the Cardinal who was back in Boston:

> We arrived home last Thursday. Your cable was awaiting me. We certainly enjoyed seeing you off. You will always be in our thoughts and prayers. HOLLER any time we can serve you. Your needs will be our needs.
>
> We were certainly happy to accompany you to New York and to leave you with your fond friends prior to your departure. I hope the flight was pleasant and that you are not too tired and that you will get a little rest.

But rest was the last thing on Tom's mind. He wanted the action to begin immediately: he wanted to be up and doing, exploring his new home, his last port of call in this world. In his previous visit he had seen some of Lima's worst features and consequently he was under no illusion about what to expect.

Lima is a strange, sad, brooding city. It is hugely over-populated with a massive estimated population of over six million souls: for many of them their souls were the least of their worries. A low, dense and depressing pall of cloud seems to hang permanently over the city as if the sun were anxious to dissociate itself from the cruel society which lives beneath. Lima has all the worst features of any over-crowded Latin-American city: air pollution, water pollution, traffic chaos, sporadic violence, a constant babble of noise. One could not imagine oneself falling in love with Lima.

The city centre, however, still retains something of the grace and elegance of old Spain: its Spanish cultural heritage is everywhere visible. The Spaniards always had an eye for beauty of design. Pizarro, Peru's *conquistador* and founder of Lima, left to posterity a beautiful and well laid-out capital city.

Originally known as *La Cuidad de los Reyes*, the city of the kings, in deference to its founding by Pizarro on the feast of the Magi, it was once a city almost without compare, a city truly fit for kings. Lima had known its glory days when it was the capital of the huge sprawing Spanish Empire of Latin America, the seat of the Viceroy (arguably the next most important man to the King of Spain in the whole Spanish-speaking world). As one looks at its magnificent central square, La Plaza de Armas, the lovely Viceroy's Palace (now the President's), the Spanish-style Cathedral, the imposing Municipalidad, one can imagine what a majestic city it must once have been.

Even today the city centre bears strong witness to its Spanish heritage. It is throbbing with life and vitality and Latin exuberance. There is constant flurry of movement. Its streets are beautifully laid-out and its shops and arcades bear every sign of opulence and wealth. The shops in Miraflores and Plaza San Martín compare in luxury with the best in any city anywhere.

The police in their bright uniforms walk with the same swagger one might see anywhere in Spain and just as numerous as in the mother-country.

The tourist, busily ticking off the sights that according to his travel agent had to be seen, sees only this Lima, the colonial heart of wealthy old Lima. He does not know that only a few miles away is a second Lima, a very different Lima, the squatters' city, the despised *barriadas* or migrant settlements, euphemistically referred to by the establishment as *pueblos jovenes*, young towns. Like flocks of migrating birds on the wing to seek warmer climates, wave after wave of migrants left the cold and misery of the Andes, seeking nothing as magical as an *Eldorado* but a much humbler objective, a place to lay down their heads with a roof over them, living conditions in keeping with their dignity as human beings, and a chance of employment. For the great majority this humble dream was a mirage. Hunted out of the city, they erected their primitive adobe huts in the wastelands on the desert sands at the foot of the Andes. Gradually, in the course of decades, the indomitable will to survive of these human scarecrows overcame all obstacles. Their haphazardly placed hovels became human settlements and some developed into reasonably comfortable *pueblos* with their own little shops and villages. These were the fortunate ones: the others still lack the basic comforts of modern society or even its basic necessities such as electricity, paved roads, piped water or elementary modern sanitary facilities. Naturally these areas became fruitful breeding-grounds for diseases such as typhoid and cholera, brought about by pollution and lack of hygiene. Unfortunately in the political sphere they became breeding-grounds for communism and all sorts of anarchy.

For long the State tried to ignore the problem. Such progress as was made in the living conditions of the migrants did not come about through any help from above but rather from the sheer hard work of the people themselves. Force of numbers and pressure from civil rights groups eventually forced the government to take notice but there was no radical or comprehensive rescue plan. Those who shouted most were listened to and the rest continued in their misery. Government assistance was only on a piecemeal basis and, given the prevailing corruption which marks all Peruvian governmental agencies, little if any assistance filtered down to those most in need.

In the circumstances the Church fared badly both among the rich and the poor. In old Lima with its magnificent old churches the Church was faced with the traditional Latin-American apathy and indifference to religion. There, Catholicism seems to flourish only on the occasion of the great fiestas held in honour of their favourite icons, *El Senor de los Milagros*, Our Lord of the Miracles, or of the two patrons, *St. Rose of Lima* and *St. Martín de Porres*. In recent times the situation has become aggravated by a crippling shortage of native priests and by the inroads of wealthy evangelical groups and by groups such as Jehovah Witnesses and Mormons.

In the *barriadas* or shanty-towns the situation was even worse. Local agitators fed the latent anti-Church and anti-clerical attitudes of the poor people. In the eyes of the poor, as a result, the Church seemed to be on the side of the rich. In such a situation it is understandable that without a priestly presence they would laugh at the very idea of a loving and caring God.

It was against this frightening background of a people lapsing into religious indifference, if not atheism, that Pope Paul VI and especially Pope John XXIII launched a crusade for help for Latin America from the better-off Catholic dioceses throughout the world. They called for material help and for help in personnel in the form of volunteer missionaries to make up the depleted ranks of local clergy.

Among those who answered the call were the Columban Fathers, the Maryknoll Fathers and the Missionary Society of St. James the Apostle founded by Cardinal Cushing for the express purpose of evangelisation in Latin America.

When Tom Duggan arrived in Lima as a member of the Society of St. James the Apostle he took up residence at the Society's headquarters in the Avenida Grau in the shopping and residential area of Miraflores. The house, built as a large-sized family home was barely adequate for the needs of the Society, then in its first glow of enthusiasm and expansion. It catered both for a residential administrative staff and as a headquarters for missionaries returning from their apostolates in need of rest and spiritual renewal.

Tom Duggan had few problems of adaptation. He related easily to people. There was no trace of racialism in his nature. The only problem was the cramped conditions of his new home. He had always valued his privacy. In the house in Lima there was no place in which he could be *incommunicado*. In a letter to the author he referred obliquely to this problem: 'If I ever succeed in dragging these ancient feet home, I'll be much less particular about my surroundings.'

The local superior of the Society in Peru was an Italian-American called Rodolfo Masciarelli, known to all and sundry as 'Rudy', a gentle, kindly and humorous man. Interviewed by the author in Lima in February 1991, thirty years after Tom Duggan's death, he still retained a very clear mental picture of Tom:

> He had the spirit of a young missionary. He related to everyone of every age – that's why we meant him to be a spiritual director. Most of the priests were very young – they needed an old head. I remember his sprightly step, he seemed on dancing feet. He was jovial and droll and very witty but beneath it all he was a very spiritual man.
>
> He always had a fresh and original approach – he'd see sides to a problem which we had overlooked. In Paul Vincent Carrol's play *Shadow and Substance* there is a portrait of an elderly Canon of the old school, very stiff and formal and grand, so much so that his curates were expected to stand up at his entrance. I mention him because Tom was the direct opposite; he never stood on ceremony. He had great wisdom. It was a shame he was with us for only so short a time. He'd have been a great help.

The Archbishop of Lima at the time, Archbishop Landazzuri, later to become a cardinal, has equally clear memories of Tom. Entertaining the author in his hospitable home he spoke warmly of him: 'Definitely a man of God,' he said, 'An outstanding Christian gentleman.'

It is clear from Fr. Masciarelli's remarks that it was not at all the Society's intention that Tom should be a mere figure-head, as if his mission had been fully accomplished simply by arriving in Peru at his advanced age. They saw him as much more than a mere publicity symbol. In spite of, or rather because of, his age they envisaged him as a sort of father-figure, the sort of patriarch the young priests of the Society could look up to as spiritual director and counsellor. Most of the priests were young Americans coming from far more pampered backgrounds than most of their Irish counterparts. Life in the raw which they encountered in the Andes among a peasant people with crude living conditions must have come as a rude shock: they would have needed shock treatment to recover. In such a situation Tom would have been a steadying and reassuring influence in the turbulent years which lay ahead following Vatican II and the rise of liberation theology.

Tom's new *confreres* knew enough about his background and reputation to expect that he would not confine himself to a purely spiritual apostolate within the four walls of the house on Avenida Grau. They knew that the world of politics and intrigue fascinated him and that he had a style of his own for dealing with bureaucracy (which in Latin America takes on a few extra layers compared to the rest of the world). They would give him a free hand, hoping perhaps that this aptitude of his could be turned to advantage. Like all predominantly North American groups, the Society of St. James had an image problem in Peru: to the Peruvians it was inconceivable that anybody should come to their country for purely altruistic motives. Tom might come in useful for dispelling their prejudices and gaining their confidence.

If he felt like involving himself in the campaign for social justice on behalf of the poor on the *barridas* his superiors would have no objection provided that he did not compromise the Society in the eyes of the government, an unlikely contingency giving his experience in walking across political tight-ropes.

Sadly, all this remained pure speculation. Tom was never given time to fulfil these bright expectations. It was only a dream which never saw the light of day, the last of a long series of might-have-beens which bedevilled his life story. The final missing chapter might have been the most entertaining and fruitful of all. As it turned out, once again people were left to wonder at the strangeness of God's ways. Tom, as always in his approach to the deity, would probably have shrugged his shoulders philosophically, and muttered something about 'Man proposing but God disposing' or, 'Tis not in mortals to command success'. He certainly was too experienced in God's ways to expect a perfect ending in this world.

The hoped-for honorary doctorate which would have been a useful status symbol in the eyes of the Peruvian establishment failed to materialise. Kevin MacNamara wrote regretfully from Maynooth:

> If Maynooth had enough flexibility and/or common sense of *comme il faut* it would jump at the opportunity of bestowing an honorary

> degree on so distinguished a son. I have made a few soundings but so far the reaction is unpromising.
>
> The fact that something has never been done in the past (Maynooth hasn't given an honorary D.D. so far) is practically sufficient reason for ruling it out.

Kevin had to content himself with sending a cable on behalf of the committee of the Maynooth Union, couched in classical Roman terms: *Perigrinantem te salutamus*, we salute you, missionary.

Tom did not neglect his study of Spanish. A lady tutor was brought in to help and Tom travelled by taxi to her home for his lessons. On his way he always passed a spacious plaza which contained two items which fascinated him – a monument to an airman called Fawcett in the form of a broken propeller – perhaps he saw it as an allegory of his own life – and an ultra-modern funnily-shaped Catholic church which he promptly nicknamed 'the dragon's egg': possibly it represented for him the remoteness of the Peruvian Church from reality.

His old tendency to criticise the Church's wasteful deployment of her clerical troops received fresh impetus from what he saw in Peru. Writing to Bishop Lucey he said:

> I am getting on fine. The anticipated difficulties are never realized. I had visions of the Equator, Summer season, fierce heat etc. Instead imagine yourself somewhere near the sea on a summer day and someone saying, 'It would be hot only for that lovely breeze'.
>
> Our quarters are comfortable, and, so far, I am fattening on the food. In fact, the only blot is the absence of Spanish. I am doing my best to soak it in but the infernal thing evaporates.
>
> As to work. Obviously the Columbans and the St. James's Society approach it from opposite view-points. The Columbans are helping an urban proletariat: they have three contiguous parishes (which form a deanery). Where they are, there was literally nothing and (how they did it the Lord knows) now they have church, rectory and schools in every parish.
>
> The St. James's Society has a H.Q. in Lima and in addition one parish. But their concentration – or rather their dispersion – is on the mountains of Peru pushing north into Ecuador and east into Bolivia. The Maryknolls follow the St. James pattern but their strength is in Bolivia.

In addition there are all sorts of miscellanies – a team from St. Louis, Poles from Wisconsin, Jesuits from the Mid-West province, etc., etc.

The whole campaign – and the components are all good men – could do with some central oganization. What they could use would be a sort of super-Nuntio.

I'd imagine an Irish team would work best on its own. Boston would help in the capital expenses, churches, rectories and schools. Then, equipped, they could get really going.

And some day there will have to be very fully considered, the question of Wastage and Insurance. In my opinion, after a five year stint everyone should go home, their contract fulfilled. Then, if a man were a conspicuous success, he could be allowed back – having rehabilitated himself in the routine work of an Irish parish for a year.

All this is not worth putting on paper because I have hardly seen anything yet.

I hope to Heaven you'll be able to read even bits of this. Why in my wasted years did I not learn (a) to type (b) *hablar Espanol* (to speak spanish).

With love and affection,

T.F.D.

Far from 'not being worth putting on paper' these ideas about the shape a future diocesan mission might take are truly prophetic, linking Tom's name very closely with the future Cork Mission to Latin America. A few years later when Bishop Lucey established his Mission he used many of these ideas as the basis of his constitution; by subtracting a little, and adding on a little, he produced the *Magna Charta* of the Cork Mission.

It is interesting to note that from his proposed centralised missionary structure Tom wanted to exclude the Irish. Was this a recognition of a basic Irish tendency towards individuality?

He had begun to post his Christmas mail. Writing to an old soldier friend, Major Ian English, he seemed to feel that he had few remaining battles to fight: 'As for myself, I feel like an old galleon, battered but sound, on the verge of dropping into port.'

A letter arrived from Cardinal Cushing on November 25:

Thanks for all the letters I received from you. I read them and re-read them.

I am glad everything looks 'bright and rosy'. The fact is you would create such an atmosphere wherever you are.

Everybody here sends you love and prayerful mementos and the best of everything. 'Holler' if I can be of service.

Tom wrote to Bishop Lucey on December 8:

I'd have written last week but:

(a) all my pens have gone back on me.

(b) I was expecting a letter.

(c) There is no news.

I can't stir an inch until I get Spanish. It is coming but slowly. I can do a lot of things which are not much good:

i) I can make sense out of bits of written Spanish. That is only Latin trans. at sight.

ii) Risking apoplexy (spelling?) I can convey a message in Spanish but...

iii) I can't understand one single word when it is being spoken, especially if the speaker is a native: it is like being under machine-gun fire and no sand-bags.

We are going to the Nuntio for lunch today.....

All that remains is to wish you, and that from the bottom of my heart, the joys and blessings of Christmas.

On 9 December he wrote a joint letter to three very old friends in the Bon Secours Hospital at Glasnevin, Mothers Euphemia, Docetae and Philomena. Mother Euphemia had been very ill and had written to him for prayers. His opening remarks are addressed to her:

Dear Mother Euphemia,

Get it right out of your mind that in the present crisis of my affairs I can have you wandering off to Heaven. For the next three years I am depending on the Holy Mother of God and yourself.

In 1965 we shall make a nice joint jubilee, mine golden, yours diamond....After that we will do a leisurely planning of our futures. In the meantime no precipitate nonsense.

Things are going grand for me. I am, of course, so far hamstrung for want of Spanish but I think it is coming....

All this a preliminary to my real business: to wish you all and through you, to every single one in Glasnevin, the joys and blessings of Christmas and 1962. *Ora pro me.* (Pray for me)

P.S. To Mother P.,
Would you ever drop a line to Sheila Acton, giving all my devotion. I'd write myself, but, if I did, I'd have to write to all in Kinsale.

The following week he was delighted to be invited by Fr. Michael Fitzgerald to preside over a Day of Recollection for the young Columban priests. He was very glad of the opportunity of giving some return to the Columbans for all the kindnesses he had received from them. He was happy also for another reason: he hoped that this was the beginning of a spiritual relationship with the Columban missionaries which would be an added justification for his own presence in Peru.

On Friday, 15 December, he telephoned Fr. Michael Crowley who was working on the mission field in Monsefu further north. Michael remembers it as being 'a marathon call'. The gist of his conversation was that he was hoping to organise a get-together with the three Cork priests over Christmas. He suggested that they meet in Lima and enjoy a few days' break together somewhere along the coast.

Saturday, 16 December, was just another working day. He wrote some letters, one of which, to Mother Raphael in the Bon Secours convent in Cork, has survived:

Dear Lady Raphael,

Your letter came today. I wish to Heaven I could write like you, I'd never stop.

I am sorry that poor Dr. James is again not so well.

[The Dr. James in question was Dr. James O'Mahony, an eminent Capuchin scholar and Professor of Philosophy in University College, Cork.] Ask him to give me a small share of his sufferings....

Would you believe it. Some demented person has put it upon me to give a four-day Retreat. They may as well have asked me to sing. 2nd, 3rd, 4th and 5th Jan. For the Lord's sake, pray.

It could be that the Lord took him at his word about giving him a share of suffering. That same Saturday evening there was some excitement at the St. James's House. Fr. Rudy Masciarelli recalls that some visitors arrived at the

Avenida Grau and were received by Tom. They had brought some Irish newspapers which they forgot to leave behind when they were going away. Tom discovered the loss very quickly and ran into the street to intercept them but their taxi was already on its way. This little incident took on wings in the telling, ending up as a most dramatic tale of Tom forgetting his breviary in a local bus, running after the bus, and collapsing on the pavement.

The story may well have some slight foundation in fact. Tom was inclined to get excited and fussy about small things: the excitement about the forgotten newspapers may well have triggered off the cardiac discomfort which he experienced later on in the night.

Spiritually he was well prepared. He had no fear of death, not even of sudden death. He had remarked once to Fr. Bobby Ormond, one of his curates in Ballyphehane, 'All I ask of God is to give me ten minutes at the end to settle my accounts'.

He never worried unduly about his health, often remarking that when he was young he was afraid he would die of a heart attack but as he grew older he was afraid he wouldn't! Another of his remarks was that he'd like to go out on a high note but unfortunately he did not know the difference between a high note and a low note!

God was good to him because he was a very poor subject for a lingering illness.

That Saturday night he had no premonition of death. He did not know that the end was very near.

He retired to bed as usual on Saturday night. The next thing that is known with certainty is that at about 6.30 a.m. he knocked at the bedroom door of Fr. George Flynn, the house-superior. Fr. George takes up the story:

> He excused himself for not feeling well enough to celebrate the Mass which had been assigned to him in a local convent. Then he asked me to anoint him. He returned to bed and while I was administering the Last Sacraments he seemed to suffer some sort of heart attack but he remained quite conscious. A doctor was summoned. I heard Fr. Duggan's confession and anointed him. He participated in the rite but was obviously in great pain and not at all chatty afterwards.
>
> He prayed silently. Other priests arrived including Fr. Frank O'Connor. When the doctor came he administered a strong injection but to no avail. Minutes later, in the doctor's presence, he collapsed and died immediately of a massive thrombosis.

Fr. Masciarelli said, 'He went out like a light'. Thinking back on the course of events Fr. George Flynn concluded that he must have felt some pain during the night but waited until it was light before disturbing anybody.

In liturgical terms, it was the third Sunday in Advent, known as *Gaudete* or *Rejoicing* Sunday because the Liturgy of the Mass of that day is dominated by St. Paul's great admonition, '*Always be joyful, then, in the Lord.* I repeat, be joyful'.* No scriptural passage could be more appropriate in the circumstances. It was indeed Tom's day of rejoicing, his *Passover* and *Transitus* to the Lord.

Cardinal Cushing was shocked when he heard the news. He described his reactions in his homily at the funeral Mass:

> Sunday morning, December 17th, while recovering from an attack of bronchial pneumonia, I received a telephone call from Peru that Fr. Tom died at 7.30 a.m. It was 'Gaudete Sunday'. For me it was Passion Sunday.

Bishop Cornelius Lucey was equally shocked. The Cardinal was in immediate touch with him and they arranged to met at Idlewild Airport in New York on the following day and to travel on to Lima together on the first available jet flight.

Fr. Michael Murphy and Fr. Paddy Leader were contacted in Bolivia. They boarded a rickety Bolivian aircraft but after a perilous journey to Lima they arrived late for the funeral.

Fr. Michael Crowley had been keeping a detailed diary. The entry for Sunday the 17th, is brief and to the point:

> I just got the sad news of Canon Duggan's death.
>
> I got on a bus at 6.30 p.m. on Sunday evening and I travelled through the night to Lima, $13^{1}/_{2}$ hours. Saw poor Duggan in morgue and had difficulty getting the embalming done and facing up to the bureaucracy.

Actually Michael Crowley's arrival spared a good deal of embarrassment. When he arrived at the mortuary to which the remains had been transferred he found a complete *impasse*. The official in charge was obstinately refusing to release the body until the necessary forms had been filled. The bureaucracy against which Tom Duggan has fought all his life seemed set to defeat him in death. Michael summed up the situation at a glance, knowing the ways of Peruvian officials. He proclaimed that he was 'family', a cousin of the deceased. To the Latin mind the

* St. Paul, Phillipians, Chapter 4, Verse 4. *The New Jerusalem Bible.*

word 'family' is sacred: it is the ultimate appeal which opens all doors. The official relaxed: it seemed to him that sanity had been restored. The forms were quickly filled, Michael answering all the questions without blinking an eyelid: father's name (which he happened to know); mother's maiden name (which he had to invent), and so on down through the remaining questions, his answers being a mixture of truth and fiction. At the end there was much hand-shaking and bowing, as the body was finally released. Duggan, being Duggan, presented problems even in death.

Michael's diary continues: 'I was up all night – a real Irish wake. It was just what Duggan would have wished.'

A quick decision had to be made regarding the place of burial. The St. James Society did not possess any burial plot of its own. Actually Tom was the first member of the Society to die in Peru. It was decided that he should be buried in what was popularly known as the Britannic cemetery, which was the usual burial place for English-speaking people who died in the area. It was situated at Callao, a few miles from Lima.

The funeral ceremonies were most impressive. Cardinal Cushing was the sole celebrant of the Mass as concelebration had not yet been introduced. In the sanctuary were Archbishop Romolo Carboni, Papal Nuncio to Peru; Archbishop Landazuri-Ricketts, Archbishop of Lima and Primate of Peru; Bishop Cornelius Lucey of the dioceses of Cork and Ross and two other Peruvian bishops. The Irish colony in Lima was present in strength. Fr. Michael Fitzgerald, in deference to his Cork origins and to Duggan's strong links with the Columbans, was given a special place in the ceremonial. Fr. Michael Crowley was the only Cork diocesan priest present.

At the cemetery Cardinal Cushing officiated. It came as a shock to him during a pause in the ceremonial to discover that the cemetery was British. His deep voice could be heard booming through the cemetery: 'I know who will be the first out of this place when the last trumpet sounds.'

Michael Crowley's diary sums up the day's events:

> Cushing and Lucey arrived today. The Cardinal said grand things about the Archdeacon in his sermon at the Mass. We laid him to rest in the Britannic cemetery. There among strangers he awaits his resurrection.

Afterwards there were several functions to be attended including a formal visit to the President's Palace where they were received by the President and his wife.

Nuncio Carboni gave a banquet in honour of the distinguished visitors. He made a long but witty speech, beginning in typical Italian style: 'At the outset I must apologise for this humble repast which is not at all equal to the many and important reasons for our being together this evening.'

He went on to reveal one of the important reasons: 'Catholics in the more fortunate parts of the world have a grave responsibility to investigate, study and help solve the serious problems that beset their co-religionists in other parts of the world.'

He did not mention Bishop Lucey by name in this context but there was no doubt that his remarks were directed towards him. Archbishop Carboni was a very determined man and at the Vatican Council he availed of every opportunity of reopening the subject whenever he encountered Bishop Lucey.

For the remaining time he spent in Peru Bishop Lucey, with Fr. Michael Fitzgerald as his guide, did his best to see for himself the conditions under which the poor in the shanty towns lived. The tiring circuit of the poverty-stricken settlements made a lasting impression on his mind, particularly one drive southwards along the Pan Americana highway in the company of Fr. Michael Crowley and Fr. Billy Francis, the Cardinal's nephew. Fr. Crowley's diary records: 'It was that run down by the coast that I regard as the most significant in the context of a future Cork mission. Bishop Lucey was very opened up by the whole sequence of events.'

They stopped at a miserable little settlement of poor people encamped near the highway and Fr. Crowley introduced the Bishop to each of them. They were so welcoming, so cheerful and uncomplaining about their miserable lot that it brought tears to Bishop Lucey's eyes. He realised then for the first time the extent of their abandonment by the State and the pathetic lack of contact with God's holy Church. Literally and heart-breakingly they were outcasts with nobody to fight their cause.

For the remainder of his short stay Bishop Lucey was in serious and thoughtful mood. Obviously he had been given much food for thought. The plight of the poor people which he had witnessed with his own eyes called for action. It seemed to him as if God had spoken. But he was not a man to make instant decisions under the impulse of emotion. As far as he was concerned God does not make his designs known by sudden revelations but by a slow and gradual process of enlightenment. Consequently he did not rush in at this stage to make any rash promises to Nuncio Carboni. There were a great many strands to be brought together; there was much consultation to be done and a great deal of quiet prayer before he finally took the plunge in 1965 and launched his own mission at Trujillo, a coastal city towards the north of Peru. As a result a desert expanse with a teeming Peruvian population became the direct responsibility of the people of the dioceses of Cork and Ross.

Tom Duggan was dead and gone before the mission opened in Trujillo but who can say that his life and death played no part in its foundation? His death occasioned Bishop Lucey's first visit to Latin America. The days the Bishop spent in Lima were crucial factors in forming his decision. It is not fanciful, therefore, to regard Archdeacon Tom Duggan as the instrument chosen by God to open up Bishop Lucey's mind to the pressing material and spiritual needs of the Peruvian people. To achieve this purpose it was necessary for Tom Duggan to die:

> Unless a wheat grain falls into the earth and dies,
> it remains only a single grain;
> but if it dies it yields a rich harvest.*

To those who believe in a caring God the sequence of events was no mere accident: it was the finger of God at work tracing out on his divine canvas the outlines of a future Cork Mission to Latin America.

Tom Duggan did not await his resurrection for very long in the Britannic cemetery. Little more than a year after his interment the St. James's Society had second thoughts about its suitability as his final resting place. It was felt that his remains might be more appropriately laid to rest in missionary soil. The Society had just established a language school in Cieneguilla in the foothills of the Andes some fifteen miles from Lima. Accordingly in the spring of 1963 Tom's remains were exhumed and transferred to Cieneguilla for burial. Unlike Bishop Shanahan's second burial there was no triumphal ceremony to mark the occasion. It was not exactly a case of 'we buried him darkly at dead of night'† but it was strictly a low-key affair.

One might have imagined that this should mark the final curtain for Tom Duggan but there was one final twist to his story. In a short time it became evident to the St. James's Society that a mistake had been made in locating the school so far away from Lima. Logistical difficulties had arisen which made it expedient to move the language school to Lima. When the transfer was made, Tom Duggan's remains were left behind. Today the place is no longer missionary territory and can hardly be described as a place of pilgrimage. It is a lonely grave,

* Gospel of St. John, 12, 24. *The New Jerusalem Bible.*

† Wolfe, Charles, *The Burial of Sir John Moore.*

'a little little obscure grave'* but no matter. Tom Duggan need have no fear. It is the soul that counts. His soul is at rest, he has reached his homeland:

Thou thy worldy task hast done,
Home art gone, and ta'en thy wages.†

* William Shakespeare, *King Richard II*, II, iii, 143.
† William Shakespeare, *Cymbeline*, IV, ii, 258.

EPILOGUE

In appearance Tom Duggan was sturdily and stockily built, inclining to corpulence, of medium height. By any standards one would not call him a handsome man. He himself joked about his looks, saying he knew he was no oil painting! There was a tradition in Farranferris that the staff presented a new president with his portrait in oils, to be subsequently hung in the refectory. This custom died with Tom Duggan. Very reluctantly he agreed to sit for his portrait. Frank Sanquest, the artist, was commissioned to do the work. He decided to begin with a charcoal sketch on which the final portrait in oils would be based. He had not reckoned with his subject's impatience. Very soon Tom grew bored and the project had to be abandoned, Tom telling the disappointed artist that he had come to the conclusion that his face lent itself more to sculpture! It reminds one of the remark attributed to Pio Nono, Pope Pius IX, when asked to sign a particularly hideous-looking portrait, 'Fear not, it is I'.

Whatever he may have lacked in looks, Tom made up for in character. There was nothing mean or petty about him. He was a big man, big in spirit, big in heart, big in mind. He thought big and his sharp mind was constantly turning out new projects.

An unusual man, his courage was legendary, matched only by his restlessness and impatience. Canon Connolly, his successor as President of Farranferris, claimed that it was only in a crisis that he became normal. Certainly crisis brought out the best in him. The citation accompanying the award of the Military Cross at Dunkirk spoke of his 'coolness, courage and example' under fire. Lucy, his sister, presented a somewhat different picture when asked to comment on the citation, 'Sure, we never knew him to be cool'.

He was intensely human and compassionate. Human misery never failed to sadden him. Travelling in the Third World he grieved at what he saw, 'Surely the good God never intended things to be like this' he said. The Irish Civil War and the death of so many brave men also affected him deeply.

There was a soft spot in his heart which made him identify with human suffering and want, and he cared very little that he was looked on as a 'soft touch'. He knew that people took advantage of his good nature but still he kept on giving, 'When the hunger bites, morals go out the door,' he would say philosophically. Generous to a fault he forced others to be generous too as his sister, Lucy, and certain well-off friends knew to their cost. There was a Robin Hood streak in him which made him eager to even out the imbalances of society as far as one individual could.

He did not possess a cultured mind, indeed he was something of a philistine. Literature, art and especially music, generally speaking, left him cold. Cardinal Newman was his favourite author and like many of the clergy of his time he admired the writings of Chesterton and Belloc. However, he by no means despised less serious-minded writers and usually within reach in his study was the latest 'thriller'. Possessed of a very sharp mind he might have become a great advocate in the secular courts had not God called him to the priesthood. He had a sharp tongue, sometimes too sharp for his own good.

Tom was no knight in shining armour. He had his faults as some people were quick to point out. Some considered him an intriguer. Perhaps he was. It is true that at times he was not above attaining his objectives by devious means, by 'indirections' as Polonius might say.* But in such instances he always had some good cause in view: it was his soft heart speaking. He looked on the ultimate good to be achieved as the over-riding consideration. He never intrigued for personal advancement or from unworthy motives. It seems true to say that in certain circumstances he believed that the end justifies the means, a strange position for a theologian to adopt. It was of course, bad theology, objectively speaking, but, subjectively, very understandable and almost forgivable in his case because the milk of human kindness underlay and explained many of his controversial actions and activities. In this context one thinks in particular of his plan to blow up the walls of Cork gaol to free I.R.A. prisoners condemned to death during the War of Independence.

Like his mentor, Walter MacDonald, he could be accused of intellectual pride. He was not one to hide his light under a bushel or to keep his opinions to himself even when it might have been wiser to do so. He sometimes antagonised people by his almost contemptuous dismissal of their opinions. On the other hand as a teacher he was surprisingly patient in his treatment of less gifted pupils, 'the afflicted of Allah' as he playfully called them.

Predictably he never attained his full potential in the Church which likes conformity in its ministers. There was a rebel streak in Tom, a non-conformalism which hindered his advancement. This did not worry him unduly: he preferred life at the fringe of the herd. According to Canon Denis Murphy, who was not one of his greatest admirers, 'He was built for opposition'. He was by no means a 'safe man' or what theologians call a 'tutiorist'. If two courses lay open before him more likely than not he would choose the more dangerous.

One begins to see why he did not reach the heights as far as advancement in

* William Shakespeare, *Hamlet*, II, i, 64.

the Church was concerned. There are certain qualities looked on as essential in aspirants to high places in the Church such as steadiness and stability of mind, common sense and *savoir faire*, emotional control which Tom lacked. Tom's trouble was that he was deficient in the virtue of prudence. He was impulsive and inclined to follow the dictates of his heart rather than those of cold reason. It seemed as if he liked to live dangerously, as if he believed that:

> One crowded hour of glorious life
> Is worth an age without a name.*

Tom failed to find complete fulfilment within the constraints of the diocesan system of his time. The reason was that both Bishop Coholan and Bishop Lucey, although extremely hard-working bishops and men of the highest principle, shared the strong conservatism of the Irish Church of the time which inhibited growth and stifled innovation. Suspicious of change and firm upholders of the *status quo*, they ruled alone in conformity with the famous expression of Pope Pius XII, 'I want executants, not collaborators'. They expected their priests to fit into traditional moulds and to engage in parish work or chaplaincies or seminary teaching, the only forms of apostolate open to them.

Though a brilliant scholar himself, Bishop Lucey seemed strangely loath to send talented young priests on intensive post-graduate courses of study. The result was a great dearth of qualified priest-specialists. The idea that a modern diocese needed trained specialists in many areas never seemed to strike him. He seems never to have entertained the thought of creating particular posts in the diocese to suit individual talents. To him that would have seemed like undue exaltation of the individual over the system.

And yet the individual should come first. The system, the structures are not sacrosanct, far from it. If the Church is to accomplish its evangelical mission properly, the *raison d'être* of its existence, it must have a certain flexibility. It must take cognisance of changes in society. There should be a constant reassessment of methods. Each individual priest is an apostle and the particular apostolate marked out for him ought to correspond to his talents.

The Church will last till the end of time but not necessarily in its present form. It must be open to change. Cardinal Newman held that 'to live is to change, and to be alive is to change often'. And Pope John believed in adaptability – in each age, he said, there should be a great leap forward.

Tom Duggan was an individualist. He needed scope and freedom. Dr. Maguire of the Columban Fathers, a wise and perspicacious man who had

* Thomas Osbert Mordaunt, Verses written during the War.

known Tom since his student days in Maynooth, had watched him at work in the United States and was greatly taken by his technique:

> I will say this: if our organisation (i.e. the Columbans) in this country had a man of the Canon's ability, versatility and persuasive powers, he would almost certainly find himself with a roving commission from the Holy Ghost. He would function as our ambassador-at-large, a man whose task it would be to explain the financial needs of our Society by word of mouth to members of the hierarchy and to prominent lay folk.

What Tom needed was freedom of action, based on the words of St. Paul: 'Am I not free? Am I not an Apostle?'* He did not want any undue emphasis on structures to come between him and his work. He did not want anyone breathing down his neck or checking up on his performance. It is surely no coincidence that the happiest and most fruitful periods of his life, i.e. his peacemaking activities in the Irish Civil War, his years as a military chaplain, his mission in the United States were all periods when he was free to exercise his own initiative and to carve out his own role outside of his diocese. It is bordering on an indictment of the whole system to say that it was only outside his diocese that he was at ease in his work. It should not have been beyond the ingenuity of man to find, or if necessary to create, some niche for him within his diocese which would have suited his restless disposition.

The welfare of the Church was a constant preoccupation with Tom Duggan. 'Zeal for his father's house'† drove him on. It seemed to him that the Irish Church of his time was working at less than its full potential. He felt that it ought to concentrate more on the lapsed and the indifferent. Perhaps, he said, there should be a re-think about the suitability of the parochial system in modern conditions, especially in urban areas. The priority should be to reach out to all the people of God, church-goers and non-church-goers alike. The present system came into being many centuries ago in a predominantly rural society. But society changes and in a changing society a static Church must lose out. The Church must get back to its real mission which is to evangelise. If there are pockets on indifference to be found in urban areas where not just individuals but the whole sheep-fold has wandered away; if there are 'no go' areas where the clergy are not welcome it is time to start thinking about new methods. There

* St Paul, 1 Cor, 9,1. *New Jerusalem Bible.*

† Psalm 69, 9. *New Jerusalem Bible.*

must not be any spirit of defeatism, any bunker mentality, any complacency in failure or acceptance of total defeat.

In his usual trenchant style Tom Duggan addressed himself to this problem, less urgent in his time than in ours:

> If pastoral responsibility is to be effective it must be exclusive and is not tolerant of over-lapping. At present we have an extraordinary position. The goodly people, who could make their way to Heaven without the assistance of anyone are sedulously being saved six times over. At the other end of the scale, and because the ground is not being methodically covered there exists all manner of odd pockets, of people resistant of grace and absolutely uncared for.

In effect, Duggan was asking what has become of Christ's evangelical principle: 'It is not the healthy who need the doctor but the sick. I came to call not the upright but sinners.'*

How did Tom Duggan propose to deal with this situation? Not by moaning or wringing of hands: the Church must not lose courage or be afraid of change or of introducing radical new measures. For instance, a dynamic new approach is needed to service the huge corporation and council estates often referred to as concrete jungles, to flood them with priests and lay helpers at least on a temporary basis, to treat them as emergency problems not solvable by traditional means. Otherwise without the saving grace of Christianity jungle law must prevail.

This would involve a fresh look at the Church's deployment of her troops. As an old soldier Tom Duggan had learned the crucial importance of deploying troops to the best advantage. He frequently pointed out that in a military campaign flash points emerge which spell danger unless attended to immediately, i.e. by powerful reinforcements. Tom believed that the Church might well learn from such flexibility.

Tom's next point was more radical and controversial. Again speaking as an old soldier he wanted unity of command at diocesan level among all those engaged in the pastoral ministry. He quoted Napoleon's dictum: 'It is easy to beat allies.' He hoped that the Council would speak out loudly and boldly on the need for pastoral unity at diocesan level under the authority of the bishop. He dreams, he says, of a clergy working with common dedication, unified and brigaded in common purpose. An effective unity of command through the bishops to the bishop of all bishops, i.e. the Roman Pontiff.

* Mark 2, 17. *New Jerusalem Bible.*

This he claimed was what Pope John was hinting at when he asked for 'a generous collaboration of the two clergies under the supervision and direction of the bishop who is pastor of all the little sheep'.*

This far-reaching suggestion meant that in the pastoral field both diocesan and religious priests would work directly under the bishop's authority, so putting an end to the duality and over-lapping which adversely affect fruitful evangelisation. Dwindling vocations among both types of clergy may well make some new form of co-operation necessary. Already considerable progress has been made in that regard in some dioceses.

In viewing the Church Tom was inclined to concentrate on the clerical wing and to regard only the clergy as the Pope's troops. There was little if any mention of lay evangelists. This was typical of the clericalism of the time. Vatican II corrected this attitude, laying down that both clergy and laity together form the People of God. Everybody in the Church is a potential evangelist.

Above all else Tom Duggan wanted the Church to fulfil its role as a sign, as a sacrament of Christ. In all times and in all places it should be a shining light 'a lumen gentium'. People should be able to see in its never-failing love and compassion the hallmark of Christ himself.

Although he made mistakes in his ecclesiology perhaps enough has been said to show that Tom Duggan's constant preoccupation was the welfare of the Church. He was a faithful follower of Christ and a willing and dutiful servant of his Church, one who might justifiably take to himself Newman's great words:

Firmly I believe and truly
God is Three, and God is One
And I next acknowledge duly
Manhood taken by the Son

And I trust and hope most fully
In that Manhood crucified;
And each thought and deed unruly
Do to death, as He has died.

And I hold in veneration,
For the love of Him alone,
Holy Church, as His creation,
And her teachings, as His own.†

* L'Osservatore Romano, 24-5-1959.

† John Henry Cardinal Newman, *The Dream of Gerontius.*

BIBLIOGRAPHY

Adam, James S. *My Private War against the Army* (privately published).

Amos, Keith, *The Fenians in Australia* 1865-1880, New South Wales/University Press.

Anderson, Jon Lee, *Guerrillas*, Harper Collins, 1993.

Andrews, C.S., *Dublin Made Me*, The Mercier Press, 1988.

Barry, General Tom, *Guerrilla Days in Ireland*, (The Mercier Press, 1955) Anvil Book edition, 1981.

Bromage, Mary, *De Valera and the March of a Nation*, Hutchinson, 1956.

Casey, John Sarsfield, *Journal of the Voyage from Portland to Australia.*

Catton, Bruce, *The Centennial History of the American Civil War*, volume three, 'Never Call Retreat', Gollancz, London, 1967.

Coogan, Tim Pat, *Michael Collins*, Hutchinson, 1990. *De Valera*, Hutchinson, 1993.

Corish, Professor P.J., *The Irish Catholic Experience*, Gill and Macmillan, 1990.

Deasy, Liam, *Towards Ireland Free*, The Mercier Press, 1973. *Brother against Brother*, The Mercier Press, 1982.

Deighton, Len, *BLITZ-Kreig*, Grafton Books, London, 1990.

Duggan, John P., *A History of the Irish Army*, Gill and Macmillan, 1991.

Dwyer, T. Ryle, *Michael Collins, the Man who Won the War*, The Mercier Press, 1990.

English, Ian R. and Lewis, P.J. *Into Battle with the Durhams*, Stamp Exchange, London, 1990.

Gaughan, J. Anthony, *Alfred O'Rahilly*, volume II, Kingdom Books, 1989. *Austin Stack, Portrait of a Separist*, Kingdom Books, 1977.

de Gaulle, Charles, *Memoirs of Hope*, translated from the French by Terence Kilmartin, Weidenfeld and Nicolson, 1971.

Hamilton, Nigel, *Monty*, Volume I, *The Making of a General*, Sceptre, 1933.

Liddell Hart, Basil, *History of the First World War*, Pan Books, 1972. *History of the Second World War*, Pan Books, 1973.

Hopkinson, Michael, *Green against Green*, Gill and Macmillan, 1988.

Horne, Alistair, *To Lose a Battle*, Macmillan, Papermac edition, 1990.

Keegan, John, *The Second World War*, Hutchinson, 1989.

Levi, Carlo, *Christ Stopped at Elboli*, translated by Frances Frenaye, King Penguin edition, 1984.

Longford, Lord, and O'Neill, Thomas P. *Eamon de Valera*, Hutchinson, 1970.
McCardle, Dorothy, *The Irish Republic*, Irish Press, 1954.
McDonald, Walter, *Reminiscences of a Maynooth Professor*, edited by Denis Gwynn, Jonathan Cape, 1925 (reprinted with a memoir by Denis Gwynn, Mercier Press, 1967).
MacEoin, *Survivors* (edited), Argentina Publications, 1968.
Montgomery, Field-Marshal Bernard, *The Memoirs of Field-Marshal Montgomery*, Collins 1958.
Neeson, Eoin, *The Civil War 1922-23*, Poolbeg Press edition, 1989.
Newman, John Henry Cardinal, *The Dream of Gerontius*, Longmans Green, 1929. *The Idea of a University*, discourse six, quoted by James J. Carey in *New Senior Prose*, Gill, 1958.
O'Broin, Leon, *The Gaelic League and the Chair of Irish at Maynooth*, Studies, Winter 1963.
O'Carroll, J.P. and Murphy John A. (edited) *De Valera and his Times*, Mercier Press, 1983.
O'Donoghue, Florence, *No Other Law*, Irish Press, 1954. *Tomas MacCurtain*, The Kerryman, 1958. *Guerilla Warfare in Ireland*, An Cosantoir, XXIII (1963)
O'Donovan Rossa, Jeremiah, *My Years in English Jails*, edited by Sean O'Cearnaigh, Anvil Books, 1967. *Rossa's Recollections*, Mariner's Harbour, New York, 1898. *Irish Rebels in English Prisons*, Brandon Books, 1991.
O'Faolain, Sean, *Vive Moi,* Little Brown, Boston, 1963.
O'Malley, *Papers* and *Notebooks*, Archives Department, University College, Dublin.
O'Maoileoin, Seamas, *B'Fhiu an Braon Fola*, Sairséal agus Dill, 1972.
O'Sullivan, John L., *By Carrigdhoun and Owenabue*, Ballyheeda Press, 1990.
Pitt, Barrie, *1918 The Last Act*, Macmillan, 1984.
Ramsey, Paul, The Just War, University Press of America, 1983.
Ryan, Meda, *The Tom Barry Story*, The Mercier Press, 1982.
Sullivan, T.D., A.M., and D.B., *Speeches from the Dock*, M.H. Gill, 1935.
Tardini, Cardinal Domenico, *PIO XII*, Tipografia Vaticana, 1960.
Terraine, John, *To Win a War, 1918*. Papermac (Macmillan), 1986. *The First World War 1914-18*, Papermac (Macmillan), 1984.
Townshend, Dr. Charles, *The British Campaign in Ireland 1919-1921*, Oxford University Press, 1975. *The Irish Republican Army and the Development of Guerrilla Warfare*, English Historical Review, XCIV (1979).
Valiulis, Maryann Gialanella, *General Richard Mulcahy,* Irish Academic Press Ltd., 1992.

Walzer, Michael, *Just and Unjust Wars*, Basic Books (Harper Collins) 1992.
de Vere White, Terence, *Kevin O'Higgins*, Anvil Books, 1986.
Younger, Calton, *Ireland's Civil War*, Frederick Muller Ltd., 1968.
Walker, Breifne, *Official Roman Catholic Teaching on Revolutionary Armed Force*, The Irish Theological Quarterly, volume 57, (1991:1).